IMPEACH BUSH!

Written by
BOB SCOTT

Illustrated by
MIKE LEFFEL

D1521050

BLATANT

IMPEACH BUSH!
by Bob Scott and Mike Leffel

IMPEACH BUSH is (C) 2006 by Blatant Comics, Bob Scott, and Mike Leffel.

Published by BLATANT COMICS
P.O. Box 110, Cresbard, SD 57435
Web: www.blatantcomics.com

ISBN 0-9722350-9-4
First Printing, August 2006
10 9 8 7 6 5 4 3 2 1

Printed in Canada

GEORGE W. BUSH WAS BORN IN NEW HAVEN, CONNECTICUT, ON JULY 6, 1946.

ONE MIGHT WONDER AT HOW EARLY A POINT IT WAS THAT PEOPLE WERE CLAIMING THAT HIS DESTINY WAS THE PRESIDENCY.

ONE MIGHT ALSO WONDER, IF HIS PATH TO THE PRESIDENCY WAS SO OBVIOUS, HOW IT WAS THAT HE DIDN'T EVEN RECEIVE THE SUPPORT OF THE MAJORITY OF VOTERS IN THE 2000 ELECTION, ONLY CLAIMING THE PRESIDENCY THROUGH LEGAL MANEUVERING ENDING WITH A CONTROVERSIAL SUPREME COURT DECISION IN HIS FAVOR.

FUTURE PRESIDENT

A COMMON REFRAIN AMONG SOME BUSH FANS BOTH BEFORE AND AFTER SEPTEMBER 11, 2001, WAS THAT BUSH WAS CHOSEN BY GOD.

FORMER NEW YORK CITY MAYOR RUDY GIULIANI

"THERE WAS SOME DIVINE GUIDANCE IN THE PRESIDENT BEING ELECTED." *

*MEET THE PRESS, DECEMBER 23, 2001.

REV. MARK CRAIG

"YOU WERE CHOSEN BY GOD... TO LEAD THE PEOPLE." *

I'M LIKE JESUS.

*"TRANSITION BEGINS; BUSH TEAM PREPS FOR WHITE HOUSE," IDAHO STATESMAN, DECEMBER 15, 2000.

BEFORE THE 2000 CAMPAIGN, EVEN BUSH HIMSELF BELIEVED GOD WOULD MAKE HIM PRESIDENT, SO THAT HE COULD DEAL WITH SOME UNKNOWN EVENT IN AMERICA'S FUTURE.

"I FEEL LIKE GOD WANTS ME TO RUN FOR PRESIDENT. I CAN'T EXPLAIN IT, BUT I SENSE MY COUNTRY IS GOING TO NEED ME. SOMETHING IS GOING TO HAPPEN... I KNOW IT WON'T BE EASY ON ME OR MY FAMILY, BUT GOD WANTS ME TO DO IT." *

DO IT! DO IT! DOOO IT!

*FROM STEPHEN MANSFIELD'S BOOK, THE FAITH OF GEORGE W. BUSH, QUOTED IN PAUL HARRIS, "BUSH SAYS GOD CHOSE HIM TO LEAD HIS NATION," THE OBSERVER, NOVEMBER 2, 2003.

SEPTEMBER 11, 2001...

THREE THOUSAND PEOPLE WERE KILLED AS TERRORIST HIJACKERS CRASHED AIRLINERS INTO THE TWO TOWERS OF THE WORLD TRADE CENTER, THE PENTAGON, AND A FIELD IN PENNSYLVANIA.

IF PRECAUTIONARY MEASURES HAD BEEN PUT IN PLACE PRIOR TO 9/11, IN RESPONSE TO AN INCREASE IN INTERCEPTED TERRORIST COMMUNICATIONS THROUGH THE SPRING AND SUMMER OF 2001, THE HORRENDOUS TRAGEDY OF 9/11 COULD HAVE BEEN AVOIDED.

ON SEPTEMBER 15, 2001, PRESIDENT BUSH OUTLINED HIS ADMINISTRATION'S POSITION REGARDING THE ATTACKS OF 9/11. THIS ARGUMENT HAS BEEN REPEATED IN VARIOUS FORMS BY BUSH AND THOSE AROUND HIM, EVEN AS IT BECAME APPARENT THAT IT WAS UTTERLY FALSE.

"NONE OF US COULD HAVE ENVISIONED THE BARBARIC ACTS OF THESE TERRORISTS." *

IN OTHER WORDS, IT'S NOT HIS FAULT, HE JUST RUNS THE COUNTRY.

*REMARKS AT CAMP DAVID, SEPTEMBER 15, 2001.

TERRORIST PLOTS INVOLVING THE CRASHING OF HIJACKED PLANES INTO SPECIFIC TARGETS HAD BEEN UNCOVERED PRIOR TO 9/11.

FOR EXAMPLE, THE FBI WAS AWARE OF A FAILED 1994 ALGERIAN TERRORIST PLOT TO CRASH A HIJACKED PLANE INTO THE EIFFEL TOWER.*

* POSNER, *WHY AMERICA SLEPT*, P. 175.

IN 1998, A WARNING WAS RECEIVED BY THE FBI AND FEDERAL AVIATION ADMINISTRATION ABOUT THE POSSIBILITY OF ARAB TERRORISTS CRASHING A PLANE LOADED WITH EXPLOSIVES INTO THE WORLD TRADE CENTER. *

WATCH OUT!

PLEASE CHECK THIS OUT AFTER LUNCH. -N

*JAMES RISEN, "THREATS AND RESPONSES: THE INVESTIGATION; U.S. FAILED TO ACT ON WARNINGS IN '98 OF A PLANE ATTACK," *THE NEW YORK TIMES*, SEPTEMBER 19, 2002, P. A1.

THE THREAT OF TERRORISTS CRASHING A PLANE INTO THE JULY 2001 G-8 SUMMIT IN GENOA, ITALY, WHICH WAS ATTENDED BY PRESIDENT GEORGE W. BUSH, WAS TAKEN SO SERIOUSLY THAT THE CIA "TASKED THE MILITARY TO RING THE CONFERENCE SITE WITH SURFACE-TO-AIR MISSILES." *

THIS SHOWS THAT JUST TWO MONTHS BEFORE 9/11, THE CIA WAS CONSIDERING THAT TERRORISTS WERE PLANNING TO CRASH A PLANE INTO A BUILDING!

WHY DID YOU BRING THESE?

BRING WHAT?

*MILLER, STONE, AND MITCHELL, *THE CELL*, P. 293.

EVEN THE WRITERS BEHIND AN X-FILES SPINOFF CALLED THE LONE GUNMEN HAD DREAMED UP THE POSSIBILITY OF A PLANE BEING CRASHED INTO THE WORLD TRADE CENTER IN THEIR FIRST EPISODE, WHICH AIRED IN MARCH 2001.

APPARENTLY, NONE OF THE EPISODE'S 13.2 MILLION VIEWERS WORKED AT THE WHITE HOUSE.

PRIOR TO 9/11, AT LEAST TWO INCIDENTS SHOWED THAT TERRORISTS WERE INTERESTED IN LEARNING TO FLY.

ON JULY 10, 2001, KENNETH WILLIAMS, AN FBI AGENT IN PHOENIX, ALERTED FBI HEADQUARTERS THAT POSSIBLE TERRORISTS WERE TRAINING AT LOCAL FLIGHT SCHOOLS, AND SUGGESTED THAT IF THIS WERE HAPPENING ELSEWHERE IN THE U.S., IT SHOULD BE INVESTIGATED.

IF THE MEMO HAD BEEN ACTED UPON, IT IS POSSIBLE THAT SOME OF THE 9/11 HIJACKERS MIGHT HAVE BEEN DISCOVERED BEFORE THEY COULD PUT THEIR DEADLY PLAN INTO ACTION. *

HMMM

LEARN TO FLY!

555-5545 ASK FOR JAY

*MILLER, STONE, AND MITCHELL, *THE CELL*, PP. 288-290.

WHILE ZACARIAS MOUSSAOUI HAD BEEN ARRESTED IN MINNEAPOLIS ON AUGUST 16, 2001, FOR OVERSTAYING HIS VISA, HE WAS CAUGHT ONLY BECAUSE A FLIGHT INSTRUCTOR HAD CONTACTED THE FBI ABOUT MOUSSAOUI'S SUSPICIOUS BEHAVIOR. BASED ON INFORMATION FROM FRENCH INTELLIGENCE INDICATING MOUSSAOUI WAS POSSIBLY A TERRORIST, MINNEAPOLIS FBI AGENTS SOUGHT A WARRANT TO SEARCH MOUSSAOUI'S COMPUTER FOR INFORMATION REGARDING ANY PLOTS HE MIGHT HAVE BEEN INVOLVED IN. *

*POSNER, *WHY AMERICA SLEPT*, PP. 172-173.

UNFORTUNATELY, THE MINNEAPOLIS AGENTS' REQUEST FOR A WARRANT WAS BLOCKED BY FBI HEADQUARTERS, AS WAS A REQUEST TO INTERROGATE MOUSSAOUI. HAD THE AGENTS BEEN ALLOWED TO INSPECT HIS COMPUTER, THEY COULD HAVE LINKED MOUSSAOUI TO MOHAMED ATTA (ONE OF THE 9/11 HIJACKERS), WHOSE PHONE NUMBER MOUSSAOUI POSSESSED, AND TO A FLIGHT SCHOOL IN NORMAN, OKLAHOMA, WHERE ANOTHER AL QAEDA MEMBER HAD PREVIOUSLY TRAINED. *

*IBID., PP. 173-174.

STILL, BUSH ADMINISTRATION OFFICIALS CLAIMED THAT NO ONE COULD HAVE GUESSED WHAT THE TERRORISTS HAD PLANNED FOR 9/11.

MAY 16, 2002:

"I DON'T THINK ANYBODY COULD HAVE PREDICTED THAT THESE PEOPLE WOULD TAKE AN AIRPLANE AND SLAM IT INTO THE WORLD TRADE CENTER, TAKE ANOTHER ONE AND SLAM IT INTO THE PENTAGON; THAT THEY WOULD TRY TO USE AN AIRPLANE AS A MISSILE, A HIJACKED AIRPLANE AS A MISSILE." *

*CONDOLEEZA RICE, NEWS CONFERENCE.

THAT THESE INCIDENTS AND OTHER WARNINGS WERE MISSED OR IGNORED IS CLEAR, AND 9/11 WAS THE RESULT.

IF BUSH HAD SPENT AS MUCH TIME SERIOUSLY CONSIDERING THE THREAT OF TERRORISM AS HE HAD SPENT ON WHAT HE THEN CONSIDERED HIS DOMESTIC PRIORITIES, SUCH AS HIS ALL-IMPORTANT TAX CUTS, AMERICA MIGHT HAVE BEEN SPARED THE TERROR OF 9/11.

ON JANUARY 31, 2001, A BIPARTISAN COMMISSION HEADED BY FORMER SENATORS GARY HART AND WARREN RUDMAN, THE U.S. COMMISSION ON NATIONAL SECURITY FOR THE 21ST CENTURY, ENDED ITS TWO YEAR STUDY OF FINDING WAYS TO INCREASE DOMESTIC SECURITY. THE COMMISSION PRESENTED THEIR CONCLUSIONS AND SUGGESTIONS TO CONGRESS AND MEMBERS OF THE BUSH ADMINISTRATION. *

*POSNER, *WHY AMERICA SLEPT*, P. 153.

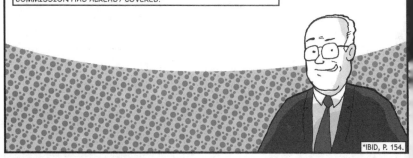

INSTEAD OF ACCEPTING THE BIPARTISAN CONCLUSIONS OF THE COMMISSION AS A BASIS FOR DOMESTIC SECURITY REFORMS, BUSH CHOSE TO HAVE VICE PRESIDENT DICK CHENEY HEAD A TASK FORCE TO INVESTIGATE THE SAME TOPICS THAT THE HART-RUDMAN COMMISSION HAD ALREADY COVERED.*

*IBID, P. 154.

IF THE ADMINISTRATION HAD ACTED ON SOME OF THE RECOMMENDATIONS OF THE COMMISSION, ISN'T IT EVEN SLIGHTLY CONCEIVABLE THAT 9/11 COULD HAVE BEEN PREVENTED?

NOT ACTING!

A PLAN DRAFTED LATE IN THE CLINTON ADMINISTRATION WAS PRESENTED TO THE BUSH ADMINISTRATION BY RICHARD CLARKE, WHO HAD BEEN CARRIED OVER BY THE NEW ADMINISTRATION AS HEAD OF THE COUNTERTERRORISM SECURITY GROUP. IF CLARKE'S PLAN HAD BEEN ENACTED, IT COULD HAVE UNDERMINED AL QAEDA IN AFGHANISTAN PRIOR TO 9/11, AS BUSH'S SIMILAR POST-9/11 PLAN WAS INTENDED TO DO. *

*FRANKEN, *LIES*, PP. 112, 114.

DURING THE ATTACKS ON SEPTEMBER 11, 2001, PRESIDENT BUSH WAS TAKING IT EASY IN SARASOTA, FLORIDA.

8:55 A.M.

THE PRESIDENT WAS IN THE HALLWAY OUTSIDE OF A CLASSROOM AT EMMA E. BOOKER ELEMENTARY SCHOOL WHEN HIS CHIEF OF STAFF, ANDREW CARD, INFORMED HIM THAT A PLANE HAD STRUCK THE NORTH TOWER OF THE WORLD TRADE CENTER. *

EXCUSE ME, SIR...

*BILL SAMMON, "SUDDENLY A TIME TO LEAD," *WASHINGTON TIMES*, OCTOBER 7, 2002, P. A1.

BUSH LATER RECALLED THAT HE WAS TOLD THAT THE FIRST PLANE TO HIT THE WORLD TRADE CENTER WAS A "LIGHT... TWIN ENGINE AIRPLANE." *

"THERE'S ONE TERRIBLE PILOT!" *

*BOTH QUOTES FROM BILL SAMMON, "SUDDENLY A TIME TO LEAD," *WASHINGTON TIMES*, OCTOBER 7, 2002, P. A1.

HOWEVER, BUSH HAS ALSO MADE THE CLAIM THAT HE SAW THE FIRST PLANE HIT THE TOWER ON A TELEVISION IN THE HALLWAY BEFORE ENTERING THE CLASSROOM, * WHICH IS IMPOSSIBLE, BECAUSE FOOTAGE OF THE FIRST PLANE'S COLLISION WAS NOT IMMEDIATELY AVAILABLE.

AND EVEN IF IT WERE POSSIBLE FOR HIM TO HAVE SEEN SUCH FOOTAGE, HE CERTAINLY WOULDN'T HAVE MISTAKEN A JETLINER FOR A "TWIN-ENGINE AIRPLANE."

*SPEECH IN ORLANDO, FLORIDA, DECEMBER 4, 2001.

*BILL SAMMON, "SUDDENLY A TIME TO LEAD," *WASHINGTON TIMES*, OCTOBER 7, 2002, A1.

SO, WHAT DID BUSH DO IN RESPONSE TO THIS NEWS?

DID HE SPRING INTO ACTION TO PLAN A RESPONSE TO THE ATTACKS, TO PUT IN MOTION A PLAN TO PREVENT FURTHER DEVASTATION?

NO.

WHATEVER BUSH WAS THINKING AT THE TIME, IT DIDN'T INVOLVE HIS LEAVING THE CLASSROOM OR DOING ANYTHING WHICH COULD BE MISTAKEN FOR ATTEMPTING TO TAKE CONTROL OF THE DIRE SITUATION.

BUSH STAYED PUT, WAITING FOR THE KIDS TO FINISH READING, TAKING THE ADVICE OF HIS PRESS SECRETARY ARI FLEISCHER, WHO FLASHED A MESSAGE TO THE PRESIDENT ON THE BACK OF A LEGAL PAD: *

DON'T SAY ANYTHING YET!

*BILL SAMMON, "SUDDENLY A TIME TO LEAD," WASHINGTON TIMES, OCTOBER 7, 2002, P. A1.

THAT THE TERRORISTS MIGHT HAVE KNOWN BUSH'S SCHEDULE FOR THAT MORNING AND CRASHED A HIJACKED JETLINER INTO BOOKER ELEMENTARY MUST NOT HAVE OCCURRED TO THE PRESIDENT OR THE SECRET SERVICE AGENTS CHARGED WITH HIS PROTECTION.

EVERYONE IN THE SCHOOL COULD HAVE BEEN KILLED IN A TERRORIST STRIKE AIMED AT THE PRESIDENT. OTHER POTENTIAL TERRORIST TARGETS THROUGHOUT THE COUNTRY WERE TOO NUMEROUS TO COUNT.

UNBELIEVABLY, WHEN EACH SECOND COULD HAVE MEANT THE DIFFERENCE BETWEEN LIFE AND DEATH FOR LARGE NUMBERS OF PEOPLE, THE PRESIDENT CHOSE TO STAY WITH THE READING CHILDREN INSTEAD OF STEPPING INTO THE ROLE OF COMMANDER IN CHIEF AND CONFIRMING THAT SUSPECT JETLINERS COULD BE SHOT DOWN TO PREVENT FURTHER TERRORIST ATTACKS.

FIVE MINUTES PASSED FROM WHEN CARD TOLD BUSH OF THE SECOND ATTACK TO WHEN BUSH LEFT THE CLASSROOM. *

*WILLIAM LANGLEY, "REVEALED: WHAT REALLY WENT ON DURING BUSH'S 'MISSING HOURS,'" TELEGRAPH.CO.UK, DECEMBER 16, 2001.

JUST AFTER 9:24 A.M., NORAD DETECTED ANOTHER POTENTIALLY HIJACKED FLIGHT, THIS TIME FLYING TOWARD WASHINGTON, D.C. NEARLY 15 MINUTES LATER, THE PLANE CRASHED INTO THE PENTAGON. EVEN IF FIGHTER JETS HAD CAUGHT UP TO IT, THEY WOULDN'T HAVE HAD THE NECESSARY PRESIDENTIAL ORDER TO SHOOT IT DOWN. *

*MIKE TAIBBI, "CHAIN OF EVENTS AT NORAD ON SEPTEMBER 11," *DATELINE NBC*, SEPTEMBER 23, 2001.

9:30 A.M.

BUSH, STILL AT BOOKER ELEMENTARY, SPEAKS BRIEFLY.

"TODAY, WE'VE HAD A NATIONAL TRAGEDY. TWO AIRPLANES HAVE CRASHED INTO THE WORLD TRADE CENTER IN AN APPARENT TERRORIST ATTACK ON OUR COUNTRY. I... HAVE ORDERED THAT THE FULL RESOURCES OF THE FEDERAL GOVERNMENT GO TO HELP THE VICTIMS AND THEIR FAMILIES, AND TO CONDUCT A FULL-SCALE INVESTIGATION TO HUNT DOWN AND TO FIND THOSE FOLKS WHO COMMITTED THIS ACT. TERRORISM AGAINST OUR NATION WILL NOT STAND."

IT WAS 9:35 A.M., NEARLY ONE HALF-HOUR AFTER HE HAD BEEN NOTIFIED OF THE SECOND ATTACK, WHEN BUSH FINALLY LEFT THE *SCHOOL* FOR THE AIRPORT WHERE AIR FORCE ONE WAS WAITING. *

*WILLIAM LANGLEY, "REVEALED: WHAT REALLY WENT ON DURING BUSH'S 'MISSING HOURS,'" TELEGRAPH.CO.UK, DECEMBER 16, 2001.

AT 9:55 A.M., PRESIDENT BUSH LEAVES SARASOTA ON BOARD AIR FORCE ONE. ONLY THEN DOES HE COMMUNICATE TO VICE PRESIDENT CHENEY THAT CIVILIAN AIRLINERS MAY BE SHOT DOWN BY THE MILITARY IF DEEMED A THREAT.

"YOU BET." *

*DAN BALZ AND BOB WOODWARD, "AMERICA'S CHAOTIC ROAD TO WAR," WASHINGTON POST, JANUARY 27, 2002.

THE REST OF THE DAY WOULD FIND BUSH FLYING TO LOUISIANA AND NEBRASKA, OUT OF FEAR OF BEING TARGETED BY TERRORISTS, BEFORE RETURNING TO THE WHITE HOUSE THAT EVENING.

JOHNNY CARSON WAS FROM NORFOLK, NEBRASKA!

AND THAT'S ALL THERE IS TO SAY OTHER THAN CORN AND FOOTBALL.

BUT WHAT REALLY HAPPENED IN THE YEARS AND MONTHS LEADING UP TO 9/11? FAMILY MEMBERS OF MANY 9/11 VICTIMS, AS WELL AS MANY OTHERS WHO FELT THAT SUCH A TRAGEDY COULD HAVE BEEN PREVENTED, SUSPECTED THAT BUSH AND MEMBERS OF HIS ADMINISTRATION WERE HIDING THE TRUTH TO SAVE THEMSELVES FROM EMBARRASSMENT AND THE PUBLIC BACKLASH THEY WOULD FACE IF THEY WERE SHOWN TO HAVE ACTED INCOMPETENTLY IN THE MONTHS LEADING UP TO 9/11.

CORN?

SECRET

THE BUSH ADMINISTRATION OPPOSED THE CREATION OF AN INDEPENDENT COMMISSION TO INVESTIGATE WHAT HAD HAPPENED. THEY WENT SO FAR AS TO SUGGEST THAT THE TRUTH WOULD HAMPER THE WAR ON TERRORISM. *

OF COURSE, IT WOULDN'T BE THE LAST TIME THAT RAISING QUESTIONS ABOUT THE ADMINISTRATION'S ACTIONS WOULD LEAD TO ACCUSATIONS OF AIDING THE TERRORISTS.

HEH! HEH!

OSAMA

DECLASSIFIED INFO TO HELP TERRORISTS DESTROY AMERICA

*BRIAN MONTOPOLI, "SCHLEP TO JUDGMENT," WASHINGTON MONTHLY, SEPTEMBER 2003, P. 38.

FINALLY, IN NOVEMBER OF 2002, BUSH ALLOWED FOR THE CREATION OF THE INDEPENDENT COMMISSION TO INVESTIGATE 9/11, BUT WITH SOME IMPORTANT DECISIONS ABOUT THE COMMISSION'S POWER AND MEMBERSHIP LEFT UP TO THE PRESIDENT.

FOR EXAMPLE, A SUBPOENA BY THE COMMISSION WOULD REQUIRE THE APPROVAL OF AT LEAST 6 OF THE GROUP'S 10 BIPARTISAN MEMBERS, THE COMMISSION'S CHAIRMAN WAS TO BE APPOINTED BY THE PRESIDENT, AND THE INVESTIGATION HAD A DEADLINE OF MAY 27, 2004. *

*BRIAN MONTOPOLI, "SCHLEP TO JUDGMENT," *WASHINGTON MONTHLY*, SEPTEMBER 2003, P. 38.

BUSH'S FIRST CHOICE TO HEAD THE COMMISSION:

FORMER SECRETARY OF STATE (AND ALLEGED WAR CRIMINAL) HENRY KISSINGER.

KISSY!

THE THUNDEROUS DIN OF CRITICISM AT SUCH AN OUTRAGEOUS AND DISINGENUOUS CHOICE TO HEAD SUCH AN IMPORTANT PANEL ONLY SUBSIDED WHEN, BECAUSE OF POTENTIAL CONFLICTS OF INTEREST, KISSINGER STEPPED DOWN AS CHAIRMAN. *

*"KISSINGER RESIGNS AS HEAD OF 9/11 COMMISSION," CNN, DECEMBER 13, 2002.

A NEW, NOT-SO-CONTROVERSIAL CHAIRMAN WAS NAMED A FEW DAYS LATER:

REPUBLICAN THOMAS KEAN, THE FORMER GOVERNOR OF NEW JERSEY. *

"NOT-SO-CONTROVERSIAL" THOMAS KEAN

NOT A WAR CRIMINAL!

*"EX-NJ GOVERNOR TO HEAD 9/11 PANEL," CBSNEWS.COM, DECEMBER 16, 2002.

BY THE TIME THE COMMISSION WAS READY TO GET TO WORK MONTHS LATER, SOME FEDERAL AGENCIES WERE LESS THAN COOPERATIVE.

IN JULY OF 2003, THOMAS KEAN COMPLAINED TO THE PRESS THAT THE COMMISSION'S INTERVIEWS WITH JUSTICE DEPARTMENT EMPLOYEES WERE OVERSEEN BY "MINDERS," * THE SAME TACTIC DECRIED AS WITNESS INTIMIDATION IN INTERVIEWS WITH IRAQI SCIENTISTS BY U.N. WEAPONS INSPECTORS IN IRAQ.

BUT WHAT BUSH HAD CALLED WRONG IN IRAQ WAS A-OK IN THE U.S.A.

*JULIAN BORGER, "9/11 INQUIRY ALLEGES WITNESS INTIMIDATION," THE GUARDIAN, JULY 10, 2003.

EVENTUALLY, THE COMMISSION STARTED TO GET THE KIND OF COOPERATION FROM MANY GOVERNMENT AGENCIES IT WOULD NEED TO REACH CONCLUSIONS BY ITS MAY 2004 DEADLINE. BUT IT WASN'T ALL CLEAR SAILING. THE WHITE HOUSE DIDN'T WANT TO GIVE THE COMMISSION COMPLETE ACCESS TO THE PRESIDENT'S DAILY SECURITY BRIEFINGS.

"IT'S IMPORTANT FOR ME TO PROTECT NATIONAL SECURITY. IT'S IMPORTANT FOR THE WRITERS OF THE PRESIDENTIAL DAILY BRIEF TO FEEL COMFORTABLE THAT THE DOCUMENTS WILL NEVER BE POLITICIZED AND/OR UNNECESSARILY EXPOSED FOR PUBLIC PURVIEW." *

*ADAM ENTOUS, "BUSH WILLING TO PROVIDE SOME DOCUMENTS TO 9/11 PANEL," REUTERS, OCTOBER 28, 2003.

BUSH AND THE COMMISSION SEEMED TO REACH AN AGREEMENT REGARDING THE BRIEFS IN NOVEMBER 2003. BUT BY THE END OF JANUARY 2004, THE WHITE HOUSE SEEMED TO REVERSE ITSELF, NOT ALLOWING NOTES TAKEN BY THE FEW COMMISSIONERS WHO HAD SEEN THE BRIEFINGS TO BE SHOWN TO THE OTHER COMMISSIONERS. THEN IN EARLY FEBRUARY, THE COMMISSION AND THE WHITE HOUSE REACHED AN AGREEMENT ONCE AGAIN, WITH THE CHAIRMAN AND VICE CHAIRMAN OF THE COMMISSION EXPRESSING SATISFACTION THAT THEY WOULD HAVE ACCESS TO THE INFORMATION THEY NEEDED. *

*"WHITE HOUSE, SEPT. 11 PANEL REACH DEAL ON BUSH PAPERS," REUTERS, FEBRUARY 10, 2004.

DECEMBER 17, 2003...

"THIS WAS NOT SOMETHING THAT HAD TO HAPPEN." *

"THERE ARE PEOPLE THAT, IF I WAS DOING THE JOB, WOULD CERTAINLY NOT BE IN THE POSITION THEY WERE IN AT THAT TIME BECAUSE THEY FAILED." *

CONTROVERSIAL STATEMENTS

9/11

*BOTH QUOTES FROM "9/11 CHAIR: ATTACK WAS PREVENTABLE," CBSNEWS.COM, DECEMBER 17, 2003.

THE NEXT DAY, IN RESPONSE TO QUESTIONS ABOUT KEAN'S REMARKS, WHITE HOUSE PRESS SECRETARY SCOTT MCCLELLAN RESTATED THE ADMINISTRATION'S RIDICULOUS CLAIM:

"THERE IS NOTHING THAT WE HAVE SEEN THAT LEADS US TO BELIEVE THAT SEPT. 11 COULD HAVE BEEN PREVENTED." *

THE WHITE HOUSE

*LAURENCE ARNOLD, "SEPT. 11 PANEL CHIEF CLARIFIES REMARKS," ASSOCIATED PRESS, DECEMBER 18, 2003.

WILL THE COMMISSION'S FINAL REPORT BE FAIR AND ACCURATE? IT'S HARD TO KNOW WITH ANY CERTAINTY, AS THE IMPARTIALITY OF SOME COMMISSIONERS HAS BEEN BROUGHT INTO QUESTION.

IN MARCH 2003, IT WAS REVEALED THAT AT LEAST SIX OF THE TEN COMMISSIONERS HAVE PREVIOUS OR CURRENT TIES TO THE AIRLINE INDUSTRY. *

THIS POTENTIAL FOR CONFLICT OF INTEREST THREATENS TO TAINT THE CREDIBILITY OF THE COMMISSION'S FINAL REPORT, AT LEAST INASMUCH AS IT DEALS WITH THE AIRLINE INDUSTRY.

*"SEPTEMBER 11 COMMISSION CONFLICTED?", CBS EVENING NEWS WITH DAN RATHER, MARCH 5, 2003.

MORE CONFLICTS OF INTEREST APPEARED IN THE NEWS IN JANUARY 2004, WHEN TWO OF THE COMMISSIONERS WERE FOUND TO HAVE BEEN INVOLVED WITH THE AGENCIES THEY WERE INVESTIGATING.

PHILIP ZELIKOW →

"PHILIP ZELIKOW, THE COMMISSION'S EXECUTIVE DIRECTOR, WORKED ON THE BUSH-CHENEY TRANSITION TEAM AS THE NEW ADMINISTRATION TOOK POWER, ADVISING HIS LONGTIME ASSOCIATE AND FORMER BOSS, NATIONAL SECURITY ADVISER CONDOLEEZA RICE, ON THE INCOMING NATIONAL SECURITY COUNCIL." *

"JAMIE S. GORELICK...WAS DEPUTY ATTORNEY GENERAL IN JANET RENO'S JUSTICE DEPARTMENT DURING THE CLINTON ADMINISTRATION." *

*SHAUN WATERMAN, "9/11 DIRECTOR GAVE EVIDENCE TO OWN INQUIRY," UNITED PRESS INTERNATIONAL, JANUARY 15, 2004.

IN JANUARY OF 2004, THE 9/11 COMMISSION ASKED FOR MORE TIME TO FINISH ITS WORK. THOUGH BUSH AT FIRST REFUSED THEIR REQUEST, BELIEVING THAT THE INFORMATION IN THE COMMISSION'S REPORT WOULD INTERFERE WITH HIS REELECTION CAMPAIGN, IN EARLY FEBRUARY, HE GAVE CONGRESS PERMISSION TO EXTEND THE COMMISSION'S REPORT DEADLINE TO THE END OF JULY 2004. BUT EVEN WITH THE PRESIDENT'S PERMISSION, THE REPUBLICAN-CONTROLLED CONGRESS COULD REFUSE TO EXTEND THE DEADLINE, FORCING THE COMMISSION TO DROP IMPORTANT PARTS OF THEIR INVESTIGATION.*

TRUTH

POLITICS

OINK OINK

*HOPE YEN, "9/11 PANEL COULD PARE DOWN INTEL PROBE," ASSOCIATED PRESS, FEBRUARY 13, 2004.

WHETHER THE COMMISSION'S FINAL REPORT IS FILLED WITH REVELATIONS THAT SHINE NEW LIGHT ON THE EVENTS OF 9/11 WILL BE SEEN WITH THE REPORTS RELEASE. PERHAPS IF THE REPORT CAN LEAD TO THE ACKNOWLEDGMENT BY ANY HIGH-LEVEL BUSH ADMINISTRATION OFFICIAL THAT THE EVENTS OF SEPTEMBER 11 WERE PREVENTABLE, THAT COULD BE COUNTED AS SOMETHING OF A VICTORY FOR THOSE WHO HAVE SOUGHT TO GET BEYOND THE ADMINISTRATION'S OVERT POLITICAL POSTURING ON THIS INCREDIBLY IMPORTANT ISSUE.

ANOTHER IMPORTANT ISSUE THAT BUSH CHOSE TO POLITICIZE WAS THE CREATION OF A DEPARTMENT OF HOMELAND SECURITY. THE DEPARTMENT WAS TO INCLUDE 22 SEPARATE GOVERNMENT AGENCIES AND NEARLY 170,000 EMPLOYEES.

FEMA

INS

USD

APHC

DEPARTMENT OF HOMELAND SECURITY

BUSH'S PLAN FOR A DEPARTMENT OF HOMELAND SECURITY REMOVED CIVIL SERVICE PROTECTIONS FROM ALL EMPLOYEES WITHIN THE NEW AGENCY.

WHEN THE DEMOCRATS DIDN'T WANT TO THROW THEIR SUPPORT BEHIND A PLAN THAT THREATENED THE RIGHTS OF SO MANY FEDERAL EMPLOYEES, BUSH RESORTED TO BULLYING TACTICS THAT PRESENTED THE DEMOCRATS AS TRAITORS TO THE CAUSE OF PROTECTING AMERICA.

"THE SENATE IS MORE INTERESTED IN SPECIAL INTERESTS IN WASHINGTON, AND NOT INTERESTED IN THE SECURITY OF THE AMERICAN PEOPLE." *

OF COURSE, THIS WAS JUST THE PRESIDENT'S WAY OF DISTRACTING THE AMERICAN PEOPLE FROM THE FACT THAT HE WAS TAKING JOB SECURITY AWAY FROM SO MANY FEDERAL EMPLOYEES.

*"BUSH AND DASCHLE COMMENTS ON SECURITY AND POLITICS," *NEW YORK TIMES*, SEPTEMBER 26, 2002, P. A17.

THE BILL CREATING THE DEPARTMENT OF HOMELAND SECURITY WAS PASSED BY THE SENATE ON NOVEMBER 20, APPROVED BY 90 SENATORS AND OPPOSED BY 9. ONE ESPECIALLY CONTROVERSIAL PROVISION OF THE BILL PREVENTED LAWSUITS AGAINST THE MANUFACTURERS OF VACCINES BELIEVED TO CAUSE AUTISM IN CHILDREN. *

THANKS, CONGRESS!

THANKS 1234567 MOUSE.

PAT PAT

BIG PHARMA

*EUNICE MOSCOSO, "SENATE OKS HOMELAND SECURITY BILL," *PALM BEACH POST*, NOVEMBER 20, 2002.

AFTER 9/11, AMERICANS HAVE FACED A DIMINUTION OF CIVIL LIBERTIES, IN PART BECAUSE OF THE USA PATRIOT ACT.

RUSHED THROUGH CONGRESS LESS THAN TWO MONTHS AFTER THE ATTACKS OF 9/11 WITH MINIMAL DEBATE, AND SIGNED INTO LAW BY PRESIDENT BUSH ON OCTOBER 26, 2001, THE USA PATRIOT ACT GREATLY EXPANDED THE POWERS OF U.S. INTELLIGENCE AGENCIES.

ACCORDING TO A GOVERNMENT WEB SITE * OUTLINING THE SUPPOSED ACCOMPLISHMENTS OF THE PATRIOT ACT AND THE JUSTICE DEPARTMENT OF ATTORNEY GENERAL JOHN ASHCROFT:

"WE HAVE EXPANDED FREEDOM OVER THE PAST TWO YEARS WHILE PROTECTING CIVIL LIBERTIES AND PROTECTING PEOPLE HERE AND AROUND THE WORLD FROM FURTHER TERRORIST ATTACKS."

SURE SOUNDS NICE! UNFORTUNATELY, IT'S NOT EXACTLY TRUE.

MINISTRY of FREEDOM

*www.lifeandliberty.gov/subs/a_terr.htm

IF ASHCROFT AND HIS ILK WOULD LIKE TO PRESENT A REASONABLE ARGUMENT SHOWING THAT INCREASING SURVEILLANCE POWER WHILE REMOVING CHECKS AND BALANCES FROM THE PROCESS SOMEHOW EXPANDS FREEDOM...

THAT CLAIMING THE RIGHT TO INVESTIGATE ANYONE THEY SUSPECT OF ANYTHING REMOTELY RELATED TO TERRORISM WITHOUT A GUARANTEE OF DUE PROCESS ENHANCES LIBERTY...

THAT TAKING AWAY FREEDOMS ONE BY ONE IN THE NAME OF FIGHTING TERRORISM BUILDS UP OUR CIVIL LIBERTIES...

WELL, THE ATTORNEY GENERAL IS FREE TO PRESENT SUCH AN ARGUMENT, BUT IT SEEMS MORE LIKELY THAT HE'LL JUST STICK TO TIRED RHETORIC THAT SINGS HOLLOW PRAISES OF BUSH'S POLICIES WHILE DISMISSING ALL CRITICISM AS HYPERBOLE AND HYSTERIA.

ONE EXAMPLE OF ASHCROFT'S DISMISSAL OF CRITICISM INVOLVED ONE PARTICULARLY CONTROVERSIAL PART OF THE PATRIOT ACT.

ASHCROFT MOCKED THOSE WHO INSISTED THAT SECTION 215 OF THE PATRIOT ACT, WHICH IN PART ALLOWS FEDERAL AGENTS TO SECRETLY GAIN ACCESS TO A PATRON'S LIBRARY RECORDS, IS A VIOLATION OF PERSONAL PRIVACY RIGHTS.

"ACCORDING TO...BASELESS HYSTERIA, SOME HAVE CONVINCED THE AMERICAN LIBRARY ASSOCIATION THAT UNDER THE BIPARTISAN PATRIOT ACT, THE FBI IS NOT FIGHTING TERRORISM. INSTEAD, AGENTS ARE CHECKING HOW FAR YOU'VE GOTTEN ON THE LATEST TOM CLANCY NOVEL." *

*ASHCROFT'S REMARKS TO THE NATIONAL RESTAURANT ASSOCIATION, SEPTEMBER 15, 2003.

ASHCROFT, BY INSINUATING THAT ANYONE SUSPICIOUS OF THE PATRIOT ACT IS AN IMBECILE, AVOIDED ADDRESSING THE ACTUAL ISSUE: LAW ENFORCEMENT OFFICIALS ARE NOW ALLOWED TO ACCESS AN INDIVIDUAL'S LIBRARY RECORDS.

WITHIN DAYS OF INSULTING HIS DETRACTORS, ASHCROFT WAS RELEASING FORMERLY CLASSIFIED INFORMATION IN AN ATTEMPT TO PROVE THAT PEOPLE WERE CRAZY NOT TO TRUST HIM AND PRESIDENT BUSH TO MAKE SOUND JUDGMENTS.

ASHCROFT INDICATED THAT SECTION 215 OF THE PATRIOT ACT HAD BEEN USED AS OF MID-SEPTEMBER 2003. *

*CURT ANDERSON, "ASHCROFT TO DECLASSIFY PATRIOT ACT DATA," ASSOCIATED PRESS, SEPTEMBER 17, 2003.

BEWARE THE PATRIOT ACT

FICTION →

MYSTERY ←

NEVER MIND THAT IN ACKNOWLEDGING THAT SECTION 215 HAD NOT YET BEEN USED, ASHCROFT WAS UNDERMINING HIS OWN ARGUMENT THAT IT WAS AN ESSENTIAL TOOL AGAINST TERRORISTS.

WHETHER IT'S BEEN USED OR NOT, THE LAW STILL EXISTS, AND ITS POTENTIAL EFFECTS ON PRIVACY ARE AS REAL AS EVER, EVEN AFTER ASHCROFT'S EMPTY REASSURANCES.

ACCORDING TO THE AMERICAN CIVIL LIBERTIES UNION, THE USA PATRIOT ACT ALLOWS FOR THE FOLLOWING ABUSES OF POWER, AMONG OTHERS:

-"SECTION 215...ALLOWS THE FBI TO FORCE ANYONE AT ALL - INCLUDING DOCTORS, LIBRARIES, BOOKSTORES, UNIVERSITIES, AND INTERNET SERVICE PROVIDERS - TO TURN OVER RECORDS ON THEIR CLIENTS OR CUSTOMERS." *

-SECTION 213 "UNCONSTITUTIONALLY...ALLOW[S] THE GOVERNMENT TO CONDUCT SEARCHES WITHOUT NOTIFYING THE SUBJECTS, AT LEAST UNTIL LONG AFTER THE SEARCH HAS BEEN EXECUTED. " *

-UNDER SECTION 218, "THE FBI CAN SECRETLY CONDUCT A PHYSICAL SEARCH OR WIRETAP ON AMERICAN CITIZENS TO OBTAIN EVIDENCE OF CRIME WITHOUT PROVING PROBABLE CAUSE, AS THE FOURTH AMENDMENT EXPLICITLY REQUIRES." *

-UNDER SECTION 214 "[WIRETAP] ORDERS ISSUED BY A JUDGE ARE NO LONGER VALID ONLY IN THAT JUDGE'S JURISDICTION, BUT CAN BE MADE VALID ANYWHERE IN THE UNITED STATES." *

-SECTION 214 ALSO ALLOWS FOR THE TRACKING OF EMAIL HEADERS, INCLUDING SUBJECT LINES, AS WELL AS THE ADDRESSES OF WEB SITES AN INDIVIDUAL VISITS. *

-THE PATRIOT ACT "ALLOWS FOR THE INDEFINITE DETENTION OF NON-CITIZENS....THE ATTORNEY GENERAL CAN ORDER DETENTION BASED ON A CERTIFICATION THAT HE OR SHE HAS 'REASONABLE GROUNDS TO BELIEVE' A NON-CITIZEN ENDANGERS NATIONAL SECURITY." *

*THESE FACTS ARE FROM AN ACLU DOCUMENT TITLED "SURVEILLANCE UNDER THE USA PATRIOT ACT," WHICH CAN BE FOUND AT WWW.ACLU.ORG/SAFEANDFREE/SAFEANDFREE.CFM?ID=12263&C=206

IN JUST A FEW SENTENCES, ASHCROFT SUGGESTS THAT HE WANTS OPEN DEBATE, BUT THEN CLAIMS THAT ANYONE ENGAGING IN SUCH A DEBATE AGAINST JUSTICE DEPARTMENT POLICY BETRAYS AMERICA TO THE TERRORISTS.

SINCE HE CAN'T PHYSICALLY MUZZLE HIS CRITICS (YET), HE JUST ACCUSES THEM OF TREASON.

MMPH!

STYMIED! MMM!

CRITIC USA

BENEDICT!

POCKET ASHCROFT →

BUT BUSH'S ATTEMPTS TO GAIN REMARKABLE POWERS FOR HIS ADMINISTRATION AFTER 9/11 WERE ONLY BEGINNING.

TERRORIST DOG!

SOB!

IN EARLY 2003, A DRAFT OF A SEQUEL TO THE PATRIOT ACT, DUBBED PATRIOT ACT II BY ITS MANY CRITICS, WAS LEAKED TO THE PUBLIC. THOUGH DISMISSED BY THE JUSTICE DEPARTMENT AS NOTHING MORE THAN A DISCUSSION DRAFT, IT WAS OBVIOUS TO MANY THAT THE DOCUMENT WAS SERIOUS, HAVING BEEN SENT TO BOTH VICE PRESIDENT CHENEY AND SPEAKER OF THE HOUSE DENNIS HASTERT. *

*CHARLES LEWIS AND ADAM MAYLE, "JUSTICE DEPT. DRAFTS SWEEPING EXPANSION OF ANTI-TERRORISM ACT," CENTER FOR PUBLIC INTEGRITY, FEBRUARY 7, 2003.

WHAT WERE SOME OF THE MOST OUTRAGEOUS PARTS OF PATRIOT ACT II?

-THE PUBLIC WOULD HAVE EXTREMELY LIMITED ACCESS TO INFORMATION REGARDING INDUSTRIES IN THEIR COMMUNITIES WHICH STORE HAZARDOUS CHEMICALS. THE REASON PRESENTED FOR CHANGING THE LAW TO KEEP PEOPLE FROM KNOWING ABOUT SUCH POTENTIAL ENVIRONMENTAL AND HEALTH THREATS IS THAT SUCH INFORMATION IS "A ROADMAP FOR TERRORISTS." *

-THE GOVERNMENT WOULD MAINTAIN A DNA DATABASE OF NONCITIZENS WHO ARE SUSPECTED OF HAVING TIES TO A TERRORIST ORGANIZATION OR OF SUPPORTING SUCH AN ORGANIZATION. *

-ACCUSED TERRORISTS COULD BE HELD WITHOUT BAIL. MERE SUSPICION THAT ONE IS A TERRORIST WOULD BE ENOUGH TO KEEP THEM LOCKED UP UNTIL THE GOVERNMENT DECIDED WHAT TO CHARGE THEM WITH. *

-AMERICAN CITIZENS ACCUSED OF ASSISTING TERRORISTS COULD BE STRIPPED OF THEIR CITIZENSHIP. SO GROUPS DESIGNATED TERRORIST ORGANIZATIONS WOULD BE OFF LIMITS TO AMERICAN CITIZENS FOR ANY REASON. CONTACT WITH SUCH A GROUP COULD LEAD TO SUSPICION OF TIES TO THE GROUP, AND SUSPICION IS ALL THAT THE ADMINISTRATION CLAIMS IS NEEDED TO INFER THAT THE CITIZEN IS WILLINGLY REVOKING THEIR CITIZENSHIP.*

*EXAMPLES FROM CHARLES LEWIS AND ADAM MAYLE, "JUSTICE DEPT. DRAFTS SWEEPING EXPANSION OF ANTI-TERRORISM ACT," CENTER FOR PUBLIC INTEGRITY, FEBRUARY 7, 2003.

AFTER THE PUBLIC BALKED AT SOME PROVISIONS OF PATRIOT ACT II, THE BILL SLITHERED BACK INTO THE SHADOWS, RETREATING FROM THE LIGHT OF DAY WHICH THREATENED TO DESTROY IT.

BUT IT DIDN'T SIGNAL THE END OF THE BUSH'S EXPANSION OF FEDERAL INVESTIGATIVE AND SURVEILLANCE POWERS.

A MEASURE STEALTHILY ATTACHED TO AN INTELLIGENCE SPENDING BILL WHICH PASSED CONGRESS IN NOVEMBER 2003 AND WAS SIGNED INTO LAW BY PRESIDENT BUSH IN JANUARY 2004 MAKES IT EASIER FOR THE FBI TO CONDUCT SEARCHES OF FINANCIAL RECORDS WITHOUT A JUDGE'S PERMISSION.

THE MEASURE REDEFINED "FINANCIAL INSTITUTIONS" THAT THE FBI CAN INVESTIGATE, "BROADEN[ING] THE DEFINITION...TO INCLUDE SUCH BUSINESSES AS INSURANCE COMPANIES, TRAVEL AGENCIES, REAL ESTATE AGENTS, STOCKBROKERS, THE U.S. POSTAL SERVICE AND EVEN JEWELRY STORES, CASINOS AND CAR DEALERSHIPS." *

*"KIM ZETTER, "BUSH GRABS NEW POWER FOR FBI," WIRED NEWS, JANUARY 6, 2004.

WAS THE PATRIOT ACT IN ITS CURRENT AND FUTURE INCARNATIONS UNSTOPPABLE?

THE JUSTICE DEPARTMENT WOULD LIKE TO THINK SO. THEIR WEB SITE AT WWW.LIFEANDLIBERTY.GOV PROUDLY PROCLAIMED THAT "[N]O PROVISION OF THE PATRIOT ACT HAS BEEN HELD UNCONSTITUTIONAL BY ANY COURT."

PATRIOT ACT JUGGERNAUT

BUT ON JANUARY 23, 2004, A FEDERAL JUDGE RULED THAT PART OF THE PATRIOT ACT EQUATING "EXPERT ADVICE OR ASSISTANCE" TO A TERRORIST GROUP WITH "MATERIAL SUPPORT" TO TERRORISTS, WAS UNCONSTITUTIONALLY VAGUE. INDIVIDUALS COULD BE CHARGED FOR PROVIDING ADVICE ABOUT PEACEFUL CONFLICT RESOLUTION TO ANY GROUP THE GOVERNMENT LABELED A TERRORIST GROUP. *

UNCONSTITUTIONAL!

THE JUSTICE DEPARTMENT, HOWEVER, SEEMED IN NO HURRY TO UPDATE THEIR WEB SITE, AS THEIR CLAIM ABOUT THE PATRIOT ACT'S CONSTITUTIONALITY REMAINED UNCHANGED FOR AT LEAST ONE MONTH AFTER THE COURT'S DECISION.

*LINDA DEUTSCH, "PART OF PATRIOT ACT RULED UNCONSTITUTIONAL," ASSOCIATED PRESS, JANUARY 26, 2004.

A FEW DAYS AFTER THE ATTACKS OF 9/11, PRESIDENT BUSH SPOKE AT THE ISLAMIC CENTER IN WASHINGTON, D.C., TO POINT OUT THAT PEOPLE SHOULD NOT BELIEVE THAT AN INDIVIDUAL'S RELIGIOUS AFFILIATION INDICATED A LINK TO TERRORISM.

THAT'S POKEMON, NOT ISLAM!

I LIKE BOTH.

"THE FACE OF TERROR IS NOT THE TRUE FAITH OF ISLAM. THAT'S NOT WHAT ISLAM IS ALL ABOUT. ISLAM IS ABOUT PEACE." *

*BUSH'S REMARKS AT THE ISLAMIC CENTER, SEPTEMBER 17, 2001.

WHILE BUSH WAS TOUTING THE GLORY OF A FAITH THAT AT LEAST ONE OF HIS OWN PERSONAL SPIRITUAL ADVISERS (FRANKLIN GRAHAM) HAS REPEATEDLY DENOUNCED, HIS ADMINISTRATION'S IMMIGRATION POLICY TRAINED ITS SIGHTS ON ARAB AND MUSLIM COMMUNITIES THROUGHOUT AMERICA.

SHORTLY AFTER SEPTEMBER 11, 2001, OVER 1,200 NONCITIZENS WERE DETAINED. INFORMATION ABOUT THESE DETAINEES WAS WITHHELD FROM THE PUBLIC, AND MANY WERE DEPORTED AFTER CLOSED IMMIGRATION HEARINGS.

YOU'RE GOING AWAY FOR A LONG TIME, FAT MAN!

I SAW THAT BEARD AND I KNEW HE WAS ONE OF **THEM!**

TIK TIK TIK

ACCORDING TO A MIGRATION POLICY INSTITUTE REPORT INVOLVING A SURVEY OF 406 INDIVIDUALS DETAINED AFTER 9/11, "OVER 46 PERCENT HAD BEEN IN THE UNITED STATES AT LEAST SIX YEARS.... ALMOST HALF HAD SPOUSES, CHILDREN, OR OTHER FAMILY RELATIONSHIPS IN THE UNITED STATES," WITH THESE SORTS OF SOCIETAL TIES DISTINGUISHING THEM FROM THE HIJACKERS. *

ANY ARAB OR MUSLIM WHO OVERSTAYED THEIR VISA COULD BE A TERRORIST, BUSH DEDUCED. AND IF THEY WEREN'T TERRORISTS, WELL, THEN THE GOVERNMENT WAS JUST ENFORCING IMMIGRATION LAW.

GOOD-BYE, POSSIBLE EVILDOERS!

GOOD-BYE, DUE PROCESS.

*CHISHTI, ET. AL., *AMERICA'S CHALLENGE*.

BUT THE BUSH ADMINISTRATION'S IMMIGRATION AGENTS IGNORED THEIR OWN NORMAL PROCEDURES. ACCORDING TO A REPORT BY THE MIGRATION POLICY INSTITUTE, OF THE 406 DETAINEES SURVEYED, "OVER HALF...WERE DETAINED FOR MORE THAN NINE MONTHS BEFORE BEING RELEASED OR EXPATRIATED." *

ALSO, "[M]ANY OF THESE DETAINEES HAD SEVERE PROBLEMS NOTIFYING OR COMMUNICATING WITH THEIR FAMILY MEMBERS AND LAWYERS OR ARRANGING FOR REPRESENTATION AT ALL." *

THE SIGHT OF FLOATING WORDS IN BOXES DOES NOT IMPROVE MY SITUATION, THOUGH IT IS A WELCOME DIVERSION!

*IBID.

THE MIGRATION POLICY INSTITUTE REPORT ALSO FOUND THAT "BY TARGETING MUSLIM AND ARAB IMMIGRANTS, THE U.S. GOVERNMENT HAS DEEPENED THE PERCEPTION ABROAD THAT THE UNITED STATES IS ANTI-MUSLIM." *

IN EFFECT, BUSH'S POST-9/11 ANTI-ARAB AND MUSLIM IMMIGRATION POLICIES REINFORCED THE BELIEFS OF TERRORIST-SPONSORING NATIONS AND TERRORIST GROUPS AROUND THE WORLD.

*IBID.

ONE LAST PIECE OF INFORMATION FROM THE MIGRATION POLICY INSTITUTE REPORT:

"IMMIGRATION ARRESTS BASED UPON TIPS, SWEEPS, AND PROFILING HAVE NOT RESULTED IN ANY TERRORISM-RELATED CONVICTIONS AGAINST THESE DETAINEES." *

YET BUSH CLAIMED THAT THE DEPORTATION OF THESE PEOPLE WAS ANOTHER SUCCESS IN THE WAR ON TERRORISM.

ANOTHER SUCCESS!

SWAT!

CHISHTI, ET. AL., *AMERICA'S CHALLENGE.*

BUT WHAT ABOUT U.S. CITIZENS? SURELY GEORGE W. BUSH WOULDN'T UNDERMINE AMERICA'S LEGAL SYSTEM TO SUCH AN EXTENT THAT HE WOULD ACTUALLY DETAIN AMERICAN CITIZENS WITHOUT CHARGES, RIGHT?

THOUGH AT ANY OTHER POINT IN AMERICAN HISTORY, SUCH DISRESPECT FOR THE BILL OF RIGHTS WOULD HAVE BEEN GREETED BY A TREMENDOUS PUBLIC OUTCRY, THE POST-9/11 ERA HAS SEEN A SHIFT TO GRANTING THE PRESIDENT THE RIGHT TO IGNORE THE RULE OF LAW, TO DO WHATEVER HE DEEMS IS NECESSARY TO DEFEAT "EVIL."

ONE CASE, INVOLVES YASER ESAM HAMDI. HAMDI WAS FIGHTING ALONGSIDE THE TALIBAN IN AFGHANISTAN WHERE HE WAS CAPTURED BY COALITION FORCES. HE WAS SENT BACK TO THE U.S. WHEN IT WAS DISCOVERED THAT HE WAS AN AMERICAN CITIZEN.

INSTEAD OF PROSECUTING HAMDI USING EXISTING LAWS, THE ADMINISTRATION DECIDED THAT HE COULD BE DETAINED INDEFINITELY AS AN "ENEMY COMBATANT," A LABEL THAT BUSH CLAIMS HE HAS THE RIGHT TO PLACE ON ANY AMERICAN CITIZEN HE SEES AS A POTENTIAL TERRORIST.

"ENEMY COMBATANTS" ARE NOT ALLOWED LEGAL REPRESENTATION, AT LEAST NOT UNTIL THEY'VE BEEN DRAINED OF ALL INTELLIGENCE VALUE, * BUT ONLY BUSH HAS FINAL SAY ON WHEN THAT POINT HAS BEEN REACHED.

BUSH AND INTELLIGENCE? THERE'S A JOKE!

*TONI LOCY AND KEVIN JOHNSON, "FEDS EXPLAIN WHY PADILLA CAN'T SEE LAWYER," *USA TODAY*, DECEMBER 17, 2003.

JOSE PADILLA, THE OTHER ENEMY COMBATANT BEING DETAINED INDEFINITELY BY THE BUSH ADMINISTRATION, IS ACCUSED OF PLOTTING A TERRORIST ATTACK WITHIN THE U.S. USING A RADIOACTIVE "DIRTY BOMB."

THE 2ND U.S. COURT OF APPEALS, HOWEVER, OVERRULED THE BUSH ADMINISTRATION'S DETENTION OF PADILLA, AS IT WAS DETERMINED THAT BUSH COULD ONLY HOLD A U.S. CITIZEN WITHOUT CHARGES WITH THE AUTHORIZATION OF CONGRESS. *

*LARRY NEUMEISTER, "BUSH OVERRULED ON 'DIRTY BOMB' SUSPECT," ASSOCIATED PRESS, DECEMBER 18, 2003.

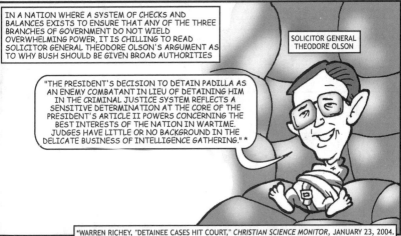

IN A NATION WHERE A SYSTEM OF CHECKS AND BALANCES EXISTS TO ENSURE THAT ANY OF THE THREE BRANCHES OF GOVERNMENT DO NOT WIELD OVERWHELMING POWER, IT IS CHILLING TO READ SOLICITOR GENERAL THEODORE OLSON'S ARGUMENT AS TO WHY BUSH SHOULD BE GIVEN BROAD AUTHORITIES

SOLICITOR GENERAL THEODORE OLSON

"THE PRESIDENT'S DECISION TO DETAIN PADILLA AS AN ENEMY COMBATANT IN LIEU OF DETAINING HIM IN THE CRIMINAL JUSTICE SYSTEM REFLECTS A SENSITIVE DETERMINATION AT THE CORE OF THE PRESIDENT'S ARTICLE II POWERS CONCERNING THE BEST INTERESTS OF THE NATION IN WARTIME. JUDGES HAVE LITTLE OR NO BACKGROUND IN THE DELICATE BUSINESS OF INTELLIGENCE GATHERING." *

*WARREN RICHEY, "DETAINEE CASES HIT COURT," *CHRISTIAN SCIENCE MONITOR*, JANUARY 23, 2004.

STEP!

OL' CONSTY

OLSON'S ARGUMENT BOILS DOWN TO THIS: BUSH KNOWS WHAT'S BEST FOR AMERICA, AND THE COURTS DON'T.

IF THAT SORT OF SIMPLE-MINDED REASONING IS ACCEPTED BY JUST FIVE OF THE NINE SUPREME COURT JUSTICES WHEN THE LEGITIMACY OF THE PRESIDENT'S DESIGNATION OF CITIZENS AS "ENEMY COMBATANTS" IS ARGUED BEFORE THE HIGH COURT, THE CONSEQUENCES COULD BE DIRE FOR THE FUTURE OF AMERICAN DEMOCRACY, AS THE EXECUTIVE BRANCH UNDER BUSH CLAIMS SOMETHING OF A DIVINE RIGHT TO DO WHATEVER IS DEEMED NECESSARY TO RID THE WORLD OF EVIL.

WHEN THE BUSH ADMINISTRATION PROUDLY ANNOUNCED THE CAPTURE OF AN AL QAEDA CELL IN LACKAWANNA, NEW YORK, THEY PORTRAYED THE SIX MEN INVOLVED AS READY TO KILL AMERICANS ON COMMAND.

THE MEN PLED GUILTY ONE BY ONE, FEARING THAT THEY MIGHT BE THE NEXT "ENEMY COMBATANTS" AND PREFERRED TO FACE A DEFINED AMOUNT OF TIME IN PRISON AS OPPOSED TO THE INDEFINITE DETENTION THEY COULD OTHERWISE FACE.

ONE OF THE MEN WHO RECRUITED THE SIX, AN AMERICAN CITIZEN BY THE NAME OF KAMAL DERWISH, WAS KILLED IN YEMEN BY A MISSILE FIRED FROM A U.S. PREDATOR DRONE. THE GOVERNMENT REFUSES TO TALK ABOUT IT, * SINCE IT'S NOT REALLY A GREAT THING TO MANY AMERICANS TO KNOW THAT AN AMERICAN CITIZEN WAS KILLED BY HIS OWN GOVERNMENT WITHOUT ANY CHARGES HAVING BEEN BROUGHT AGAINST HIM.

WHO NEEDS DUE PROCESS WHEN YOU CAN JUST KILL PEOPLE?

*MICHAEL POWELL, "NO CHOICE BUT GUILTY: LACKAWANNA CASE HIGHLIGHTS LEGAL TILT," *WASHINGTON POST*, JULY 29, 2003, P. A1.

ANOTHER SIGN OF THE BUSH'S CONTEMPT FOR EVEN-HANDED JUSTICE IS THE WAY THAT HIS ADMINISTRATION TREATS THOSE ACCUSED OF CRIMES LINKED, HOWEVER TENUOUSLY, TO TERRORISM.

IN ONE CASE, ATTORNEY GENERAL JOHN ASHCROFT DESIGNATED STEPHEN J. HATFILL A "PERSON OF INTEREST" IN THE ANTHRAX MAILINGS CASE. HATFILL'S IDENTITY WAS DISCOVERED BY THE PRESS, WHICH QUICKLY UNCOVERED INFORMATION RAISING QUESTIONS ABOUT HIS CHARACTER, THOUGH NOT ABOUT THE LIKELIHOOD THAT HE WAS THE ANTHRAX MAILER. *

ALTHOUGH HE IS CHARGED WITH NO CRIME, HATFILL IS THE ONLY PLAINLY VISIBLE INDIVIDUAL THAT THE FBI HAS FOCUSED ON IN THE ANTHRAX MAILINGS CASE. HIS REPUTATION HAS BEEN IRREPARABLY DAMAGED BY THE UNFAVORABLE PRESS COVERAGE BROUGHT ABOUT BY THE FBI'S INVESTIGATION OF HIM.

IF MAKING THE PUBLIC PERCEIVE HATFILL AS AN ALL-AROUND BAD GUY WAS JOHN ASHCROFT'S GOAL, PERHAPS THE PERFECT DISTRACTION FROM THE LACK OF ANY DEFINITIVE CONCLUSIONS AS TO THE IDENTITY OF THE ANTHRAX MAILER, HE HAS BEEN LARGELY SUCCESSFUL.

*JOHN DUDLEY MILLER, "SMALLPOX EXPERT DECRIES TREATMENT OF TWO SCIENTISTS," WWW.THE-SCIENTIST.COM, SEPTEMBER 5, 2003.

WHILE U.S. COMMERCIAL FLIGHTS WERE GROUNDED IN THE DAYS AFTER 9/11, MEMBERS OF THE BIN LADEN FAMILY FROM VARIOUS U.S. CITIES WERE ALLOWED TO FLY TO BOSTON ON A SAUDI-CHARTERED AIRLINER.

THE FBI ONLY QUESTIONED EACH BIN LADEN FAMILY MEMBER BRIEFLY ON THE DAY THAT THEY DEPARTED. *

WHILE IT BECAME COMMON TO HOLD IMMIGRATION VIOLATORS FROM ARABIC NATIONS FOR MONTHS ON END WITHOUT DEPORTING THEM, BUSH WAS KEEN TO MAKE SURE THAT THE BIN LADENS COULD BE ON THEIR WAY BEFORE ANY ANTI-BIN LADEN SENTIMENT MIGHT FIND THEM.

THEN, ONLY A WEEK AFTER THE ATTACKS, THEY WERE ON THEIR WAY TO SAUDI ARABIA. *

NEVER MIND, OF COURSE, THAT BEING RELATED TO SOMEONE SOMETIMES MEANS YOU KNOW CERTAIN THINGS ABOUT THEM, THAT YOU MIGHT HAVE HAD CONTACT WITH THEM.

..BUT A METEOR..

DIDN'T YOU HEAR ME? ONLY **BIN LADENS** CAN FLY TODAY! **BELIEVE IT!**

*BYRON YORK, "THE GREAT ESCAPE," *NATIONAL REVIEW*, SEPTEMBER 30, 2002.

JUST LIKE "WINGS"

BIN LADEN AIRLINES

*IBID.

FBI SPOKESMAN BILL CARTER RESORTED TO REPEATING ONE PHRASE WHEN ASKED WHY THE BIN LADENS WERE ALLOWED TO LEAVE THE COUNTRY WITHOUT BEING MORE FULLY INVESTIGATED.

"WE WERE GIVEN FULL ACCESS TO THE INDIVIDUALS ON THAT PLANE, AND WE WERE SATISFIED THAT WE DID NOT BELIEVE ANY OF THOSE INDIVIDUALS HAD ANYTHING TO DO WITH THE 9/11 PLOTS." *

BILL CARTER

*IBID.

OF COURSE! HOW FOOLISH OF ANYONE TO THINK THAT THE FBI SHOULD HAVE QUESTIONED THE BIN LADENS THOROUGHLY. MAYBE THEY DIDN'T HAVE ANYTHING TO DO WITH THE 9/11 ATTACKS.

BUT THEY WERE RELATED TO THE GUY WHO HAD EVERYTHING TO DO WITH THOSE ATTACKS. THEY MIGHT HAVE BEEN THE MOST VALUABLE SOURCES OF INFORMATION ON OSAMA BIN LADEN AT THE TIME OF THE ATTACKS. THEY ALMOST CERTAINLY WOULD HAVE KNOWN MORE THAN MOST OF THE OVER 1,000 INDIVIDUALS DETAINED ON IMMIGRATION VIOLATIONS.

BUT BUSH DID A FAVOR FOR THE SAUDI GOVERNMENT, AND FOR THE BIN LADEN FAMILY. WHAT DID THE BIN LADENS KNOW? COULD THEY HAVE REVEALED INFORMATION LEADING TO THE EARLY CAPTURE OR DEATH OF OSAMA BIN LADEN?

BECAUSE OF BUSH'S DECISION TO LET THE BIN LADENS RETURN TO SAUDI ARABIA WITHOUT ALLOWING THEM TO BE QUESTIONED THOROUGHLY, AMERICANS WILL NEVER KNOW THE ANSWERS TO THESE AND OTHER QUESTIONS.

BUSH AND HIS ADMINISTRATION PROCLAIM THE
WONDROUS MAJESTY OF THEIR ANTI-TERRORISM
PROGRAMS, AND SAY THAT THEY'RE DEDICATED TO
SECURING AMERICA FROM TERRORISTS.

BUT AS IS OFTEN THE CASE, ACTIONS
SPEAK LOUDER THAN WORDS. BUSH'S
HOMELAND SECURITY POLICY SEEMS
TO BE TO MAKE SUPERFICIAL CHANGES
THAT MAKE AMERICANS FEEL SAFER.
HOWEVER, THE APPEARANCE OF SAFETY
IS NOT THE SAME AS ACTUAL SAFETY.

DESPITE HIS REPEATED DEDICATION TO THE DEFENSE
OF AMERICA FROM FURTHER TERRORIST ATTACKS, BUSH
REJECTED ANY HOMELAND SECURITY SPENDING BEYOND
AN ARBITRARY $20 BILLION CAP THAT HE PROPOSED IN
LATE 2001, AND THREATENED TO VETO ANY BILL THAT
AUTHORIZED MORE MONEY. *

BUSH'S INSISTENCE ON FISCAL
RESPONSIBILITY WHEN IT COMES TO
HOMELAND SECURITY IS ESPECIALLY
STRIKING WHEN COMPARED TO HIS
OWN LACK OF ANY DISCIPLINE WHEN
IT COMES TO CUTTING TAXES FOR
THE WEALTHY.

*JONATHAN CHAIT, "THE 9/10 PRESIDENT," *THE NEW REPUBLIC*, MARCH 10, 2003.

INSTEAD OF REGULATING INDUSTRIES WHICH COULD BE TARGETED BY TERRORISTS, BUSH LEAVES IT TO THE BUSINESSES TO CHOOSE WHETHER THEY WILL TAKE STEPS TO PREVENT FUTURE TERRORIST ATTACKS. IN DOING SO, BUSH IGNORES BOTH THE ECONOMIC AND PSYCHOLOGICAL IMPACT THAT A TERRORIST ATTACK ANYWHERE IN THE UNITED STATES WOULD HAVE ON THE NATION AS A WHOLE. *

NOW **THAT'S** SELF-REGULATIN' INDUSTRY AT IT'S **BEST!**

DEADLY CHEMICALS

*JONATHAN CHAIT, "THE 9/10 PRESIDENT," *THE NEW REPUBLIC*, MARCH 10, 2003.

TO SAFEGUARD NUCLEAR FACILITIES IN THE UNITED STATES, IN 2002 BUSH APPROVED FUNDING EQUAL TO ONLY 7 PERCENT OF THE AMOUNT REQUESTED BY HIS OWN ADMINISTRATION'S ENERGY SECRETARY. *

50 POINTS

*IBID.

BUT DOESN'T THE LACK OF ANOTHER TERRORIST ATTACK MEAN THAT THE BUSH ADMINISTRATION IS DOING SOMETHING RIGHT?

NOT IF YOU CONSIDER THAT TWO YEARS AFTER 9/11, A 20-YEAR OLD COULD SNEAK WEAPONS ONTO A PLANE, EVEN WITH THE INCREASED AIRPORT SECURITY. *

NOTSOSAFE AIRLINES

HMMM..

*CURT ANDERSON, "FBI: PLANE-SECURITY PERPETRATOR LOCATED," ASSOCIATED PRESS, OCTOBER 17, 2003.

THEN THERE'S A REPORT FROM THE TERRORISM-FOCUSED GILMORE COMMISSION, LED BY REPUBLICAN JAMES GILMORE, THE FORMER GOVERNOR OF VERMONT, THAT QUESTIONED THE BUSH ADMINISTRATION'S PROGRESS IN DEVELOPING A COMPREHENSIVE ANTI-TERROR STRATEGY. *

I SAID WE'LL GET THE EVIL DOERS.. AIN'T THAT **ENOUGH?**

*DEBORAH CHARLES, "PANEL SEES SLOWDOWN IN U.S. FIGHT AGAINST TERROR," REUTERS, DECEMBER 15, 2003.

THOUGH ONE WOULD EXPECT THAT SECURITY AT U.S. PORTS WOULD HAVE IMPROVED SINCE 9/11, VERY LITTLE HAS CHANGED. IN HIS 2003 AND 2004 BUDGETS, BUSH ALLOTTED NOTHING TO ENHANCE PORT SECURITY. *

*MICHAEL HIRSH, "HOW MUCH SAFER ARE WE?", *NEWSWEEK*, SEPTEMBER 15, 2003, P. 46.

AS OF SEPTEMBER 2003, THE BUSH ADMINISTRATION HAD FAILED TO SCREEN AS MANY AS 20,000 AIRPORT WORKERS, * RAISING QUESTIONS ABOUT THE VULNERABILITY OF AIRPORTS AND PLANES TO INFILTRATION BY TERRORISTS.

EMPLOYEE ENTRANCE

TIK TIK TIK TIK

*IBID.

JUST HOW SERIOUS IS GEORGE W. BUSH ABOUT MAKING AMERICA SAFER AFTER SEPTEMBER 11? MEASURED IN THE NUMBER OF DAYS HE'S TAKEN VACATION, HE'S ULTRA-SERIOUS!

I'M ULTRA SERIOUS!!!

BY AUGUST OF 2003, BUSH HAD SPENT A FULL 27 PERCENT OF HIS PRESIDENCY AT HIS RANCH IN CRAWFORD, TEXAS, CAMP DAVID, OR KENNEBUNKPORT, MAINE. *

I'M JUST LETTING TIME TAKE ITS COURSE IN SMOKING OSAMA BIN LADEN OUT OF HIS HOLE!

*MIKE ALLEN, "BUSH ACES PHYSICAL, BEGINS A MONTH AT RANCH," *WASHINGTON POST*, AUGUST 3, 2003, P. A05.

ADD IN THE TIME THAT BUSH SPENDS CAMPAIGNING FOR HIMSELF AND REPUBLICAN CANDIDATES THROUGHOUT THE COUNTRY, AND YOU MIGHT GET THE FEELING THAT BUSH HAS ACTUALLY SPENT MORE TIME ON POLITICS THAN ON IMPORTANT ISSUES LIKE TERRORISM.

BY THE BEGINNING OF APRIL 2004, BUSH HAD RAISED A RECORD $182 MILLION FOR HIS 2004 REELECTION CAMPAIGN. *

IF I DIDN'T SPEND ALL THAT TIME RAISING MONEY FOR MY REELECTION, THEN I WOULDN'T BE REELECTED, AND AMERICA WOULD NO LONGER BE SAFE! BECAUSE FOR SOME REASON, PEOPLE EQUATE ME WITH SAFETY!

*ADAM ENTOUS, "BUSH CAMPAIGN TOPS GOAL OF RECORD $170 MILLION," REUTERS, APRIL 2, 2004.

SO, AFTER 250 DAYS OF VACATION BY AUGUST OF 2003, * AND COUNTLESS FUNDRAISING EVENTS UP THROUGH 2004, IS AMERICA SAFER?

THOUGH HE DOESN'T KNOW, HE SURE AS HELL SAYS IT IS!

MY POLICY OF UNRELENTING LONG VACATIONS IS WORKING TO UNDERMINE TERRORISM BY MAKING THE TERRORISTS WONDER WHERE THE HELL THE PRESIDENT OF THE UNITED STATES IS WHEN HE SHOULD BE DOING MORE THAN JUST SAYING THAT HE'S TOUGH ON TERROR!

*MIKE ALLEN, "BUSH ACES PHYSICAL, BEGINS A MONTH AT RANCH," *WASHINGTON POST*, AUGUST 3, 2003, P. A05.

IN MAY 2000, THE BOSTON GLOBE RAN A PIECE ABOUT HOW GEORGE W. BUSH HAD SKIPPED AT LEAST 12 MONTHS OF SERVICE IN THE TEXAS AIR NATIONAL GUARD. *

*WALTER V. ROBINSON, "ONE-YEAR GAP IN BUSH'S NATIONAL GUARD DUTY," *BOSTON GLOBE*, MAY 23, 2000.

AT FIRST THE BUSH CAMP SIMPLY DENIED THE AWOL (AWAY WITHOUT LEAVE) ACCUSATIONS, FAILING TO DISPROVE THE STORIES WITH ANY DOCUMENTARY EVIDENCE.

I DON'T KNOW ANYBODY WITH THE NAME AWOL.

LATER, A SINGLE TORN DOCUMENT WAS PRESENTED BY BUSH'S CAMPAIGN, WHICH THEY CLAIMED WAS PROOF THAT BUSH HAD MET HIS OBLIGATIONS TO THE AIR NATIONAL GUARD. HOWEVER, IT WAS IMPOSSIBLE TO KNOW IF IT REFERRED TO GEORGE W. BUSH, AS THE SOCIAL SECURITY NUMBER HAD BEEN REDACTED, AND THE ONLY PART OF THE NAME ON THE SHEET WHICH HADN'T BEEN TORN OFF WAS THE LETTER W. *

W... MORE MYSTERIOUS THAN X!

*ERIC BOEHLERT, "BUSH'S MISSING YEAR," SALON.COM, FEBRUARY 5, 2004.

IN 1968, UPON GRADUATING FROM YALE, GEORGE W. BUSH APPLIED FOR A PILOT POSITION WITH THE TEXAS AIR NATIONAL GUARD TO AVOID BEING DRAFTED INTO SERVICE TO FIGHT IN VIETNAM. HE WAS ACCEPTED, DESPITE A WAITING LIST OF 500 OTHER CANDIDATES. *

EXCUSE ME! FUTURE PRESIDENT COMING THROUGH!

*WALTER V. ROBINSON, "ONE-YEAR GAP IN BUSH'S NATIONAL GUARD DUTY," *BOSTON GLOBE*, MAY 23, 2000.

WAS BUSH TREATED FAVORABLY AT THE EXPENSE OF THOSE ON THE WAITING LIST? BOTH GEORGE W. AND HIS FATHER, WHO WAS AT THE TIME A HOUSTON CONGRESSMAN, HAVE REPEATEDLY CLAIMED THAT THEY DID NOT SEEK PREFERENTIAL TREATMENT.

IN 1999, HOWEVER, IT BECOME CLEAR THAT SID ADGER, A CLOSE FRIEND OF THE BUSHES, CONTACTED BEN BARNES, THEN SPEAKER OF THE TEXAS HOUSE, ASKING FOR HELP IN GETTING GEORGE W. BUSH INTO THE GUARD. BARNES CONTACTED GENERAL JAMES ROSE, COMMANDER OF THE TEXAS GUARD AT THE TIME, AND APPARENTLY SUCCEEDED IN INFLUENCING THE GENERAL TO KNOCK BUSH TO THE TOP OF THE CANDIDATE WAITING LIST. *

SEEKIN' AIN'T THE SAME AS GETTIN'!

*SCOTT BALDAUF, "COMMANDER IN CHIEF: VETERANS NEED NOT APPLY," *CHRISTIAN SCIENCE MONITOR*, OCTOBER 20, 1999.

WHO ELSE WAS ACCEPTED TO THE UNIT BUSH FOUND HIMSELF IN?

THE SON OF A FORMER U.S. SENATOR, THE SON OF A FORMER TEXAS GOVERNOR, AND SEVERAL MEMBERS OF THE DALLAS COWBOYS FOOTBALL TEAM * WERE SOME OF THE MOST BLATANT EXAMPLES, INDICATING THAT POLITICAL AND SOCIAL INFLUENCES WERE AT WORK BEHIND THE ACCEPTANCE OF AT LEAST SOME INDIVIDUALS INTO THE TEXAS AIR NATIONAL GUARD.

*ANDREW GUMBEL, "PROFILE: GEORGE W. BUSH - THIS CHARMED MAN," *INDEPENDENT* (UK), NOVEMBER 4, 2000.

SO, BUSH WAS QUICKLY ACCEPTED TO THE AIR NATIONAL GUARD, RECEIVING PREFERENTIAL TREATMENT FROM THE START. HE WAS COMMISSIONED AS A SECOND LIEUTENANT EVEN BEFORE ATTENDING BASIC TRAINING. *

FFICERS CLUB

WAY TO HAVE A LAST NAME, BUDDY!

*WALTER V. ROBINSON, "ONE-YEAR GAP IN BUSH'S NATIONAL GUARD DUTY," *BOSTON GLOBE*, MAY 23, 2000.

BUSH WAS ACCEPTED FOR FLIGHT TRAINING, WITH A SCORE OF ONLY 25 PERCENT ON HIS PILOT APTITUDE TEST - THE LOWEST POSSIBLE PASSING SCORE. *

*WALTER V. ROBINSON, "ONE-YEAR GAP IN BUSH'S NATIONAL GUARD DUTY," *BOSTON GLOBE*, MAY 23, 2000.

BUSH TRAINED TO FLY FROM NOVEMBER 1968 TO JUNE 1970. HE THEN JOINED THE 111TH FIGHTER-INTERCEPTOR SQUADRON AT ELLINGTON FIELD IN HOUSTON, TEXAS. THERE HE FLEW AN F-102 FIGHTER JET UNTIL APRIL 1972. IN HIS BIOGRAPHY, A CHARGE TO KEEP, HOWEVER, BUSH WROTE, "I CONTINUED FLYING WITH MY UNIT FOR THE NEXT SEVERAL YEARS." *

22 MONTHS EQUALS SEVERAL YEARS? SOUNDS A BIT FUZZY...

I WIN!

SEVERAL!

NOW WHO'S USING FUZZY MATH?

GORE CAN SPELL

*IBID.

ACTUALLY, BUSH LEFT FOR ALABAMA IN MAY 1972 TO WORK WITH WINTON BLOUNT'S U.S. SENATE CAMPAIGN. ONE OF HIS SUPERIORS IN HOUSTON, COLONEL RUFUS MARTIN, TRIED TO GET BUSH A JOB WITH THE 9921ST AIR RESERVE SQUADRON IN MONTGOMERY, A SQUADRON REQUIRING "THE LEAST PARTICIPATION OF ANY TYPE OF UNIT." *

STOP RUSTLING THOSE PAPERS! CAN'T YOU SEE IT'S NAP TIME?

*"DEMOCRATS ATTACK BUSH'S MILITARY SERVICE," *FLORIDA TIMES UNION*, NOVEMBER 4, 2000.

BUSH LEFT FOR ALABAMA AND ATTEMPTED TO JOIN THE 9921ST, BUT HIS APPLICATION TO THE UNIT WAS REJECTED BY A HIGHER OFFICE OF THE GUARD. APPARENTLY, BUSH DIDN'T SEEK TO RECTIFY THE MATTER, AS MONTHS WENT BY WITHOUT A REQUEST TO JOIN ANOTHER UNIT.*

IN JULY 1972 BUSH FAILED TO SHOW UP FOR A REQUIRED MEDICAL EXAM, WHICH WOULD HAVE INCLUDED A DRUG TEST.*

DID HE HAVE SOMETHING TO HIDE, OR WAS IT JUST HIS WAY OF SHIRKING THE RESPONSIBILITIES AND AVOIDING THE RISKS OF REMAINING A PILOT?

HE WANTS TO JOIN THAT UNIT AFTER ALL HIS FLIGHT TRAINING? DENIED!

*WALTER V. ROBINSON, "ONE-YEAR GAP IN BUSH'S NATIONAL GUARD DUTY," *BOSTON GLOBE*, MAY 23, 2000.

*TOM RHODES, "BUSH FLIES INTO AN AIR FORCE COCAINE CLOUD," *SUNDAY TIMES OF LONDON*, JUNE 18, 2000.

REGARDLESS OF HIS REASONING, BUSH WAS GROUNDED ON AUGUST 1, 1972, FOR MISSING HIS ANNUAL PHYSICAL. HE COULD HAVE REGAINED HIS FORMER FLYING STATUS AT A LATER DATE BY SUBMITTING TO A PHYSICAL, BUT CHOSE NOT TO. *

BUSH HAS CLAIMED THAT ONE OF THE REASONS HE CHOSE NOT TO TAKE HIS PHYSICAL WAS THAT THE F-102S WHICH HE FLEW WERE OBSOLETE AND NO LONGER BEING FLOWN. HOWEVER, THE BOSTON GLOBE POINTED OUT THAT "HIS UNIT'S RECORDS SHOW THAT GUARD PILOTS LOGGED THOUSANDS OF HOURS IN THE F-102 IN 1973." *

*"DEMOCRATS ATTACK BUSH'S MILITARY SERVICE," *FLORIDA TIMES UNION*, NOVEMBER 4, 2000.

*WALTER V. ROBINSON, "ONE-YEAR GAP IN BUSH'S NATIONAL GUARD DUTY," *BOSTON GLOBE*, MAY 23, 2000.

IN SEPTEMBER 1972, BUSH WAS GRANTED PERMISSION TO SERVE FOR THREE MONTHS WITH THE 187TH TACTICAL RECON GROUP IN MONTGOMERY, ALABAMA. BUT IT APPEARS THAT BUSH NEVER REPORTED FOR DUTY THERE. *

BUSH SHOULD BE HERE

*WALTER V. ROBINSON, "ONE-YEAR GAP IN BUSH'S NATIONAL GUARD DUTY," *BOSTON GLOBE*, MAY 23, 2000.

NEITHER GENERAL WILLIAM TURNIPSEED, COMMANDER OF THE 187TH AT THE TIME, NOR HIS ADMINISTRATIVE OFFICER KENNETH K. LOTT, COULD RECALL BUSH REPORTING FOR DUTY.

"HAD HE REPORTED IN, I WOULD HAVE HAD SOME RECALL, AND I DO NOT. I HAD BEEN IN TEXAS, DONE MY FLIGHT TRAINING THERE. IF WE HAD A FIRST LIEUTENANT FROM TEXAS, I WOULD HAVE REMEMBERED." *

GEN. WILLIAM TURNIPSEED

*QUOTED IN IBID.

WHAT EVIDENCE DID BUSH PRESENT THAT HE WORKED WITH THE GUARD IN ALABAMA?

HIS FRIENDS FROM THE BLOUNT CAMPAIGN SAID THAT THEY RECALLED BUSH TELLING THEM HE WAS GOING TO GUARD DUTY IN MONTGOMERY. *

I HEARD FROM THAT GUY THAT HE SAW BUSH TELL SOMEONE THAT HE WAS GOING TO TELL SOMEONE ELSE THAT HE WAS GOING!

*"DEMOCRATS ATTACK BUSH'S MILITARY RECORD," *FLORIDA TIMES UNION*, NOVEMBER 4, 2000.

DID BUSH REPORT FOR DUTY IN ALABAMA AT ALL? DURING THE 2000 PRESIDENTIAL CAMPAIGN, THERE WAS NO EVIDENCE THAT HE DID. EVEN RETIRED COLONEL ALBERT LLOYD JR., WHO IN 1999, AT THE REQUEST OF THE BUSH CAMPAIGN SCOURED BUSH'S GUARD RECORDS, FAILED TO FIND ANY EVIDENCE THAT BUSH HAD SERVED IN ALABAMA.

"WE CANNOT FIND THE RECORDS TO SHOW THAT HE FULFILLED THE REQUIREMENTS IN ALABAMA."*

*QUOTED IN WALTER V. ROBINSON, "ONE-YEAR GAP IN BUSH'S NATIONAL GUARD DUTY," *BOSTON GLOBE*, MAY 23, 2000.

DESPITE THE OFFERING BY A GROUP OF ALABAMAN VIETNAM VETERANS OF A $3,500 REWARD IN 2000 TO ANYONE WHO COULD PROVE THAT BUSH SERVED WITH THE GUARD IN ALABAMA, NO ONE CAME FORWARD TO CLAIM THE PRIZE. *

SO, BUSH WAS AWOL FOR THE SIX MONTHS THAT HE WAS IN ALABAMA - FROM MAY 1972 TO NOVEMBER 1972. BUT IT DIDN'T APPEAR TO END THERE.

EVEN AFTER HE RETURNED TO HOUSTON IN DECEMBER 1972, THERE WAS NO EVIDENCE THAT BUSH REPORTED FOR DUTY UNTIL MONTHS LATER.

MY TIME'S TOO VALUABLE TO DO STUFF THAT I'M SUPPOSED TO DO!

So LONELY..

FREE MONEY $$$$

WALTER V. ROBINSON, "QUESTIONS REMAIN ABOUT BUSH'S SERVICE AS GUARD PILOT," *BOSTON GLOBE*, OCTOBER 31, 2000.

TWO OF BUSH'S SUPERVISORS AT ELLINGTON WROTE IN AN ANNUAL EFFICIENCY REPORT ON MAY 2, 1973, THE FOLLOWING:

"LT. BUSH HAS NOT BEEN OBSERVED AT THIS UNIT DURING THE PERIOD OF REPORT. A CIVILIAN OCCUPATION MADE IT NECESSARY FOR HIM TO MOVE TO MONTGOMERY, ALABAMA. HE CLEARED THIS BASE ON 15 MAY 1972 AND HAS BEEN PERFORMING EQUIVALENT TRAINING IN A NON-FLYING STATUS WITH THE 187 TAC RECON GP, DANELLY ANG BASE, ALABAMA." *

WHERE'S DUBYA?

SO BUSH'S SUPERVISORS BELIEVED BUSH WAS STILL IN ALABAMA EVEN AFTER HE'D RETURNED TO HOUSTON. PROBABLY NOT THE SORT OF MISTAKE THEY'D MAKE IF BUSH HAD ACTUALLY REPORTED FOR DUTY.

*QUOTED IN WALTER V. ROBINSON, "ONE-YEAR GAP IN BUSH'S NATIONAL GUARD DUTY," *BOSTON GLOBE*, MAY 23, 2000.

AFTER THE ISSUE HAD LITTLE IMPACT THROUGHOUT THE SUMMER OF 2000, IT RETURNED SHORTLY BEFORE ELECTION DAY. THE BOSTON GLOBE RAN ANOTHER STORY, THIS TIME ASSERTING THAT BUSH MAY HAVE FAILED TO REPORT FOR DUTY IN HOUSTON AT ALL AFTER RETURNING FROM ALABAMA IN LATE 1972, RIGHT UP THROUGH SEPTEMBER 1973, WHEN HE WENT TO HARVARD BUSINESS SCHOOL. *

HARVARD
BUSINESS
SCHOOL

I GUESS ALL THAT AWOL-ING PAID OFF!

*WALTER V. ROBINSON, "QUESTIONS REMAIN ON BUSH'S SERVICE AS GUARD PILOT," *BOSTON GLOBE*, OCTOBER 31, 2000.

THERE ARE NO WITNESSES WHO CLAIM TO HAVE SEEN BUSH SERVING AT ELLINGTON IN HOUSTON FROM DECEMBER 1972 TO THE TIME HE WAS DISCHARGED IN SEPTEMBER 1973, SOMETHING EVEN BUSH'S CAMPAIGN DID NOT DISPUTE.*

I DON'T REMEMBER SEEING HIM IN '73.

ART SCHOOL
"ANY BOOB CAN DRAW"

*WALTER V. ROBINSON, "QUESTIONS REMAIN ON BUSH'S SERVICE AS GUARD PILOT," *BOSTON GLOBE*, OCTOBER 31, 2000.

IF BUSH SKIPPED HIS GUARD DUTY FROM MAY 1972 TO SEPTEMBER 1973, HOW COULD HE RECEIVE AN HONORABLE DISCHARGE EIGHT MONTHS BEFORE HIS OBLIGATION TO THE GUARD WAS FULFILLED?

ACCORDING TO MILITARY LAW ATTORNEY GRANT LATTIN:

"IF GEORGE BUSH JR. IS IN YOUR UNIT, YOU'RE GOING TO BEND OVER BACKWARD NOT TO OFFEND THAT FAMILY. IT ALL COMES DOWN TO WHO YOU KNOW." *

HE'S MUCH HANDSOMER THAN THIS.

*QUOTED IN ERIC BOEHLERT, "BUSH'S MISSING YEAR," SALON.COM, FEBRUARY 5, 2004.

BUSH'S TIME WITH THE TEXAS AIR NATIONAL GUARD BEGAN AND ENDED FAVORABLY FOR HIM. HE WAS TREATED AS THOUGH HE'D FULFILLED HIS DUTY, EVEN AFTER HE MAY HAVE FAILED TO REPORT FOR DUTY FOR NEARLY A YEAR AND A HALF.

YOUNG HAIRDO

NO COMMENT. OH, ALL RIGHT, HE'S HANDSOMER TOO.

VIP

IN 1992, THEN-PRESIDENT GEORGE H.W. BUSH, GEORGE W.'S FATHER, DEMANDED THAT DEMOCRATIC PRESIDENTIAL CANDIDATE BILL CLINTON RELEASE HIS RECORDS PERTAINING TO VIETNAM, * AND IT WAS SHOWN THAT CLINTON HAD DODGED THE DRAFT.

SHOULDN'T GEORGE W. BUSH BE HELD TO THE SAME STANDARDS THAT HIS FATHER SET FOR CANDIDATE CLINTON IN 1992? PERHAPS HE PREFERS THE PERCEPTION THAT HE HAS SOMETHING TO HIDE TO WHAT THE RECORDS WOULD ACTUALLY SHOW.

> I DID NOT HAVE SEXUAL RELATIONS WITH THE DRAFT!

*ERIC BOEHLERT, "BUSH'S MISSING YEAR," SALON.COM, FEBRUARY 4, 2004.

IN 2000, WHEN BUSH CAMPAIGN SPOKESMAN DAN BARTLETT WAS TOLD BY WALTER V. ROBINSON OF THE BOSTON GLOBE OF HOW ONE VIETNAM VETERAN HAD QUESTIONED BUSH'S CHARACTER BASED ON THE AWOL ACCUSATIONS, BARTLETT AVOIDED THE ACTUAL ISSUE ENTIRELY IN HIS RESPONSE.

> "...YOU MEAN TO TELL ME HE HAS NO PROBLEM WITH BILL CLINTON'S AVOIDANCE OF MILITARY SERVICE?" *

WAY TO CHANGE THE TONE, MR. BARTLETT!

*QUOTED IN WALTER V. ROBINSON, "QUESTIONS REMAIN ON BUSH'S SERVICE AS GUARD PILOT," BOSTON GLOBE, OCTOBER 31, 2000.

AS MENTIONED, THE ISSUE DIDN'T SEEM TO RESONATE IN THE 2000 PRESIDENTIAL CAMPAIGN, BUT IT RESURFACED IN THE 2004 CAMPAIGN, AND FOR A TIME, THE WHITE HOUSE WAS PLAYING DEFENSE TO MAKE THE ISSUE GO AWAY, OR AT LEAST SPIN IT SO THAT IT WOULD LOOK LIKE IT HAD BEEN DEALT WITH, AND THAT THE WHOLE ISSUE WAS A POLITICAL ONE, AND NOT ONE OF WHETHER PRESIDENT BUSH IS A CHRONIC LIAR.

> I'M A REAL DUBYA!

WOOOOOOP!

AT A RALLY FOR DEMOCRATIC PRESIDENTIAL CANDIDATE WESLEY CLARK IN JANUARY 2004, DOCUMENTARY FILMMAKER MICHAEL MOORE BROUGHT UP BUSH'S MILITARY SERVICE, OR LACK OF IT.

> "I WANT TO SEE THAT DEBATE: THE GENERAL VERSUS THE DESERTER!"

AT A DEMOCRATIC PRESIDENTIAL DEBATE NOT LONG THEREAFTER, PETER JENNINGS, ONE OF THE SO-CALLED MODERATORS OF THE DEBATE, TOOK OFFENSE AT MOORE'S REMARKS, DEMANDING AN EXPLANATION AS TO HOW CLARK COULD ALLOW MOORE TO SPEAK OUT LIKE THAT AGAINST A GUY AS GREAT AS PRESIDENT BUSH.

"THAT'S A RECKLESS CHARGE NOT SUPPORTED BY THE FACTS. AND I WAS CURIOUS TO KNOW WHY YOU DIDN'T CONTRADICT HIM, AND WHETHER OR NOT YOU THINK IT WOULD'VE BEEN A BETTER EXAMPLE OF ETHICAL BEHAVIOR TO HAVE DONE SO." *

*DEMOCRATIC PRESIDENTIAL CANDIDATE DEBATE, JANUARY 22, 2004.

UH OH! WESLEY CLARK WAS BEING UNETHICAL BY NOT DISTANCING HIMSELF FROM A SUPPORTER'S REMARK! BUT IT WASN'T AS IF CLARK HAD ACTUALLY ENDORSED MOORE'S OPINION JUST BY LETTING HIM SPEAK. HIS RESPONSE TO JENNINGS WAS STRAIGHTFORWARD ENOUGH.

"WELL, I THINK MICHAEL MOORE HAS THE RIGHT TO SAY WHATEVER HE FEELS ABOUT THIS." *

HISS!

*IBID.

BUT THIS DIDN'T SATISFY JENNINGS. WITH HIS WELL-KNOWN PSYCHIC PROWESS, JENNINGS WAS READING CLARK'S MIND, AND CONTINUED HIS CRITICISM OF GENERAL CLARK.

"...[S]INCE THIS QUESTION AND ANSWER IN WHICH YOU AND MR. MOORE WAS INVOLVED IN, YOU'VE HAD A CHANCE TO LOOK AT THE FACTS. DO YOU STILL FEEL COMFORTABLE WITH THE FACT THAT SOMEONE SHOULD BE STANDING UP IN YOUR PRESENCE AND CALLING THE PRESIDENT OF THE UNITED STATES A DESERTER?" *

SEE THE
JENNINGS
SUPER WONDERFUL
MENTALIST

*IBID.

CLARK'S RESPONSE PUT AN END TO JENNINGS'S INSISTENCE THAT CLARK IS RESPONSIBLE FOR WHAT MOORE SAID, AND OF THE RESPONSIBILITY WE ALL HAVE TO NEVER ALLOW PRESIDENT BUSH TO BE BESMIRCHED BY ANYONE.

"TO BE HONEST WITH YOU, I DID NOT LOOK AT THE FACTS, PETER. YOU KNOW, THAT'S MICHAEL MOORE'S OPINION. HE'S ENTITLED TO SAY THAT. I'VE SEEN... HE'S NOT THE ONLY PERSON WHO'S SAID THAT." *

WESLEY CLARK

BUT IF JENNINGS'S INTENT WAS TO MAKE THE ISSUE OF BUSH'S SERVICE IN THE TEXAS AIR NATIONAL GUARD GO AWAY, IT HAD THE OPPOSITE EFFECT. THE ISSUE OF BUSH'S GUARD DUTY WAS BACK FOR 2004.

*IBID.

WHEN TIM RUSSERT WENT TO THE WHITE HOUSE FOR A ONE-ON-ONE INTERVIEW WITH GEORGE W. BUSH ON FEBRUARY 8, 2004, HE RAISED THE AWOL ISSUE.

"HOW DO YOU RESPOND [TO CHARGES THAT YOU WERE AWOL IN ALABAMA]?"*

PRESIDENT BUSH RESPONDED IN A BLATANTLY MANIPULATIVE WAY.

"POLITICAL SEASON IS HERE. I WAS -- I SERVED IN THE NATIONAL GUARD. I FLEW F-102 AIRCRAFT. I GOT AN HONORABLE DISCHARGE."*

TIM RUSSERT

*MEET THE PRESS, FEBRUARY 8, 2004.

BUSH HAD MORE TO SAY, STEERING HIS REPLY TO HIS OWN POLITICAL ENDS, STILL AVOIDING ANY TALK OF HIS TIME AWOL FROM THE GUARD.

"I WOULD BE CAREFUL NOT TO DENIGRATE THE GUARD. IT'S FINE TO GO AFTER ME, WHICH I EXPECT THE OTHER SIDE WILL DO. I WOULDN'T DENIGRATE THE GUARD, THOUGH."*

MEET THE LI'L PRESS

WOW! SO ALL THIS TIME, PEOPLE HADN'T BEEN TALKING ABOUT BUSH'S RECORD, THEY'D JUST BEEN INSULTING THE GUARD! OF COURSE. A MOMENT'S GLANCE AT ANY OF THE AWOL ACCUSATIONS SAYS NOTHING TO SMEAR THE GUARD'S PRESTIGE. IT WAS ALL ABOUT BUSH AND WHAT HE HAD OR HAD NOT DONE IN THE GUARD IN ALABAMA AND TEXAS. BUT BUSH JUST COULDN'T RESIST REDEFINING THE ARGUMENT TO MAKE IT LOOK LIKE PEOPLE WEREN'T JUST ATTACKING HIM, BUT WERE ATTACKING THE GUARD.

IF BUSH HAS SO MUCH RESPECT FOR THE GUARD, IT BEGS THE QUESTION: WHY WAS HE AWOL?

*IBID.

THERE'S ANOTHER BIT OF THE RUSSERT INTERVIEW OF BUSH WHICH CANNOT GO UNMENTIONED.

"WOULD YOU AUTHORIZE THE RELEASE OF EVERYTHING [IN YOUR MILITARY RECORDS] TO SETTLE THIS?" *

"YES, ABSOLUTELY. WE DID SO IN 2000, BY THE WAY." *

THERE IT WAS. BUSH TOLD AN EXTRAORDINARY LIE. THE ONLY DOCUMENTS RELEASED IN 2000 WERE THOSE RELEASED UNDER THE FREEDOM OF INFORMATION ACT. BUSH NEVER RELEASED ANY OF HIS PRIVATE MILITARY FILES. YET HERE HE WAS ON MEET THE PRESS TELLING THE AMERICAN PEOPLE THAT HE DID RELEASE HIS RECORDS WHEN IT'S A PLAIN FACT THAT HE DID NOT.

*MEET THE PRESS, FEBRUARY 8, 2004.

*IBID.

THE DAY AFTER BUSH LIED ON MEET THE PRESS, SOME OF HIS PAYROLL RECORDS SURFACED, SHOWING THAT HE HAD BEEN PAID FOR SOME DAYS IN LATE 1972 AND EARLY 1973.

IT BECAME CLEAR RATHER QUICKLY, HOWEVER, THAT THESE RECORDS DIDN'T PROVE THAT BUSH HAD SERVED ON THE DAYS LISTED, BUT SIMPLY THAT HE HAD BEEN PAID. EVEN WHITE HOUSE OFFICIALS WOULDN'T CLAIM THAT THE NEW RECORDS PROVED THAT BUSH HAD SHOWN UP ON THE DAYS FOR WHICH HE WAS PAID. *

FORMER NATIONAL GUARDS-MAN RICHARD COHEN OF THE WASHINGTON POST WROTE OF HOW HE AVOIDED NEARLY TWO YEARS WORTH OF DUTY AND STILL GOT PAID, JUST A FEW YEARS BEFORE BUSH'S TIME IN THE GUARD, * MAKING IT PLAIN THAT INDICATION OF PAYMENT WAS NOT INDICATION OF SERVICE.

IF I MADE MONEY, I MUST HAVE DONE SOMETHING!

*SCOTT LINDLAW, "WHITE HOUSE RELEASES BUSH MILITARY RECORD," ASSOCIATED PRESS, FEBRUARY 10, 2004.

*RICHARD COHEN, "FROM GUARDSMAN...", WASHINGTON POST, FEBRUARY 10, 2004.

WHITE HOUSE PRESS SECRETARY SCOTT MCCLELLAN, WHO AT TIMES COULD EASILY BE MISTAKEN FOR A BROKEN RECORD PLAYER, DIDN'T EXACTLY CLEAR THINGS UP AT THE FEBRUARY 11, 2004, WHITE HOUSE PRESS BRIEFING.

"YOU KEEP SAYING [BUSH] SERVED -- HE FULFILLED HIS DUTY, HE MET HIS REQUIREMENTS. YOU'RE NOT SAYING, HE DRILLED, HE SHOWED UP, HE ATTENDED. IS THAT INTENTIONAL?"

"NO, HE RECALLS PERFORMING HIS DUTIES, BOTH IN ALABAMA AND TEXAS."

SCOTT MCCLELLAN

BUT THE PAYROLL DOCUMENTS DIDN'T PROVE IT, AND THE PRESIDENT'S RECOLLECTION OF WHAT HE DID OR DIDN'T DO WAS NOT OBJECTIVE EVIDENCE. QUESTIONS WERE NOT BEING ANSWERED. A REPORTER INQUIRED AS TO WHAT DUTIES BUSH PERFORMED WITH HIS ALABAMA GUARD UNIT.

"DEFINE THAT."

"WELL, AGAIN, I DON'T HAVE A MINUTE-BY-MINUTE BREAKDOWN OF EVERY SINGLE THING HE DID THROUGHOUT THAT TIME PERIOD."

"YOU KEEP SAYING THE WORD, 'SERVE.' DEFINE 'SERVE.'"

"HE MET -- HE SERVED BOTH IN ALABAMA, AND HE SERVED BOTH IN TEXAS."

WHAT HAD BUSH DONE IN ALABAMA? HE MET. HE SERVED. WHAT DOES "SERVE" MEAN? HE MET. HE SERVED. MCCLELLAN WAS REFUSING TO OFFER ANY DETAILS OF WHAT BUSH ACTUALLY DID WHEN HE WAS WITH THE AIR NATIONAL GUARD IN BOTH ALABAMA AND TEXAS. AND STILL THE WHITE HOUSE ACTED SHOCKED THAT THE STORY WOULDN'T DIE.

MAP of "AREA"

BUSH WAS

HERE

AND SO THE PRESS CONFERENCE WENT ON, WITH MCCLELLAN REPEATING VARIATIONS OF THE PHRASES "THE PRESIDENT FULFILLED HIS DUTIES," "THE PRESIDENT SERVED," "THE PRESIDENT RECALLS SERVING," AND "THE PRESIDENT MET HIS REQUIREMENTS," MORE THAN 50 TIMES IN LESS THAN 45 MINUTES.

FULFILLED DUTIES... HONORABLY DISCHARGED... MET REQUIREMENTS...

THE NEXT DAY, THE WHITE HOUSE WAS SHOWING ITS IMMENSE DISPLEASURE AT THE PERSISTENCE OF THE ISSUE OF BUSH'S GUARD SERVICE.

"I THINK WHAT YOU'RE SEEING NOW IS THAT SOME ARE NOT INTERESTED IN THE FACTS. SOME ARE MORE INTERESTED IN TROLLING FOR TRASH FOR POLITICAL GAIN. AND THAT'S JUST UNFORTUNATE THAT WE'RE SEEING THAT THIS EARLY IN AN ELECTION YEAR. THIS IS NOTHING BUT GUTTER POLITICS." *

*WHITE HOUSE PRESS BRIEFING, FEBRUARY 11, 2004.

BUT STILL, THE STORY WOULDN'T GO AWAY.

LATER IN THE DAY ON FEBRUARY 11, THE WHITE HOUSE RELEASED A DENTAL RECORD SHOWING THAT BUSH HAD SEEN A DENTIST AT THE BASE WHERE HE SUPPOSEDLY SERVED IN MONTGOMERY, ALABAMA. BUT IT ONLY SERVED TO RAISE EVEN MORE QUESTIONS, AS THE EXAM TOOK PLACE ON JANUARY 6, 1973. IT HAD PREVIOUSLY BEEN ESTABLISHED THAT HE HAD LEFT ALABAMA FOR HOUSTON AT THE END OF NOVEMBER 1972. *

THOSE TEETH HAVE TO GO!

*DEB RIECHMANN, "WHITE HOUSE RELEASES '73 BUSH DENTAL EXAM," ASSOCIATED PRESS, FEBRUARY 11, 2004.

AS IF TO VERIFY THAT THEY HAD NO IDEA WHAT THEY WERE DOING, THE WHITE HOUSE INCLUDED WITH THE RELEASE OF THE DENTAL RECORDS A REPORT FROM BUSH'S PRESENT-DAY DOCTOR, STATING THAT BUSH WAS "FIT" TO SERVE IN THE GUARD. THIS WAS BASED UPON MEDICAL RECORDS THAT THE WHITE HOUSE HAD OBTAINED WITH THE DENTAL RECORDS, BUT WHICH THEY CHOSE NOT TO RELEASE, * APPARENTLY THINKING THAT WHEN THE PUBLIC HEARD BUSH'S PERSONAL DOCTOR'S REASSURING COMMENTS, THE SCALES WOULD FALL FROM THE EYES OF THE UNBELIEVERS, AND ALL WOULD FINALLY BE MADE CLEAR.

FIT!

A DOCTOR

*IBID.

BUT THE PICTURE BEING PAINTED OF BUSH'S SERVICE IN THE GUARD WAS EVEN MURKIER THAN BEFORE. WITH THE RELEASE OF EACH NEW PIECE OF INFORMATION, WITH BUSH'S REFUSAL TO DESCRIBE ANYTHING HE HAD DONE WHILE SERVING IN ALABAMA, AND WITH THE LACK OF A SINGLE EYEWITNESS WHO COULD ATTEST TO BUSH'S ATTENDANCE AT ANY GUARD MEETING AFTER APRIL 1972, THE MYSTERY DEEPENED.

DID BUSH HAVE SOMETHING TO HIDE? IF NOT, WHY WAS HE SO PROTECTIVE OF HIS RECORDS, WHERE OTHER PRESIDENTIAL CANDIDATES HAD BEEN MORE FORTHRIGHT?

ALLEGATIONS OF DESTRUCTION OF DOCUMENTS RELATING TO BUSH'S GUARD SERVICE BEGAN TO SURFACE IN THE MAINSTREAM PRESS AROUND THIS TIME.

ACCORDING TO WITNESS BILL BURKETT, IN THE SUMMER OF 1997, JOE ALLBAUGH, THEN GOVERNOR BUSH'S CHIEF OF STAFF, CONTACTED THE COMMANDER OF THE TEXAS GUARD AT THE TIME, MAJOR GENERAL DANIEL JAMES III, AND ASKED THAT BUSH'S GUARD RECORDS BE CLEANSED OF EMBARRASSING INFORMATION. *

*DAVE MONIZ AND JIM DRINKARD, "EX-OFFICER: BUSH FILE'S DETAILS CAUSED CONCERN," *USA TODAY*, FEBRUARY 11, 2004.

SUDDENLY, ON FEBRUARY 13, 2004, THE WHITE HOUSE RELEASED WHAT IT CLAIMED TO BE ALL AVAILABLE DOCUMENTS RELATING TO BUSH'S TIME IN THE GUARD, WITH THE EXCEPTION OF HIS MEDICAL RECORDS, WHICH WERE GIVEN TO A GROUP OF REPORTERS TO BROWSE FOR ABOUT 20 MINUTES. *

IT'S GREAT THAT ALL THESE MEDICAL DOCUMENTS REFER TO PERIODS PRIOR TO 1972!

*STEVE HOLLAND, "BUSH RELEASES NATIONAL GUARD FILES," REUTERS, FEBRUARY 13, 2004.

THE NEW DOCUMENTS STILL DIDN'T SHOW WHERE BUSH HAD SERVED, BUT SHOWED THAT HE HAD SERVED ON THE SAME DATES THAT THE PAYROLL FORMS INDICATED. THERE WAS NO INDICATION THAT BUSH HAD SERVED ANYWHERE BETWEEN APRIL 16, 1972, AND OCTOBER 28, 1972.

AND FOR THE DAYS THAT HE DID SERVE, THERE WAS STILL VERY LITTLE INDICATION OF WHERE HE HAD SERVED AND WHAT HE HAD ACTUALLY DONE, IF ANYTHING.

I WAS IN AN UNDISCLOSED LOCATION.

BUT THEN THERE WAS TALK OF A WITNESS! SOMEONE HAD SEEN BUSH AT DANELLY, SERVING WITH THE 187TH TACTICAL RECONNAISSANCE GROUP IN 1972-1973.

THIS WITNESS WAS BILL CALHOUN, AN OFFICER AT DANELLY AT THE TIME BUSH WAS SUPPOSED TO SHOW UP. CALHOUN CLAIMED THAT BUSH SHOWED UP FOR DUTY BETWEEN 8 AND 10 TIMES FROM MAY TO OCTOBER 1972, READING TRAINING MANUALS IN CALHOUN'S OFFICE. *

HE'S HERE AGAIN!

HMM..

HOW TO LOSE YOUR FLIGHT STATUS BY SKIPPING YOUR YEARLY PHYSICAL
A USER'S GUIDE

GWB

*MIKE ALLEN AND LOIS ROMANO, "AIDES STUDY PRESIDENT'S SERVICE RECORDS," *WASHINGTON POST*, FEBRUARY 13, 2004, P. A8.

BUT THIS WENT AGAINST WHAT THE DOCUMENTS RELEASED BY THE WHITE HOUSE SAID!

ACCORDING TO THE RECORDS, BUSH ONLY SERVED TWO DAYS AT THE END OF OCTOBER 1972, WITH NO OTHER RECORDED SERVICE IN THE PERIOD DURING WHICH CALHOUN RECALLS SEEING BUSH.

YOU'RE GEORGE W. BUSH!

BILL C.

AS CALHOUN APPEARED, SAYING THAT HE HAD SEEN BUSH IN 1972, THREE OTHER MEMBERS OF THE 187TH AT THAT TIME -- BOB MINTZ, PAUL BISHOP, AND WAYNE RAMBO -- CAME FORWARD TO SAY THAT THEY HADN'T SEEN BUSH AT DANELLY WHEN HE WAS SUPPOSEDLY THERE, DESPITE THE RELATIVELY SMALL NUMBER OF PILOTS THERE AT THE TIME -- 25 TO 30, ACCORDING TO MINTZ.*

JUST FOR THE RECORD, I NEVER SAW HIM, EITHER. AND I DIDN'T APPRECIATE BEING MISTAKEN FOR HIM!

*JACKSON BAKER, "ON GUARD -- OR AWOL?", *MEMPHIS FLYER*, FEBRUARY 16, 2004.

THE SUPERFICIAL ISSUE HERE IS WHETHER BUSH SERVED AT ALL IN THE AIR NATIONAL GUARD FROM MAY 1972 TO THE TIME OF HIS HONORABLE DISCHARGE ON OCTOBER 1, 1973. THIS IS AN IMPORTANT ISSUE TO SOME, AND SHOULD NOT BE DOWNPLAYED.

BUT THE UNDERLYING ISSUE IS GEORGE W. BUSH'S HONESTY AND INTEGRITY. WHY HAS HE TRIED TO KEEP HIS PAST WITH THE GUARD UNDER WRAPS FOR SO LONG?

AND DOES HE STILL HAVE SOMETHING TO HIDE?

I HEARD THAT *GEORGE W. BUSH'S* RECORDS SHOW THAT HE'S A WEREWOLF!

I HEARD THAT HE'S MADE OF WEAPONS OF MASS DESTRUCTION!

IN 1975, GEORGE W. BUSH ENTERED THE OIL BUSINESS IN MIDLAND, TEXAS.

HE WENT STRAIGHT TO A FAMILY FRIEND, MARTIN ALLDAY, WHO SAW TO IT THAT BUSH WAS TRAINED IN THE WAYS OF THE OIL BUSINESS. BEFORE LONG, BUSH WAS ACTING AS A FREELANCE LANDMAN, LEASING DRILLING RIGHTS FROM PRIVATE LANDOWNERS. *

*GEORGE LARDNER, JR. AND LOIS ROMANO, "THE LIFE OF GEORGE W. BUSH: THE TURNING POINT; AFTER COMING UP DRY, FINANCIAL RESCUES," *WASHINGTON POST*, JULY 30, 1999, P. A1.

BUSH FOUNDED HIS OWN OIL COMPANY, ARBUSTO ENERGY, IN MIDLAND IN 1977. HOWEVER, ARBUSTO (SPANISH FOR "BUSH") DIDN'T ACTUALLY DO ANY BUSINESS UNTIL MARCH 1979, MONTHS AFTER BUSH'S FAILED 1978 RUN FOR HIS DISTRICT'S CONGRESSIONAL SEAT. *

*IBID.

BUSH FAILED TO MAKE MUCH MONEY FINDING OIL. INSTEAD, HE FOUND PLENTY OF MONEY FROM FRIENDS OF FAMILY MEMBERS AND THOSE INTERESTED IN NURTURING PROMISING CONNECTIONS WITH A POWERFUL POLITICAL FAMILY. ALL CONTRIBUTORS COULD ALSO CLAIM HUGE TAX WRITE-OFFS IF THEIR INVESTMENTS RESULTED IN SUBSTANTIAL LOSSES. *

*IBID.

IN 1979, GEORGE H. W. BUSH WAS CONSIDERING RUNNING FOR PRESIDENT, AND LATER FOR RONALD REAGAN'S VICE PRESIDENT, AND SOME OF THOSE FUNDING HIS CANDIDACY ALSO PROVIDED FUNDING TO GEORGE W. BUSH'S BUSINESS. LATER, SOME OF THOSE WHO FUNDED BUSH'S BUSINESS WOULD FIND THEMSELVES REWARDED WITH POLITICAL APPOINTMENTS IN THE ADMINISTRATIONS OF RONALD REAGAN AND GEORGE H. W. BUSH.*

*IBID.

FOR EXAMPLE, WILLIAM H. DRAPER III CONTRIBUTED $93,000 TO ARBUSTO AND WAS APPOINTED AS PRESIDENT OF THE IMPORT-EXPORT BANK DURING REAGAN'S PRESIDENTIAL TERM, WHILE JOHN D. MACOMBER, WHO CONTRIBUTED $79,000 TO ARBUSTO, WAS APPOINTED TO THE SAME POST DURING THE PRESIDENCY OF GEORGE H. W. BUSH. *

JUST 'CAUSE IT LOOKS LIKE THEY WERE REWARDED FOR MONETARY CONTRIBUTIONS DOESN'T MEAN THEY WEREN'T QUALIFIED. ESPECIALLY IF YOU CONSIDER SHOWERING MY FAILING BUSINESS VENTURES WITH MONEY A QUALIFICATION!

*GEORGE LARDNER, JR. AND LOIS ROMANO, "THE LIFE OF GEORGE W. BUSH: THE TURNING POINT; AFTER COMING UP DRY, FINANCIAL RESCUES," WASHINGTON POST, JULY 30, 1999, P. A1.

FROM THE START OF 1979 TO THE END OF THE YEAR, THE PRICE OF OIL MORE THAN DOUBLED, BUT ARBUSTO FAILED TO MAKE MUCH MONEY, WITH A SUCCESSFUL DRILLING RATE OF AROUND 50% -- AVERAGE FOR THE AREA. *

WHAT AM I DOIN' WRONG?

*IBID.

BUT ARBUSTO WAS KEEPING SOME MONEY FOR ITSELF, LEAVING THOSE WHO INVESTED IN THE COMPANY WITH MASSIVE LOSSES EVEN WHILE REWARDING ITSELF FOR ITS FAILURE AS A VIABLE BUSINESS.

ACCORDING TO THE WASHINGTON POST, "BUSH'S COMPANY COLLECTED $678,000 IN FEES AND CASH DISTRIBUTIONS ON AN INVESTMENT OF ONLY $102,000." *

THAT LOOKS ABOUT RIGHT!

BALANCE SHEET

$678,000.00

*IBID.

IN 1982, THE PRICE OF OIL WAS ON ITS WAY BACK DOWN, AND ARBUSTO WAS IN SERIOUS FINANCIAL TROUBLE, WITH NEW FUNDING SOURCES HARDER TO FIND THAN BEFORE.

THEN A MYSTERIOUS INVESTOR BY THE NAME OF PHILIP UZIELLI APPEARED. A PRINCETON CLASSMATE OF JAMES BAKER III (A BUSH-FAMILY CONFIDANT AND POLITICAL ALLY FOR MANY YEARS), UZIELLI OFFERED $1 MILLION FOR 10% OF ARBUSTO, A SHARE VALUED AT LESS THAN $40,000. *

IN OTHER WORDS, HE WAS PAYING MORE THAN 25 TIMES BOOK VALUE FOR 10% OF A COMPANY THAT HAD REPEATEDLY PROVEN TO BE A MONETARY BLACK HOLE.

THANKS A MILLION!

*IVINS AND DUBOSE, SHRUB, PP. 24-26.

THOUGH SOPHISTICATION MAY HAVE BEEN THE HALLMARK OF MR. UZIELLI'S OTHER INVESTMENTS, IT CERTAINLY DIDN'T SEEM TO PLAY ANY PART IN HIS INVESTMENT IN ARBUSTO.

ARBUSTO WENT PUBLIC SHORTLY AFTER UZIELLI'S INVESTMENT, SEEKING TO RAISE FUNDS THROUGH SELLING STOCK. AFTER RAISING LESS THAN 20% OF A $6 MILLION GOAL, BUSH CHANGED THE COMPANY'S NAME TO BUSH EXPLORATION* IN A BID TO ATTRACT PUBLIC INVESTORS TO HIS NAME, AS HIS FATHER WAS THEN VICE PRESIDENT.

"HE'S A SOPHISTICATED INVESTOR." *

FERGOT MY TROUSERS.

*QUOTED IN GEORGE LARDNER, JR. AND LOIS ROMANO, "THE LIFE OF GEORGE W. BUSH: THE TURNING POINT; AFTER COMING UP DRY, FINANCIAL RESCUES," *WASHINGTON POST*, JULY 30, 1999, P. A1.

SORRY, BUT WE'S IN THE OIL BUSINESS!

BUSH EXPLORATION

DASH AND BOTHER!

THE HUMBLE IS IN

*IBID.

THE NEW NAME DIDN'T DRAW IN THE THRONGS OF INVESTORS THAT BUSH HAD EXPECTED, AND UZIELLI'S INVESTMENT COULDN'T KEEP THE COMPANY GOING BEYOND 1984. SUCH WERE THE CIRCUMSTANCES UNDER WHICH BUSH EXPLORATION WAS PURCHASED BY SPECTRUM 7, A TEXAS OIL EXPLORATION COMPANY.

THE HEADS OF SPECTRUM 7 - WILLIAM O. DEWITT, JR. AND MERCER REYNOLDS III - BOUGHT OUT BUSH EXPLORATION, MAKING BUSH THEIR COMPANY'S CHAIRMAN AND CEO. BUSH GOT 16.3 PERCENT OF SPECTRUM 7'S STOCK OUT OF THE DEAL, AS WELL AS A YEARLY SALARY OF $75,000. *

WITH GEORGE H. W. BUSH AS REAGAN'S VICE PRESIDENT AND POTENTIALLY THE NEXT PRESIDENT, GEORGE W.'S POSITION WITH SPECTRUM 7 SEEMED TO BE BASED MOSTLY ON THE VALUE OF HAVING HIS NAME ASSOCIATED WITH THE COMPANY. *

I NEVER KNEW FAILING WAS SUCH A GOOD BUSINESS DECISION!

GOOD THING I DIDN'T CHANGE MY NAME!

HEY KIDS! IT'S
GEORGE W.
ToasterOven
Von Cabbage!

*IBID.

*IBID.

AFTER A SHORT PERIOD OF PROFITABILITY, SPECTRUM 7'S FUTURE LOOKED BLEAK. SO IN SEPTEMBER 1986, HARKEN ENERGY STEPPED IN, PURCHASING SPECTRUM 7 WITH SHARES OF HARKEN STOCK. HARKEN'S MAIN INTEREST WAS IN THE WEIGHT OF BUSH'S NAME AND THE FINANCIAL CONNECTIONS HE BROUGHT WITH HIM. *

I'M LIKE A MAGNET TO PEOPLE WITH MONEY!

*BYRON YORK, "GEORGE'S ROAD TO RICHES," *AMERICAN SPECTATOR*, JUNE 5, 1999.

BUSH RECEIVED $500,000 IN HARKEN STOCK AND WAS MADE A MEMBER OF HARKEN'S BOARD OF DIRECTORS. BUSH ALSO RECEIVED YEARLY CONSULTING FEES FROM $80,000 TO $120,000, EVEN WHILE HE WORKED FULL-TIME ON HIS FATHER'S PRESIDENTIAL CAMPAIGN. *

GUESS I DON'T NEED TO BE **CEO** IF I CAN MAKE MORE MONEY DOIN' PRACTICALLY NOTHING!

*JOHN DUNBAR, "A BRIEF HISTORY OF BUSH, HARKEN AND THE SEC," CENTER FOR PUBLIC INTEGRITY, OCTOBER 2002.

BEFORE BUSH COMMITTED HIMSELF TO HIS FATHER'S PRESIDENTIAL CAMPAIGN, HIS MERE PRESENCE AT HARKEN SEEMED TO BRING GOOD FORTUNE TO THE COMPANY. THE MANAGEMENT COMPANY FOR THE HARVARD ENDOWMENT INVESTED $20 MILLION IN HARKEN JUST A MONTH AFTER BUSH JOINED THE COMPANY. *

RIGHT HERE!

HARKEN

*IBID.

AFTER WORKING FOR HIS FATHER'S PRESIDENTIAL CAMPAIGN FROM JUNE 1987 TO LATE 1988, BUSH RETURNED TO HARKEN.

A SHORT TIME LATER, THE COMPANY FOUND ITSELF IN THE RED, AND COMPANY OFFICIALS SEEMED INTENT ON HIDING THE COMPANY'S ACTUAL FINANCIAL STATUS.

LOOKS LIKE MY WORK HERE IS NEARLY DONE!

WHRRRRR

THEN OPPORTUNITY KNOCKED FOR GEORGE W. BUSH ONCE AGAIN, THIS TIME IN THE FORM OF A CHANCE TO BUY A SHARE OF THE TEXAS RANGERS BASEBALL TEAM. BUSH HELPED BRING TOGETHER A GROUP OF INVESTORS (INCLUDING DEWITT AND REYNOLDS, HIS SPECTRUM 7 PALS) TO BUY THE TEAM FOR A TOTAL OF $86 MILLION IN APRIL 1989. BUSH BOUGHT INTO THE TEAM WITH $606,302, A 1.8 PERCENT SHARE WHICH WOULD LATER GROW TO 11.8 PERCENT AFTER THE OTHER INVESTORS HAD MADE BACK THEIR INITIAL INVESTMENTS IN THE TEAM. *

*CHARLES LEWIS, "BUSH'S DEAL FOR THE TEXAS RANGERS," TOMPAINE.COM, JANUARY 19, 2000.

ALTHOUGH BUSH HAD BEEN NAMED A GENERAL MANAGING PARTNER FOR THE RANGERS WHEN HE BOUGHT INTO THE TEAM, HE REMAINED ON HARKEN'S BOARD OF DIRECTORS, AND WAS A MEMBER OF AN AUDIT COMMITTEE WHICH OVERSAW THE COMPANY'S FINANCIAL CONDITION. *

*BYRON YORK, "GEORGE'S ROAD TO RICHES," AMERICAN SPECTATOR, JUNE 5, 1999.

IT WAS FROM HIS POSITION ON THESE BOARDS, ESPECIALLY THE AUDIT COMMITTEE, THAT BUSH HAD ACCESS TO INSIDER KNOWLEDGE OF THE COMPANY'S IMPENDING FINANCIAL TROUBLES, WHICH WERE NOT KNOWN TO THE PUBLIC AT THE TIME. ON JUNE 22, 1990, BUSH SOLD TWO-THIRDS OF HIS SHARES OF HARKEN STOCK AT $4 A SHARE, A TRANSACTION VALUED AT $848,000. *

HARKEN'S STOCK PRICE PER SHARE DIPPED AS LOW AS $1.25 BY THE END OF THAT YEAR.

*MICHAEL KRANISH AND BETH HEALY, "BOARD WAS TOLD OF RISKS BEFORE BUSH STOCK SALE," BOSTON GLOBE, OCTOBER 30, 2002, P. A1.

BUSH SOLD DESPITE HAVING SIGNED A "LOCKUP" LETTER IN EARLY APRIL 1990, PLEDGING NOT TO SELL ANY OF HIS SHARES FOR THE FOLLOWING SIX MONTHS BECAUSE OF AN EXISTING HARKEN PLAN TO PUBLICLY OFFER COMMON STOCK. ALTHOUGH THE PUBLIC OFFERING NEVER OCCURRED BECAUSE OF THE DETERIORATING FINANCIAL SITUATION AT HARKEN, * THAT BUSH SIGNED THE LETTER INDICATES THAT ANY INSISTENCE THAT HE SOLD IN JUNE BASED ON A LONG-STANDING PLAN TO RID HIMSELF OF DEBT -- WHEN ANY OTHER MOMENT MIGHT HAVE PROVEN TO BE LESS CONSPICUOUS -- HAS ALL THE CREDIBILITY OF THE AVERAGE ENRON BIGWIG'S CLAIM OF IGNORANCE ABOUT THEIR OWN COMPANY'S OPERATIONS.

IT'S NOT LIKE MY DOING SOMETHING ILLEGAL ACTUALLY **MATTERS**— I'LL JUST SAY I'VE MADE MISTAKES IF I'M CAUGHT!

*PETE YOST, "BUSH SIGNED 'LOCKUP' LETTER," ASSOCIATED PRESS, JULY 16, 2002.

NORMALLY, WHEN THERE'S NOTHING TO HIDE, AN INDIVIDUAL IS COOPERATIVE AND WORKS TO GET AN INVESTIGATION OVER WITH.

WHEN THE SEC OPENED AN INVESTIGATION IN APRIL 1991 TO FIND WHY BUSH HAD FAILED TO FILE THE NECESSARY PAPERWORK UNTIL 8 MONTHS AFTER HIS INSIDER HARKEN STOCK TRADE, BUSH WAS ANYTHING BUT COOPERATIVE. HE WASN'T EVEN INTERVIEWED BY THE SEC FOR THE INVESTIGATION, NOT THAT THERE'S ANY INDICATION THAT THEY EVER SOUGHT TO QUESTION HIM PERSONALLY. INSTEAD, THEY TALKED TO HIS LAWYERS AND EVENTUALLY ENDED THE INVESTIGATION IN OCTOBER 1993, JUST A MONTH BEFORE BUSH ANNOUNCED HIS GUBERNATORIAL CANDIDACY IN TEXAS. *

WELL, I SEE NOTHING WRONG WITH WHAT HE DID!

WHEN YOU'RE THE PRESIDENT'S SON, CAN YOU DO WRONG?

*GEORGE LARDNER, JR. AND LOIS ROMANO, "THE LIFE OF GEORGE W. BUSH: THE TURNING POINT; AFTER COMING UP DRY, FINANCIAL RESCUES," *WASHINGTON POST*, JULY 30, 1999, P. A1.

IN OCTOBER 1994, WITH THE TEXAS GUBERNATORIAL ELECTION JUST AROUND THE CORNER, BUSH ADDRESSED THE ISSUE OF HIS INSIDER TRADE. OR, MORE ACCURATELY, HE BLATANTLY LIED ABOUT THE ISSUE.

"THE SEC FULLY INVESTIGATED THE STOCK DEAL. I WAS EXONERATED." *

*IBID.

BUT A LETTER RECEIVED BY BUSH'S ATTORNEYS AT THE END OF THE SEC INVESTIGATION INDICATED JUST THE OPPOSITE, INDICATING THAT IT "MUST IN NO WAY BE CONSTRUED AS INDICATING THAT THE PARTY HAS BEEN EXONERATED OR THAT NO ACTION MAY ULTIMATELY RESULT FROM THE STAFF'S INVESTIGATION." *

WHAT!?
SAYIN' THE EXACT OPPOSITE OF THE TRUTH IS THE SAME AS **LYING?!**

I'M SHOCKED AND AWED!

*STATEMENT FROM SEC DIRECTOR FOR ENFORCEMENT BRUCE A. HILFER, QUOTED IN GEORGE LARDNER, JR. AND LOIS ROMANO, "THE LIFE OF GEORGE W. BUSH: THE TURNING POINT; AFTER COMING UP DRY, FINANCIAL RESCUES," *WASHINGTON POST*, JULY 30, 1999, P. A1.

DURING THE TIME THAT BUSH WAS AT HARKEN, IT IS HIGHLY PROBABLE THAT BUSH SIGNED OFF ON SOME SHADY DEALINGS THAT HAD ONLY ONE INTENDED EFFECT: KEEPING DEBT OFF THE BOOKS, HIDDEN FROM PUBLIC INVESTORS.

IF IT'S GOOD FOR THE COMPANY, IT'S GOOD FOR THE INVESTORS!

HA! HA! HA! HA!

IN 1989, IN ONE SUCH DEAL, HARKEN INSIDERS LOANED THEMSELVES $11 MILLION TO PURCHASE 80% OF ALOHA PETROLEUM, A HARKEN SUBSIDIARY, WITH HARKEN DECLARING A $7.9 MILLION GAIN FROM THE TRANSACTION. THE SEC WOULD LATER FORCE THE COMPANY TO CORRECT THEIR EARNINGS STATEMENT FOR 1989, RESULTING IN A DOWNWARD REVISION OF $9.3 MILLION. *

*JOHN DUNBAR, "A BRIEF HISTORY OF BUSH, HARKEN AND THE SEC," CENTER FOR PUBLIC INTEGRITY, OCTOBER 2002.

IN DECEMBER 1990, IN ANOTHER SHADY DEAL OVERSEEN BY BUSH, HARKEN AND HARVARD UNIVERSITY FORMED THE HARKEN ANADARKO PARTNERSHIP. THIS PARTNERSHIP ALLOWED HARKEN TO EFFECTIVELY HIDE $20 MILLION IN DEBT, AS THE RULES AFFECTING PARTNER-SHIPS DID NOT DEMAND DISCLOSURE OF ITS FINANCES TO THE PUBLIC. THE RESULT WAS A FALSE PUBLIC PERCEPTION THAT HARKEN'S FINANCIAL SITUATION WAS IMPROVING WHEN IT WAS ACTUALLY DETERIORATING. *

*"NEW EVIDENCE REGARDING IMPROPER FINANCIAL MANEUVERS AT HARKEN ENERGY DURING THE BUSH ERA," HARVARDWATCH, OCTOBER 2002.

IN LATE 1990, BUSH TURNED HIS ATTENTION TO THE TEXAS RANGERS BASEBALL TEAM. HE AND HIS PARTNERS THREATENED TO MOVE THE TEAM AWAY FROM ARLINGTON UNLESS THE CITY PROVIDED $135 MILLION FOR A NEW STADIUM, WITH ANOTHER $50 MILLION TO BE PAID BY THE RANGERS MANAGEMENT. *

*CHARLES LEWIS, "BUSH'S DEAL FOR THE TEXAS RANGERS," TOMPAINE.COM, JANUARY 19, 2000.

UNLESS YOU PONY UP SOME DOUGH, WE'RE OUTTA HERE, PARDNER...

MAYOR

SO IT WAS THAT ARLINGTON RESIDENTS VOTED 2-TO-1 IN FAVOR OF A HALF-CENT SALES-TAX ON THEMSELVES TO FUND THE BALLPARK AT ARLINGTON. TOTAL TAXPAYER SUBSIDIZATION OF THE RANGERS AMOUNTED TO MORE THAN $200 MILLION.*

TAX INCREASES ARE GOOD FOR BUSINESS WHEN THEY INVOLVE ME MAKING MONEY!

*IBID.

THE $50 MILLION OF THEIR OWN MONEY THAT THE RANGERS MANAGEMENT HAD PLEDGED TO INVEST IN THE NEW STADIUM'S CONSTRUCTION COSTS WAS ACTUALLY RAISED THROUGH A $1 SURCHARGE ON TICKET SALES, PASSING ON THE COST TO THE FANS, AND ALLOWING THE MANAGEMENT TO GET A NEW STADIUM, A SOURCE OF MASSIVE AMOUNTS OF INCOME, WITH NO CAPITAL INVESTMENT OF THEIR OWN NECESSARY. *

THEY'LL MAKE THE MONEY BACK IN ENTERTAINMENT VALUE!

RATS.

*IBID.

BUSH AND THE OTHER MANAGERS ALSO WORKED TO CREATE THE ARLINGTON SPORTS FACILITIES DEVELOPMENT AUTHORITY. THE SOLE PURPOSE OF THIS ENTITY WAS TO SEIZE PRIVATE PROPERTY SURROUNDING THE BALLPARK, INCREASING THE VALUE OF THE STADIUM FOR THE RANGERS.*

WE ONLY WANTED TO TAKE THE LAND AT UNFAIR PRICES TO DEMONSTRATE HOW IMPORTANT PROPERTY RIGHTS ARE!

YELLOW!

42

*IBID.

IF PROPERTY HOLDERS REFUSED TO SELL AT THE PRICE THE AUTHORITY OFFERED, THEIR LAND WAS CONDEMNED AND TAKEN FOR UNBELIEVABLY LOW PRICES. LATER COURT SETTLEMENTS REGARDING UNDERPAYMENT FOR THE PRIVATE PROPERTY AMOUNTED TO $11 MILLION, WHICH THE RANGERS EXPECTED THE TAXPAYERS TO PAY AS WELL, AS THE AUTHORITY WAS CREATED AS A PUBLIC ENTITY, EVEN THOUGH IT ONLY EXISTED TO INCREASE THE HOLDINGS OF THE RANGERS.*

BAM BAM BAM

CONDEMNED!

*CHARLES LEWIS, "BUSH'S DEAL FOR THE TEXAS RANGERS," TOMPAINE.COM, JANUARY 19, 2000.

ONE POSSIBLE USE OF SOME OF THE LAND SURROUNDING THE BALLPARK HAS RECENTLY COME TO LIGHT: IT MAY BE THE FUTURE LOCATION OF THE GEORGE W. BUSH PRESIDENTIAL LIBRARY.*

THE RANGERS WOULD GLADLY DONATE THE LAND THAT THEY NEVER HAD TO PAY FOR TO BUSH, THE MAN WHO GOT THE LAND FOR THE TEAM IN THE FIRST PLACE.

POSSIBLE FUTURE SITE OF GEORGE W. BUSH PRESIDENTIAL LIBRARY

YOU CAN BUILD IT, BUT HE'S DUMB!

*DAVE MONTGOMERY, "TEXAS RANGERS OFFER LAND AS SITE FOR BUSH LIBRARY," KNIGHT-RIDDER/TRIBUNE NEWS SERVICE, MARCH 4, 2004.

BUSH HELD HIS SHARE IN THE RANGERS UNTIL THE TEAM WAS SOLD TO THOMAS HICKS IN 1998 FOR A TOTAL OF $250 MILLION. BUSH'S SHARE BROUGHT HIM $14.9 FROM HIS INITIAL INVESTMENT OF JUST OVER $600,000.*

NOW THAT I'M A MILLIONAIRE, MAYBE I CAN **FINALLY** CATCH A BREAK FROM **LIFE'S HARDSHIPS!**

I WISH I WAS A MILLIONAIRE-THESE BANANAS IS HARD TO AIM INTO MY FACE-HOLE!

HE CAN'T AFFORD A BANANA AIMER!?

NOT IN **THIS** ECONOMY!

LIFE'S HARDSHIPS

*CHARLES LEWIS, "BUSH'S DEAL FOR THE TEXAS RANGERS," TOMPAINE.COM, JANUARY 19, 2000.

HOW HAVE SOME OF THE INDIVIDUALS WHO HAVE SEEN BUSH THROUGH THE HARD TIMES AND THE BETTER TIMES BEEN REWARDED?

MANY HAVE BEEN APPOINTED TO COZY POSITIONS BY BUSH SINCE HE ASSUMED THE PRESIDENCY.

I KNIGHT THEE.. OOP!

ONE EXAMPLE IS BUSH'S APPOINTMENT OF WILLIAM O. DEWITT, JR. -- THE FORMER SPECTRUM 7 MANAGER WHO BOUGHT OUT BUSH EXPLORATION -- TO A TWO-YEAR TERM ON AN INTELLIGENCE ADVISORY BOARD.*

THANKS FOR HELPING ME OUT BACK IN THE BEFORE TIMES!

*CARL WEISER, "BUSH TAPS DEWITT FOR INNER CIRCLE," CINCINNATI ENQUIRER, OCTOBER 10, 2003.

DEWITT, WHO LACKS ANY INTELLIGENCE EXPERIENCE, AND OBVIOUSLY LACKS INDEPENDENCE FROM THE PRESIDENT THAT HE WILL BE ADVISING, HAD AN ODD PERSPECTIVE ON THE SITUATION.

"INDEPENDANCE IS CLEARLY CRITICAL. I WOULD CERTAINLY VALUE THAT CHARACTERISTIC."*

OBEY BUSH

BUSH IS SUPER A-ONE!

DEWITT

BUSH

*QUOTED IN IBID.

IT'S SAFE TO SAY THAT MOST PEOPLE WOULD VALUE INDEPENDENCE IN SUCH AN ADVISORY POSITION. IT'S PROBABLY EQUALLY SAFE TO SAY THAT A FRIEND AND FORMER BUSINESS PARTNER WHO CONTINUES TO RAISE MONEY FOR THE PRESIDENT'S CAMPAIGNS DOESN'T FIT THE CLASSIC DEFINITION OF "INDEPENDENT ADVISOR."

WELL, Mr. PRESIDENT, I THINK WHAT YOU ARE ABOUT TO SAY IS EXACTLY RIGHT, AND INCREDIBLY WISE, I MIGHT ADD.

YOU SEE, THIS IS WHY I NEED PEOPLE I CAN TRUST AROUND ME!

ACCORDING TO TEXANS FOR PUBLIC JUSTICE, DEWITT RAISED OVER $100,000 FOR BUSH'S PRESIDENTIAL CAMPAIGN IN 2000 AND HAS ALREADY RAISED OVER $200,000 FOR BUSH'S 2004 REELECTION CAMPAIGN. ADDITIONALLY, DEWITT'S WIFE KATHERINE WAS APPOINTED BY BUSH TO THE NATIONAL COUNCIL ON THE ARTS. *

MERCER REYNOLDS III -- ALSO FROM SPECTRUM 7 AND THE TEXAS RANGERS VENTURE -- WAS APPOINTED U.S. AMBASSADOR TO SWITZERLAND BY BUSH IN 2001, THOUGH HE RESIGNED THE POST IN APRIL 2003. REYNOLDS RAISED OVER $100,000 FOR BUSH IN 2000, AND IS CURRENTLY FINANCE CHAIR FOR BUSH'S 2004 REELECTION CAMPAIGN. *

IT'S **ART** HOW I APPOINTED YOU BOTH AFTER YOU HELPED ME OUT SO MUCH IN THE PAST.!!

YOU'RE ABSOLUTELY RIGHT!

YOU DONE GOOD!

GLEH!

EW.

*TEXANS FOR PUBLIC JUSTICE, BUSH DONOR PROFILES, WWW.TPJ.ORG.

*IBID.

SOME MIGHT ARGUE THAT THERE'S NOTHING WRONG WITH A PRESIDENT HANDING OUT APPOINTMENTS TO INDIVIDUALS WHO HAVE RAISED MASSIVE AMOUNTS OF MONEY FOR THAT PRESIDENT'S CAMPAIGNS, THAT THERE'S NOTHING WRONG WITH THE PRESIDENT REWARDING THOSE WHO BAILED OUT HIS OWN FAILING BUSINESS VENTURES.

MAYBE IT'S NOT ILLEGAL, BUT IT SMACKS OF CRONYISM.

IF GEORGE W. BUSH IS MORE INTERESTED IN REPAYING THE OLD BUDDIES WHO HELPED HIM OUT IN THE PAST THAN HE IS IN PLACING QUALIFIED INDIVIDUALS IN VARIOUS GOVERNMENT POSITIONS, HE THREATENS TO UNDERMINE THE FUNCTIONALITY OF GOVERNMENT.

BUT AS SEEMS EVIDENT IN SO MANY AREAS, PERHAPS THAT IS EXACTLY BUSH'S GOAL: LESS GOVERNMENT REGULATION OF BUSINESS, DRAMATIC TAX CUTS FOR THE WEALTHY, AND MORE CASH TO STUFF INTO HIS OWN ALREADY-BULGING POCKETS.

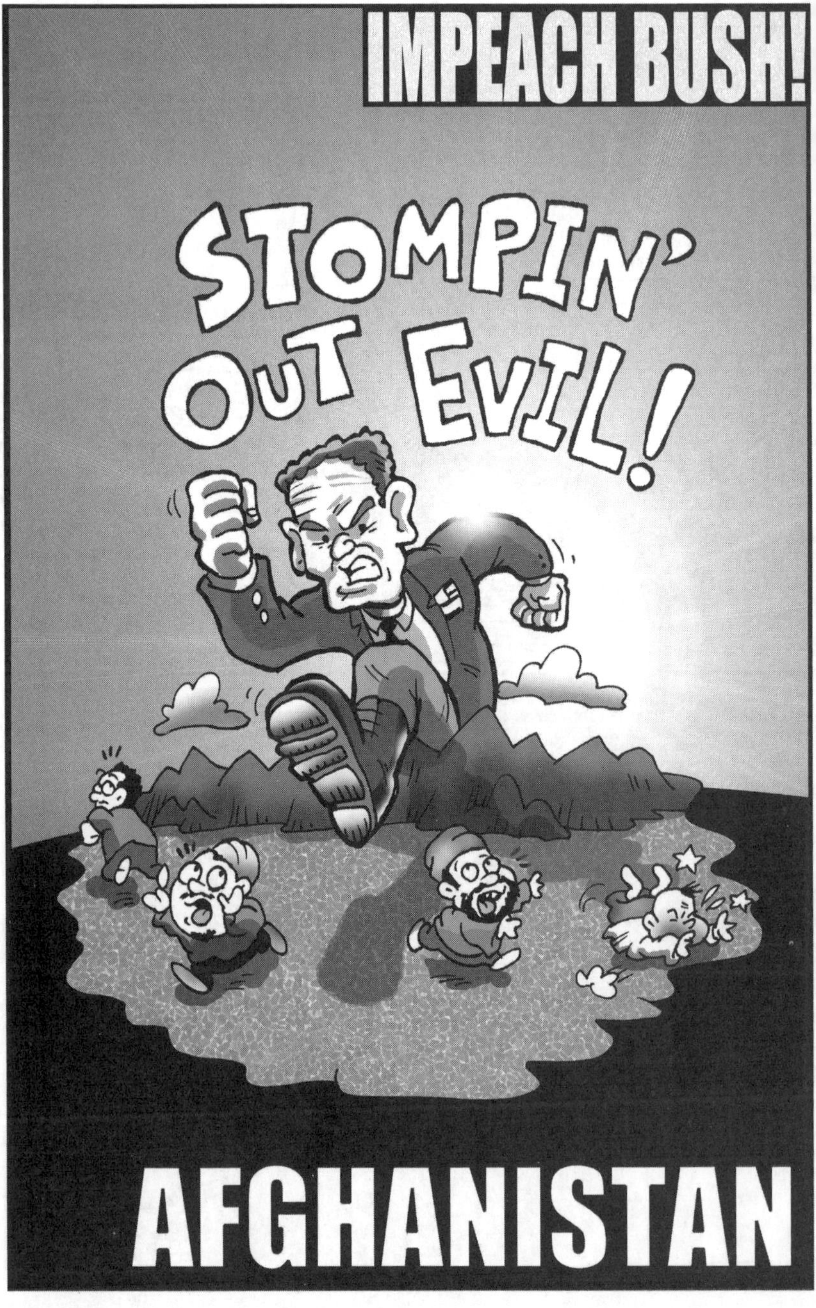
IMPEACH BUSH!
STOMPIN' OUT EVIL!
AFGHANISTAN

IMMEDIATELY AFTER THE ATTACKS OF 9/11, IT WAS APPARENT THAT GEORGE W. BUSH WAS GOING TO DO WHAT ANY PRESIDENT WOULD HAVE DONE UNDER THE CIRCUMSTANCES:

HE WOULD TAKE AMERICA TO WAR.

SEND TROOPS **THERE!**

ACTUALLY, THAT'S THE TREASURE MAP FROM A BOX OF YOUR BREAKFAST CEREAL, SIR..

TREASURE OATS

HEY KIDS! FIND ME BOOTY!

I ALREADY HAVE A SHIP IN THE AREA, COMMANDER!

THE DIFFERENCE BETWEEN HOW PRESIDENT GEORGE W. BUSH TOOK AMERICA TO WAR AND HOW ANY OTHER PRESIDENT MIGHT HAVE DONE THE SAME IS ALSO APPARENT:

MOST WOULDN'T DEFINE IT AS A WAR TO ERADICATE EVIL.

EVIL! STOP

BUT THEN GEORGE W. BUSH ISN'T LIKE MOST PRESIDENTS.

"MY ADMINISTRATION HAS A JOB TO DO, AND WE'RE GOING TO DO IT. WE WILL RID THE WORLD OF THE EVIL-DOERS." *

*REMARKS BY GEORGE W. BUSH, SEPTEMBER 16, 2001.

SUPPORT FOR BUSH IN AMERICA WAS SO STRONG THAT EVEN BUSH'S OPPONENT IN THE 2000 RACE FOR THE PRESIDENCY, AL GORE, STEPPED FORWARD WITH WORDS OF UNITY.

"GEORGE W. BUSH IS MY COMMANDER-IN-CHIEF. THIS COUNTRY IS MORE UNITED THAN AT ANY TIME I CAN REMEMBER IN MY LIFETIME." *

USA

*STEVE KRASKE, "IN IOWA ADDRESS, GORE URGES CITIZENS TO STAND BY BUSH'S LEADERSHIP," *KANSAS CITY STAR*, SEPTEMBER 30, 2001.

IT SEEMED AS IF THE WORLD UNITED BEHIND BUSH AS HE LED THE WAY TO WAR IN AFGHANISTAN.

A PRIME EXAMPLE OF JUST HOW UNITED THE U.S. WAS WITH THE INTERNATIONAL COMMUNITY AFTER 9/11 WAS FRENCH PRESIDENT JACQUES CHIRAC STANDING SIDE BY SIDE WITH BUSH AT THE WHITE HOUSE, PLEDGING FRANCE'S SUPPORT.

"I WANT TO TELL PRESIDENT BUSH, WHO IS MY FRIEND, THAT WE STAND IN TOTAL SOLIDARITY -- WE BRING YOU THE TOTAL SOLIDARITY OF FRANCE AND THE FRENCH PEOPLE." *

*REMARKS BY PRESIDENT BUSH AND FRENCH PRESIDENT CHIRAC AT THE OVAL OFFICE.

BUT SUCH UNITY CANNOT LAST FOREVER, ESPECIALLY WHEN THE LEADER OF THE COALITION WORKS TO UNDERMINE THE TRUST OF ITS MEMBERS.

AS THE FIRST BOMBS WERE DROPPING ON AFGHANISTAN, SOME ARAB NATIONS THAT HAD VOICED SUPPORT FOR THE U.S. OPERATION WERE SHOWING DISCOMFORT AT THE U.S. SUGGESTION THAT OTHER NATIONS -- INCLUDING IRAQ -- MIGHT BE TARGETED AS THE WAR ON TERROR EXPANDED. *

*JULIAN BORGER AND IAN BLACK, "BOMBING GOES ON AS U.S. HINTS AT ATTACK ON IRAQ," THE GUARDIAN, OCTOBER 9, 2001.

BY MID-DECEMBER 2001, THE TALIBAN HAD BEEN DEPOSED FROM POWER BY THE COMBINED FORCE OF U.S. SPECIAL FORCES, AIR STRIKES, AND AFGHAN NORTHERN ALLIANCE FORCES.

HOWEVER, THE PRIME TARGETS -- AL QAEDA LEADER OSAMA BIN LADEN AND TALIBAN LEADER MULLAH MUHAMMAD OMAR -- ESCAPED IMPRISONMENT OR DEATH, AND AS OF AS LATE AS MARCH 2004, ARE STILL AT LARGE, CONTINUING IN THE PURSUIT OF THEIR MURDEROUS AGENDAS.

ALTHOUGH QUICK, THE REMOVAL OF THE TALIBAN FROM POWER IN AFGHANISTAN WAS NOT THE CLEAN AND QUICK OPERATION THAT MERITED THE RESULTS *GEORGE W. BUSH* CLAIMED IN HIS 2002 STATE OF THE UNION ADDRESS.

"IN FOUR SHORT MONTHS, OUR NATION HAS COMFORTED THE VICTIMS, BEGUN TO REBUILD NEW YORK AND THE PENTAGON, RALLIED A GREAT COALITION, CAPTURED, ARRESTED, AND RID THE WORLD OF THOUSANDS OF TERRORISTS, DESTROYED AFGHANISTAN'S TERRORIST TRAINING CAMPS, SAVED A PEOPLE FROM STARVATION, AND FREED A COUNTRY FROM BRUTAL OPPRESSION."

WHEN HE SPOKE OF SAVING AFGHANS FROM STARVATION, IT'S PROBABLY SAFE TO SAY HE WASN'T THINKING ABOUT THE INCIDENTS INVOLVING AFGHAN CIVILIANS BEING KILLED BY UNEXPLODED CLUSTER BOMBS THAT WERE THE SAME COLOR AS AIR-DROPPED FOOD PACKETS. *

*DAVID TARRANT, "FOOD PACKETS, UNEXPLODED BOMBS EASY TO CONFUSE," *DALLAS MORNING NEWS*, NOVEMBER 2, 2001.

WHAT? BOMBS MAKE FOR GOOD EATIN'!

BLOW EM UP A NOTCH!

NOR WAS HE THINKING OF THE U.S. BOMBING OF A CLEARLY-MARKED RED CROSS FACILITY IN KABUL -- TWICE IN A PERIOD OF TEN DAYS -- WIPING OUT FOOD AND BLANKETS THAT THE AID ORGANIZATION HAD INTENDED TO DISTRIBUTE TO THOUSANDS OF AFGHAN CIVILIANS IN NEED OF ASSISTANCE. *

WE MADE MISTAKES!

*ELIZABETH BECKER AND ERIC SCHMITT, "U.S. PLANES BOMB A RED CROSS SITE FOR A SECOND TIME," *NEW YORK TIMES*, OCTOBER 27, 2001.

WHEN BUSH SPOKE OF THE DEAD AND CAPTURED TERRORISTS, HE PROBABLY ISN'T SPEAKING OF THE 8,000 TALIBAN MEMBERS WHO, AFTER SURRENDERING, WERE PACKED INTO CONTAINER TRUCKS IN SWELTERING DESERT HEAT TO BE TRANSPORTED TO THE PRISON AT SHIBERGHAN IN AFGHANISTAN. *

TOO GOOD FOR 'EM!

*LUKE HARDING, "AFGHAN MASSACRE HAUNTS PENTAGON," *GUARDIAN*, SEPTEMBER 13, 2002.

BUSH CERTAINLY ISN'T PROUDLY REFERRING TO HOW AIR-HOLES WERE SHOT INTO THE LOADED CONTAINERS FOR THOSE INSIDE TO BREATHE THROUGH, AND HOW WHEN THE TRUCKS WERE OPENED AT THEIR DESTINATION, AS MANY AS 2,000 TO 3,000 OF THE TALIBAN PRISONERS HAD DIED AND WERE BURIED IN MASS GRAVES. *

THE ONLY MASS GRAVES I'M INTERESTED IN TALKING ABOUT ARE IN IRAQ!

*LUKE HARDING, "AFGHAN MASSACRE HAUNTS PENTAGON," *GUARDIAN*, SEPTEMBER 13, 2002.

IN THE 2002 STATE OF THE UNION SPEECH, BUSH WAS OBVIOUSLY SPEAKING OF HIS PERCEPTION OF AN AFGHANISTAN FREE FROM THE BRUTAL REPRESSION OF THE TALIBAN.

BUT HE CERTAINLY DIDN'T WANT TO BE BOTHERED WITH THE DETAILS OF REPRESSION IN UZBEKISTAN, ONE OF THE U.S. ALLIES IN THE WAR ON THE TERROR, WHERE POLITICAL DISSIDENTS ARE JAILED, TORTURED, AND SOMETIMES EXECUTED.*

MAYBE SHE'S EVIL OR SOMETHING?

*JIM LOBE, "UZBEK LEADER BECOMING EMBARRASSMENT TO WEST," *ONEWORLD US*, DECEMBER 8, 2003.

IN THE SAME STATE OF THE UNION SPEECH, BUSH HAD SOME WORDS ON THE PRECISION WEAPONS AMERICA USED IN THE WAR IN AFGHANISTAN.

"AFGHANISTAN PROVED THAT EXPENSIVE PRECISION WEAPONS DEFEAT THE ENEMY AND SPARE INNOCENT LIVES..."

TARGET ACQUIRED.

$ $ $

NO!

ACCORDING TO A STUDY BY MARC W. HEROLD OF THE UNIVERSITY OF NEW HAMPSHIRE, RELYING ON MEDIA AND NON-GOVERNMENTAL ORGANIZATION REPORTS, AFGHAN CIVILIAN CASUALTIES FROM OCTOBER 7, 2001, TO FEBRUARY 6, 2002, TOTALED BETWEEN 3,300 AND 3,600.*

YOU'RE USIN' NUMBERS!

‹MAMA..›
‹PAPA..›

*MARC W. HEROLD, "DEAD AFGHAN CIVILIANS: DISROBING THE NON-COUNTERS," WWW.CURSOR.ORG, AUGUST 20, 2002.

IN THE PERIOD DURING WHICH THESE CIVILIAN CASUALTIES OCCURRED, THE NUMBER OF TALIBAN AND AL QAEDA MEMBERS ESTIMATED KILLED IN ACTION TOTALED 5,000. *

THESE NUMBERS SHOW THAT OF THE TOTAL NUMBER OF PEOPLE KILLED IN THE FIRST FEW MONTHS OF THE U.S. CAMPAIGN IN AFGHANISTAN, 4 IN 10 WERE CIVILIANS. PERHAPS BUSH NEEDS A REFRESHER COURSE IN SIMPLE MATHEMATICS IF HE BELIEVES THAT THE NUMBERS DON'T REFUTE THE BLATANTLY FALSE CLAIM THAT AMERICAN WEAPONS "SPARE INNOCENT LIVES."

WHAT IS IT WITH PEOPLE AND NUMBERS?!

*ROMESH RATNESAR, "GRADING THE OTHER WAR," *TIME* (CANADIAN EDITION), OCTOBER 14, 2002, P. 32.

CIVILIAN CASUALTIES DIDN'T END WITH THE REMOVAL OF THE TALIBAN FROM POWER. AS U.S. FORCES CONTINUED TO ACT IN OPERATIONS AGAINST TALIBAN AND AL QAEDA MILITANTS THROUGHOUT AFGHANISTAN, MORE CIVILIANS WOULD DIE.

IN ONE SUCH INCIDENT IN JULY 2002, U.S. PLANES, CLAIMING THAT THEY HAD BEEN FIRED UPON, BOMBED A WEDDING CELEBRATION, KILLING 48 CIVILIANS. *

BOOM! BLAM! POW!

WEDDINGS TODAY — FUNERALS TOMORROW

*CARLOTTA GALL, "AFGHAN VILLAGERS TORN BY GRIEF AFTER U.S. RAID KILLS 9 CHILDREN," NEW YORK TIMES, DECEMBER 8, 2003.

IN ANOTHER INCIDENT, NINE CHILDREN AND ONE ADULT WERE KILLED IN A DECEMBER 2003 RAID WHICH HAD BEEN INTENDED TO KILL A TALIBAN MEMBER WHO HAD LEFT THE VILLAGE WEEKS EARLIER. *

*IBID.

THREE MONTHS LATER, AFTER AN OFFICIAL INVESTIGATION, U.S. OFFICIALS DEFENDED THIS RAID WHICH FAILED TO KILL A SINGLE TALIBAN OR TERRORIST AND ONLY SUCCEEDED IN KILLING INNOCENT CIVILIANS. *

BUT THEN DEFENDING THE INDEFENSIBLE IS SOMETHING OF A HALLMARK OF THE MILITARY ESTABLISHMENT UNDER PRESIDENT GEORGE W. BUSH.

LOOK, IF AMERICA DOES SOMETHING, IT'S JUSTIFIED BY GOD!

*STEPHEN GRAHAM, "U.S. DEFENDS RAID THAT KILLED AFGHAN KIDS," ASSOCIATED PRESS, MARCH 10, 2004.

MANY OF THE SUSPECTED TERRORISTS AND TALIBAN TAKEN PRISONER IN AFGHANISTAN WERE SENT TO A U.S. NAVAL BASE AT GUANTANAMO BAY. THOUGH IT IS U.S. PROPERTY, IT IS ON FOREIGN SOIL, ALLOWING FOR THOSE DETAINED TO BE HELD WITHOUT THE RIGHTS THEY WOULD BE ALLOWED WERE THEY BEING HELD IN THE UNITED STATES.

THOUGH INTERNATIONAL ORGANIZATIONS CALLED ON BUSH TO DEFINE THESE PRISONERS AS PRISONERS OF WAR PROTECTED BY THE GENEVA CONVENTIONS, * IT BECAME CLEAR EARLY ON THAT BUSH WAS RESOLUTE TO DO EVERYTHING IN HIS POWER TO TRAMPLE WELL-ESTABLISHED INTERNATIONAL LAW.

WELCOME TO SUNNY GUANTANAMO BAY STAY FOR THE PIE!

*"UN SPEAKS OUT ON AFGHAN DETAINEES," BBCNEWS, FEBRUARY 12, 2002.

WHEN BUSH SPOKE OF THE DETAINEES AT GUANTANAMO SHORTLY AFTER HE HAD DECIDED TO HAVE THEM SHIPPED THERE, HE LOST HIS VERBAL FOOTING FOR A SECOND, BUT QUICKLY RECOVERED.

"...WE'RE IN TOTAL AGREEMENT ON HOW TO -- ON WHETHER OR NOT -- ON HOW THESE PRISONERS -- OR DETAINEES, EXCUSE ME, OUGHT TO BE TREATED. AND THEY'LL BE TREATED WELL." *

*BUSH REMARKS IN ROSE GARDEN, JANUARY 28, 2002.

TREATED WELL OR OTHERWISE, BUSH HAS DEMANDED THAT THESE "DETAINEES" BE HELD UNTIL AT LEAST ONE OF THE FOLLOWING CONDITIONS IS MET:

-THE DETAINEE WOULD NOT POSE A THREAT TO THE U.S. IF RELEASED,

-THE DETAINEE IS NO LONGER OF INTELLIGENCE VALUE TO THE U.S.,

OR

-HOSTILITIES IN THE "WAR ON TERROR" CEASE.

OF COURSE, THE FINAL DECISION ON WHETHER A DETAINEE IS RELEASED RESTS WITH PRESIDENT BUSH.

LET'S SEE.. WE'LL KEEP THESE ONES... AND LET **THIS** ONE GO. HE'S GOT A GOOD, INNOCENT-SOUNDING NAME!

ENRON O'REILLY

PRISONER LIST

EVEN WITH SUCH CONDITIONS IN PLACE, OFFICIALS WITHIN THE BUSH ADMINISTRATION HAVE AS MUCH AS CONCEDED THE OBVIOUS: THEY HAVE NO WAY OF KNOWING WHETHER RELEASED DETAINEES WILL POSE A FUTURE THREAT.

"WHAT WILL HAPPEN? WE'LL FIND OUT OVER TIME. WE'LL SEE WHAT HAPPENS." *

WHEN ASKED ABOUT FIVE BRITISH DETAINEES WHO WERE TRANSFERRED TO THE CUSTODY OF THE BRITISH GOVERNMENT IN MARCH 2004 (AND RELEASED FROM CUSTODY ALTOGETHER A SHORT TIME LATER), DEFENSE SECRETARY DONALD RUMSFELD SUGGESTED THAT THEY MAY STILL POSE A THREAT AFTER RELEASED.

NO, REALLY! WHERE'S DONALD RUMSFELD? WHO IS THIS GUY?

SOME CARICATURE, LOSER!

SOB!

*DEFENSE DEPARTMENT BRIEFING, MARCH 9, 2004.

EVIDENCE IS FOR EVIL-DOERS! WE'LL LOCK 'EM UP FOREVER 'CAUSE I SAY SO!

CSI: BUSH?

ONLY A FEW MONTHS AFTER THE FIRST DETAINEES ARRIVED AT GUANTANAMO, ANONYMOUS ADMINISTRATION SOURCES WERE LEAKING TO THE PRESS THAT BUSH WANTED TO TRY SOME DETAINEES ON CHARGES OF WAR CRIMES WITHOUT HAVING TO PRODUCE WITNESS OR DOCUMENT EVIDENCE OF THE ALLEGED CRIME. *

SO, FIRST A DETAINEE IS HELD WITHOUT BEING CHARGED. THEN, IF HE EVER IS CHARGED, THE PROSECUTORS MIGHT NOT EVEN HAVE TO PRODUCE BASIC EVIDENCE THAT HE COMMITTED A CRIME.

THAT'S FAIRNESS IN GEORGE W. BUSH COUNTRY.

*NEIL A. LEWIS, "U.S. WEIGHING NEW DOCTRINE FOR TRIBUNALS," NEW YORK TIMES, APRIL 21, 2002.

MORE THAN TWO YEARS AFTER THE FIRST PRISONERS ARRIVED AT GUANTANAMO, NOT A SINGLE DETAINEE HAS BEEN BROUGHT BEFORE THE PROMISED MILITARY TRIBUNALS. BUSH AND HIS ADVISORS CONTINUALLY TRY TO PAINT THE PROCESS TO LOOK MORE LEGITIMATE, EVEN AS THEIR CONTINUED FAILURE TO BRING FORWARD A SINGLE CASE REVEALS THAT THEY HAVE NO IDEA WHAT THEY'RE DOING.

SLOT A INTO TAB B? WUH? THESE DARN TRIBUNALS IS HARD!

HE THINKS THAT MODEL KIT IS THE BASIS FOR THE TRIBUNALS...

MODEL ROBOT

AND IT'S ALWAYS REASSURING TO KNOW THAT WHATEVER HAPPENS AT GUANTANAMO, DESPOTS EVERYWHERE ARE WATCHING TO FIND OUT HOW THEY, TOO, CAN IGNORE THE RULE OF LAW AND POINT TO THE U.S. PRESIDENT AS A SOURCE OF INSPIRATION FOR THEIR ACTIONS.

ONLY $19.95! FANTASTIC!

I TOOK THE GEORGE W. BUSH **PISS ON THE LAW** COURSE, AND GOT A DEGREE IN JUST FIFTEEN MINUTES! NOW I'M OPPRESSING PRISONERS --OH, I MEAN "DETAINEES"-- LIKE A PRO! THANK YOU, GEORGE W. BUSH!

ACTUAL DESPOTIC DICTATOR-TYPE TESTIMONIAL!

OUTSIDE ORGANIZATIONS STARTED PROTESTING BUSH'S RUNAROUND OF THE LAW ALMOST IMMEDIATELY. EVEN FORMER U.S. GOVERNMENT OFFICIALS CAME FORWARD TO DENOUNCE BUSH'S ACTIONS.

"THESE PRISONERS STAND IN A KIND OF PURGATORY. THEY ARE BEYOND THE REACH OF THE RULE OF LAW WHICH IS THE VERY ESSENCE OF AMERICA'S ROLE IN THE WORLD." *

*QUOTED IN SUE PLEMING, "GROUPS URGE SUPREME COURT TO ACT ON GUANTANAMO," REUTERS, OCTOBER 9, 2003.

William D. Rogers
former assistant secretary of state

THIS IS ONE SLIPPERY SLOPE THAT I GLADLY ACCEPT!

THE INTERNATIONAL COMMITTEE OF THE RED CROSS, THE ONLY OUTSIDE ORGANIZATION ALLOWED CONTACT WITH THE GUANTANAMO DETAINEES, MADE IT A POINT TO WARN THAT "DILUTING [DOMESTIC LEGAL] STANDARDS [IN THE FIGHT AGAINST TERRORISM] WOULD MEAN SETTING FOOT ON A SLIPPERY SLOPE WITH NO END IN SIGHT." *

*"RED CROSS WARNS AGAINST EROSION OF BASIC RIGHTS IN WAR ON TERROR," AGENCE FRANCE PRESSE, DECEMBER 3, 2004.

THE SUPREME COURT IS EXPECTED TO RULE BEFORE JULY 2004 AS TO WHETHER THE DETAINEES CAN CHALLENGE THEIR CAPTIVITY IN THE AMERICAN LEGAL SYSTEM. *

IF THE COURT RULES IN FAVOR OF THE DETAINEES, BUSH'S DETAINMENT OF THE ALLEGED AL QAEDA AND TALIBAN MEMBERS WOULD BE OPEN TO REVIEW BY ANY COURT THAT WOULD HEAR THE DETAINEES' CHALLENGES.

IF THE COURT RULES IN FAVOR OF BUSH'S ADMINISTRATION, THE WORLD CAN EXPECT THE DETENTIONS TO CONTINUE INDEFINITELY.

WELL, I KNOW THAT AT LEAST **FIVE** OF THE JUSTICES HAVE A SOFT SPOT FOR ME!

*JAMES VICINI, "SUPREME COURT TO DECIDE GUANTANAMO DETAINEES' CASES," REUTERS, NOVEMBER 10, 2003.

PRISONERS BEING HELD BY U.S. FORCES IN AFGHANISTAN MAY BE IN A SITUATION SIMILAR TO THOSE BEING HELD AT GUANTANAMO. BRAD ADAMS OF HUMAN RIGHTS WATCH HAS INDICATED THAT "†CIVILIANS ARE BEING DETAINED IN A LEGAL BLACK HOLE -- WITH NO TRIBUNALS, NO LEGAL COUNSEL, NO FAMILY VISITS, AND NO BASIC LEGAL PROTECTIONS." *

HELLO?

*QUOTED IN "AFGHANISTAN: ABUSES BY U.S. FORCES," HUMAN RIGHTS WATCH, MARCH 8, 2004.

ACCORDING TO A HUMAN RIGHTS WATCH REPORT, MOST OF THE OVER 1,000 PRISONERS DETAINED IN AFGHANISTAN WEREN'T EVEN CAPTURED DURING HOSTILITIES, * AND THE LACK OF DUE PROCESS DOES NOT ALLOW THOSE ARBITRARILY ARRESTED TO PROTEST THEIR CASE TO ANY OUTSIDE ARBITER.

BUT I'M JUST A FARMER!

*JIM LOBE, "U.S. SETS 'TERRIBLE EXAMPLE' IN AFGHANISTAN," ONEWORLD.NET, MARCH 8, 2004.

ALSO, TACTICS AKIN TO TORTURE ARE PRACTICED WITHIN U.S.-OPERATED DETENTION CENTERS IN AFGHANISTAN. ACCORDING TO HUMAN RIGHTS WATCH, "RELEASED DETAINEES HAVE SAID THAT U.S. FORCES SEVERELY BEAT THEM, DOUSED THEM WITH COLD WATER AND SUBJECTED THEM TO FREEZING TEMPERATURES. MANY SAID THEY WERE FORCED TO STAY AWAKE, OR TO STAND OR KNEEL IN PAINFUL POSITIONS FOR EXTENDED PERIODS OF TIME." *

IF'N HE'S INNOCENT, THIS'LL BUILD HIS CHARACTER!

SO.. TIRED..

*"AFGHANISTAN: ABUSES BY U.S. FORCES," HUMAN RIGHTS WATCH, MARCH 8, 2004.

EVEN THE DEATHS OF THREE DETAINEES WHILE IN U.S. CUSTODY HAVE GONE UNEXPLAINED BY DEFENSE OFFICIALS, DESPITE TWO OF THOSE DEATHS BEING QUALIFIED AS HOMICIDES BY U.S. INVESTIGATORS. *

*"AFGHANISTAN: ABUSES BY U.S. FORCES," HUMAN RIGHTS WATCH, MARCH 8, 2004.

FOR PURPOSES OF INTELLIGENCE GATHERING, U.S. POLICY HAS SHIFTED TO ALLOW FOR THE PASSING OF SOME TERROR SUSPECTS TO COUNTRIES WHICH USE TORTURE TECHNIQUES ON PRISONERS. *

SO U.S. OFFICIALS AREN'T ENGAGING IN TORTURE, THEY'RE JUST FACILITATING IT -- AND TAKING NOTES.

MAYBE PRESIDENT BUSH NEEDS HIS MORAL COMPASS READJUSTED...

*POSNER, WHY AMERICA SLEPT, P. 186.

IN ONE CASE, BUSH'S JUSTICE DEPARTMENT, UNDER THE LEADERSHIP OF ATTORNEY GENERAL JOHN ASHCROFT, DEPORTED MAHER ARAR, A CANADIAN CITIZEN, TO SYRIA, HIS BIRTH NATION, WHEN HE FAILED TO ADMIT TO U.S. IMMIGRATION OFFICIALS THAT HE WAS A MEMBER OF AL QAEDA. *

*"HIS YEAR IN HELL," 60 MINUTES II, JANUARY 21, 2004.

AFTER A YEAR OF TORTURE, SYRIA RETURNED ARAR TO CANADA. THROUGH TORTURING HIM, THEY FOUND NO EVIDENCE OF THE AL QAEDA CONNECTION THAT THE U.S. HAD CLAIMED WAS THE REASON FOR DETAINING AND DEPORTING HIM TO SYRIA IN THE FIRST PLACE. *

*IBID.

HOW WERE THINGS SHAPING UP IN AFGHANISTAN AFTER THE REMOVAL OF THE TALIBAN FROM GOVERNMENT?

CERTAINLY THINGS ARE MUCH WORSE THAN THEY MIGHT BE IF GEORGE W. BUSH HAD NOT SHIFTED RESOURCES AND ATTENTION SO COMPLETELY FROM AFGHANISTAN TO IRAQ THROUGH MUCH OF 2002 AND 2003.

AFGHANISTAN HAD BECOME SO NEGLECTED BY BUSH THAT BY LATE 2003, SOME IN THE MEDIA HAD TAKEN TO CALLING THE CONFLICT "THE FORGOTTEN WAR," * UNFORTUNATELY USURPING THE TITLE FROM THE KOREAN WAR, LEAVING IT TO BE CALLED "THE FORGOTTEN WAR OF THE 20TH CENTURY."

*TIME, THE INDEPENDENT, AND EVEN VFW MAGAZINE HAVE RUN ARTICLES DESCRIBING THE WAR IN AFGHANISTAN AS A "FORGOTTEN WAR."

SO LONG, EVENT!

YANK!

YIKES!

AFGHANISTAN

SHOOP!

IN HIS 2004 STATE OF THE UNION ADDRESS, PRESIDENT GEORGE W. BUSH LAID OUT HOW EVERYTHING IN AFGHANISTAN WAS ON THE RIGHT TRACK.

"[AFGHANISTAN] HAS A NEW CONSTITUTION, GUARANTEEING FREE ELECTIONS AND FULL PARTICIPATION BY WOMEN."

BUSH'S WORDS MAKE IT SOUND LIKE THINGS ARE GOING RELATIVELY WELL. BUT IF THERE'S ONE LESSON TO BE LEARNED FROM THE SPEECHES OF GEORGE W. BUSH, IT'S THAT HE'LL ALWAYS SAY WHAT HE'D LIKE EVERYONE TO THINK IS GOING ON, NOT WHAT'S ACTUALLY GOING ON.

TOO OFTEN, PEOPLE ACCEPT HIS ROSY SCENARIOS AS REALITY WHEN THE FACTS ON THE GROUND INDICATE OTHERWISE.

THANKS TO MY HUMBLE POLICIES, AMERICA CAN NOW BREATHE UNDERWATER!

SO IN AFGHANISTAN, THOUGH BUSH POINTS OUT THAT THE CONSTITUTION DRAFTED AND AGREED TO IN JANUARY 2004 INCLUDES GUARANTEES FOR WOMEN, HE FAILS TO MENTION THAT IT IS BASED ON SHARIA LAW, WHICH IF INTERPRETED BY EXTREME CONSERVATIVE MUSLIMS, COULD RESULT IN THE EMERGENCE OF WHAT ONE U.S. AMBASSADOR REFERRED TO AS "TALIBAN-LITE."*

IT'S LIKE EVERY DAY IS FREEDOM DAY!

HAVE SOME FREEDOM!

*TOM HENEGHAN, "AFGHAN ENVOY DEFENDS NEW CONSTITUTION ON RIGHTS," REUTERS, JANUARY 8, 2004.

JUST FIVE WEEKS AFTER THE FIRST U.S. BOMBS FELL ON AFGHANISTAN, FIRST LADY LAURA BUSH ACTED AS THOUGH WOMEN ALL OVER AFGHANISTAN WERE SUDDENLY FREE, AS IF BY MAGIC.

"BECAUSE OF OUR RECENT MILITARY GAINS IN MUCH OF AFGHANISTAN, WOMEN ARE NO LONGER IMPRISONED IN THEIR HOMES. THE FIGHT AGAINST TERRORISM IS ALSO A FIGHT FOR THE RIGHTS AND DIGNITY OF WOMEN." *

TOO LATE!

*QUOTED IN MARIAM RAWI, "RULE OF THE RAPISTS," *GUARDIAN* (UK), FEBRUARY 12, 2004.

BUT THINGS HAVEN'T REALLY CHANGED ALL THAT MUCH, ACCORDING TO AN AMNESTY INTERNATIONAL REPORT, WHICH STATES THAT "THE RISK OF RAPE AND SEXUAL VIOLENCE BY MEMBERS OF ARMED FACTIONS AND FORMER COMBATANTS IS STILL HIGH. FORCED MARRIAGE, PARTICULARLY OF GIRL CHILDREN, AND VIOLENCE AGAINST WOMEN IN THE FAMILY ARE WIDESPREAD IN MANY AREAS OF THE COUNTRY."*

WIFE!

BOING!

*IBID.

DESPITE ADVANCES IN WOMEN'S RIGHTS IN SOME OF THE MAJOR AFGHAN CITIES, IN THE VAST RURAL AREAS, OPPRESSION OF WOMEN IS WIDESPREAD. ONE STARTLING INDICATOR OF THIS OPPRESSION IS THAT THE MONTHLY SUICIDE RATE AMONG GIRLS IS ACTUALLY HIGHER TODAY THAN IT WAS UNDER TALIBAN RULE. *

*IBID.

EVEN AS THE AFGHAN GOVERNMENT PRESENTS ITSELF AS PRO-WOMENS' RIGHTS, MUCH OF THIS PRESENTATION HIDES THE TRUTH.

ACCORDING TO MARIAM RAWI OF THE REVOLUTIONARY ASSOCIATION OF WOMEN OF AFGHANISTAN, "WOMEN CANNOT FIND JOBS, AND GIRLS' SCHOOLS OFTEN LACK THE MOST BASIC MATERIALS... THERE IS NO LEGAL PROTECTION FOR WOMEN, AND THE OLDER LEGAL SYSTEMS PROHIBIT THEM FROM GETTING HELP WHEN THEY NEED IT. FEMALE SINGERS ARE NOT ALLOWED ON KABUL TELEVISION, AND WOMEN'S SONGS ARE NOT PLAYED, WHILE SCENES IN FILMS OF WOMEN NOT WEARING THE HIJAB ARE CENSORED." *

WOMEN'S INDUSTRIES

WOMEN NEED NOT APPLY

*IBID.

WHAT OF THE FREE ELECTIONS GUARANTEED BY THE NEW AFGHAN CONSTITUTION?

SCHEDULED FOR JUNE 2004, THE LACK OF SECURITY CONDITIONS SUITABLE FOR ELECTIONS THROUGHOUT MUCH OF THE COUNTRY HAS LED MANY OBSERVERS TO BELIEVE THAT THE ELECTIONS WILL HAVE TO BE POSTPONED. *

VOTE!

HELLO, MY NAME IS: THE TALIBAN

*MIKE COLLETT-WHITE, "ATTACKS RAISE FRESH DOUBTS OVER AFGHAN ELECTIONS," REUTERS, JANUARY 10, 2004.

ONE OF THE MAIN REASONS THAT THE ELECTIONS CANNOT BE HELD AS EARLY AS JUNE 2004 IS THAT REGISTRATION OF VOTERS IS NOT PROGRESSING QUICKLY ENOUGH. IN TWO MONTHS OF VOTER REGISTRATION, LESS THAN 10% OF 10.5 MILLION ELIGIBLE VOTERS HAD BEEN REGISTERED, WITH MOST OF THESE VOTERS LOCATED IN THE MORE-SECURE CITIES, AND ONLY 2% OF ELIGIBLE WOMEN REGISTERED. *

VOTER REGISTRATION

BOING!

*PAMELA CONSTABLE, "AFGHAN ELECTIONS COULD BE DELAYED," WASHINGTON POST, FEBRUARY 17, 2004, P. A16.

POSTPONING THE ELECTIONS WOULD MAKE THE SITUATION IN AFGHANISTAN LOOK WORSE THAN BUSH HAS SUGGESTED IT TO BE. SOME SEE BUSH CONTINUING TO PUSH FOR ELECTIONS IN JUNE 2004, DESPITE THE DANGERS, IN ORDER TO PROP UP HIS OWN REELECTION CAMPAIGN. *

THE PERCEPTION THAT THINGS ARE GOING JUST AS BUSH SAYS THEY ARE IS MORE IMPORTANT TO HIM THAN ENSURING AFGHANISTAN'S FUTURE AS A STABLE DEMOCRACY.

MISSION ACCOMPLISHED!

FOUR MORE YEARS!

BOING!

I DON'T REPRESENT THE POPULATION AND ALL I GOT WAS THIS GOVERNMENTAL POSITION!

*STEVEN R. WEISMAN, "U.S. AIDES HINT AFGHAN VOTING MAY BE PUT OFF," NEW YORK TIMES, FEBRUARY 16, 2004.

BEFORE THE WAR, THE TALIBAN HAD BANNED OPIUM PRODUCTION IN AFGHANISTAN. THE U.S. INVASION AND REMOVAL OF THE TALIBAN FROM POWER HAS ALLOWED FOR OPIUM PRODUCTION TO DRASTICALLY INCREASE, SO MUCH SO THAT AFGHAN OPIUM SALES ACCOUNT FOR ONE-THIRD OF WORLDWIDE NARCOTICS PROCEEDS. *

AFGHAN OPIUM NARCOTICS PROCEEDS

OTHER INTERNATIONAL NARCOTICS PROCEEDS

YUMMY OPIUM PIE!

ME WANTY!!

*FIDA HUSSEIN, "SINCE U.S. WAR, AFGHANS BACK IN OPIUM BIZ," INTER PRESS SERVICE, JANUARY 26, 2004.

THE PROBLEM OF INCREASING OPIUM PRODUCTION REMAINS ESSENTIALLY UNCHALLENGED BY GEORGE W. BUSH. SOME HAVE SUGGESTED THAT THE DRUG TRADE IS BEING IGNORED IN EXCHANGE FOR SUPPORT FROM THE MANY WARLORDS OF AFGHANISTAN FOR A SECURE AND UNITED COUNTRY. *

JUST A SECURE AND UNITED COUNTRY FULL OF POPPY FIELDS...

RE-ELECTION FOR ME OR SECURITY FOR AFGHANISTAN? RE-ELECTION, I CHOOSE YOU!

PTOO!

*RICHARD NORTON-TAYLOR, "NATO HAPPY TO IGNORE EXPLOSION IN AFGHAN OPIUM OUTPUT, SAYS RUSSIA," *GUARDIAN* (UK), FEBRUARY 9, 2004.

ODDLY, IT WAS PRESIDENT GEORGE W. BUSH WHO, IN MAY 2001, GAVE THE TALIBAN GOVERNMENT OF AFGHANISTAN A $43 MILLION REWARD FOR REDUCING OPIUM PRODUCTION THERE. *

BUSH WAS FUNDING THE REGIME THAT WAS THEN KNOWN TO BE HARBORING OSAMA BIN LADEN AND REFUSING TO TURN HIM OVER. HE WAS LINING THE POCKETS OF THE TALIBAN GOVERNMENT, RESPONSIBLE FOR ALL MANNER OF HUMAN RIGHTS ABUSES. THIS WAS, OF COURSE, THE SAME GEORGE W. BUSH WHO CONSTANTLY DEMANDS RESULTS FROM OTHER GOVERNMENTS THAT RECEIVE U.S. AID.

WHAT THE HELL WAS BUSH THINKING TO SO BLATANTLY SUPPORT ONE OF THE WORST REGIMES IN THE WORLD? TO SUBSIDIZE EVIL IS TO BECOME ENTANGLED IN EVIL, SO PERHAPS BUSH SHOULD START REFERRING TO HIMSELF AS ONE OF THE EVIL-DOERS.

*"BUSH ADMINISTRATION APPROVES AID TO THEOCRATIC AFGHANISTAN," CHURCH AND STATE, JULY 1, 2001, P. 18.

FOR REFUGEES WHO RETURNED TO AFGHANISTAN AFTER THE U.S. WAR OUSTED THE TALIBAN FROM POWER, LIFE IS INCREDIBLY DIFFICULT. MANY REFUGEES LIVE IN OLD, ABANDONED, AND POTENTIALLY UNSAFE ABANDONED GOVERNMENT BUILDINGS. FOOD AND MONETARY ASSISTANCE OFTEN DO NOT REACH THE NEEDIEST, EVEN IN THE CAPITAL CITY OF KABUL. *

*ILENE PRUSHER, "FOR AFGHANS, LIFE GETS WORSE AND WORSE," ONEWORLD.NET, DECEMBER 23, 2003.

TO MAKE MATTERS WORSE, GOVERNMENT OFFICIALS HAVE THREATENED TO EVICT SOME OF THE REFUGEES FROM THESE BUILDINGS -- THEIR ONLY SHELTER FROM THE ELEMENTS. *

*IBID.

FOR MANY OF THE POOREST AFGHANIS, LIVING WITHOUT BASIC CONVENIENCES SUCH AS WATER, HEAT AND ELECTRICITY IS THE NORM. SENDING A CHILD TO SCHOOL COSTS MORE THAN MOST OF THESE FAMILIES CAN AFFORD. *

*IBID.

AID IS BEING PROVIDED IN THE FORM OF CONSTRUCTION MATERIALS TO SOME REFUGEES, WHO ARE THEN EXPECTED TO BUILD THEIR OWN HOMES, EVEN THOUGH MANY OF THEM DON'T OWN LAND ON WHICH TO BUILD A HOME. *

*IBID.

WHAT ABOUT OSAMA BIN LADEN, THE LEADER OF AL QAEDA, THE REALLY BAD GUY THAT KEEPS TELLING MUSLIMS TO TAKE UP ARMS AGAINST THE UNITED STATES AND CIVILIZATION AS WE KNOW IT?

ON SEPTEMBER 17, 2001, GEORGE W. BUSH MADE CLEAR HIS INTENTIONS REGARDING BIN LADEN:

"I WANT JUSTICE. AND THERE'S AN OLD POSTER OUT WEST, AS I RECALL, THAT SAID, 'WANTED: DEAD OR ALIVE.'" *

*REMARKS AT THE PENTAGON, SEPTEMBER 17, 2001.

WHEN ASKED TO CLARIFY HIS STATEMENT, BUSH EMPHASIZED HIS DESIRE FOR JUSTICE TO BE SERVED THROUGH THE CAPTURE OR DEATH OF BIN LADEN:

"ALL I WANT AND AMERICA WANTS HIM BROUGHT TO JUSTICE. THAT'S WHAT WE WANT." *

*IBID.

BY MARCH 2002, BUSH WAS SINGING A DIFFERENT TUNE:

"HE'S A PERSON WHO'S NOW BEEN MARGINALIZED. HIS NETWORK, HIS HOST GOVERNMENT HAS BEEN DESTROYED. HE'S THE ULTIMATE PARASITE WHO FOUND WEAKNESS, EXPLOITED IT, AND MET HIS MATCH." *

*PRESS CONFERENCE, MARCH 13, 2002.

BUT BIN LADEN HAD NOT BEEN MARGINALIZED, AS EVIDENCED BY HIS REAPPEARANCE IN VIDEO AND AUDIO RECORDINGS URGING JIHAD AGAINST AMERICA AND ITS ALLIES.

BUSH WOULD EVENTUALLY RETURN TO BIN LADEN AS PUBLIC ENEMY NUMBER ONE, BUT FIRST HE WANTED TO TURN THE WORLD'S ATTENTION TO IRAQ AND ANOTHER "EVIL-DOER":

SADDAM HUSSEIN.

GEORGE W. BUSH WAS THE REPUBLICAN FRONTRUNNER NEARLY A YEAR BEFORE THE FIRST PRIMARY IN THE 2000 U.S. PRESIDENTIAL RACE. *

BUT EVEN BEFORE HE HAD OFFICIALLY LAUNCHED HIS CAMPAIGN, BUSH WAS SAYING AND DOING THINGS THAT SHOULD HAVE SET OFF ALARMS IN THE MINDS OF VOTERS.

HOW TO RUIN AMERICA

*HUGO GURDON, "INTERNATIONAL: PARTIES SET FOR BUSH AND GORE SHOWDOWN," *DAILY TELEGRAPH* (UK), FEBRUARY 25, 1999, P. 21.

WHEN GEORGE W. BUSH'S CAMPAIGN FOUND THE PARODY SITE WWW.GWBUSH.COM DIDN'T FURTHER THEIR CAUSE OF PUSHING THEIR CANDIDATE ON THE WORLD, BUSH BROKE AWAY FROM HIS HANDLERS AND SAID SOMETHING REMARKABLE, WHICH SOMEHOW DIDN'T SEEM TO HURT HIS CHANCES IN THE RACE FOR THE PRESIDENCY.

"THERE OUGHT TO BE LIMITS TO FREEDOM." *

SOUNDS LIKE HE WAS MAKING PLANS FOR A POST-9/11 SOCIETY WAY BACK THEN!

*WAYNE SLATER, "BUSH CRITICIZES WEB SITE AS MALICIOUS," *DALLAS MORNING NEWS*, MAY 22, 1999.

WHEN THE ISSUE OF WHETHER BUSH HAD EVER USED ILLEGAL DRUGS WAS RAISED, BUSH, AT FIRST, REFUSED TO ANSWER.

"I'VE MADE MISTAKES IN THE PAST, AND I'VE LEARNED FROM MY MISTAKES." *

*NANCY GIBBS, "'I'VE MADE MISTAKES...'", *TIME*, AUGUST 30, 1999, P. 32.

AH, BUT BUSH DIDN'T WANT TO LOOK HYPOCRITICAL. HE CAME BACK TO THE ISSUE TO PROVE THAT HE COULD MEET THE STANDARDS THAT WERE SET FOR THOSE HIRED BY THE WHITE HOUSE.

"AS I UNDERSTAND IT, THE CURRENT [FBI] FORM ASKS THE QUESTION, 'DID SOMEBODY USE DRUGS WITHIN THE LAST SEVEN YEARS?' AND I WILL BE GLAD TO ANSWER THAT QUESTION, AND THE ANSWER IS NO." *

SUCH DIGNITY! BUSH HADN'T USED ILLEGAL DRUGS ANYTIME FROM HIS LATE-FORTIES TO EARLY-FIFTIES! AMERICA WAS AMAZED AT THIS MAN'S WILLINGNESS TO PRESENT ONLY ABSOLUTE TRUTH.

*IBID.

BUT HE WASN'T DONE YET! THERE WAS STILL MORE FROM THIS SPECTACULAR TRUTH-TELLER.

LESS THAN 24 HOURS AFTER SAYING HE HADN'T USED ILLEGAL DRUGS IN THE LAST SEVEN YEARS, BUSH WAS READY TO GIVE THOSE BLOODTHIRSTY REPORTERS MORE OF WHAT THEY WANTED.

"NOT ONLY COULD I PASS THE BACKGROUND CHECK AND THE STANDARDS APPLIED TO TODAY'S WHITE HOUSE, BUT I COULD HAVE PASSED THE BACKGROUND CHECK...WHEN MY DAD WAS PRESIDENT OF THE UNITED STATES, A 15-YEAR PERIOD." *

*NANCY GIBBS, "'I'VE MADE MISTAKES...'", *TIME*, AUGUST 30, 1999, P. 32.

SIMPLY AMAZING! BUSH HADN'T USED ILLEGAL DRUGS SINCE 1974, WHEN HE WAS 28 YEARS OLD. THAT THE ENTIRE COUNTRY DIDN'T DROP WHATEVER THEY WERE DOING UPON HEARING THIS TO APPLAUD THIS PRINCIPLED MAN FOR BEING SO STRAIGHTFORWARD IS UTTERLY ASTONISHING.

BUT SERIOUSLY, WHY WOULDN'T HE JUST TOSS OUT A BLANKET DENIAL OF DRUG USE?

OKAY!

"I DON'T WANT TO SEND THE SIGNAL TO CHILDREN THAT WHATEVER I MAY HAVE DONE IS O.K." *

Ok!

OK!

*IBID.

SO, IF GEORGE W. BUSH DIDN'T USE ILLEGAL DRUGS BEFORE 1974, HE WOULDN'T SAY.

OOPS! I MADE A MISTAKE!

IF BUSH DID USE DRUGS BEFORE 1974, HOWEVER, THE FACT THAT HE HAD BECOME A PRESIDENTIAL CANDIDATE A FEW DECADES LATER WOULD BE A PERMISSION SLIP FOR TODAY'S YOUTH TO SEEK THEIR OWN DRUG-PAVED PATH TO THE PRESIDENCY.

WHAT DID YOU DO?

DON'T LOOK! YOU'LL DO IT TOO IF YOU SEE!

WISE OLD GEORGE W. BUSH HAD MADE MISTAKES IN HIS YOUTH. HE DIDN'T WANT TO TELL ANYONE WHAT THESE MISTAKES WERE FOR FEAR THAT HIS ERRORS WOULD SOMEHOW SPAWN A NEW GENERATION OF DANGEROUS COPYCAT MISTAKE-MAKERS.

WHEN REPUBLICAN PRESIDENTIAL CANDIDATE JOHN MCCAIN'S CAMPAIGN APPEARED TO BE GAINING STEAM IN NEW HAMPSHIRE, WITH MCCAIN CATCHING UP TO BUSH'S LEAD IN THE POLLS, A DEVIOUS WHISPER CAMPAIGN BEGAN.

MCCAIN, A U.S. SENATOR FROM ARIZONA, WAS HELD AS A PRISONER OF WAR IN NORTH VIETNAM FOR 5 ½ YEARS DURING THE VIETNAM WAR. THE DARK WHISPER CAMPAIGN AGAINST MCCAIN SOUGHT TO PORTRAY HIM AS MENTALLY UNSTABLE AS A RESULT OF THE TORTURE HE SUFFERED WHILE IN CAPTIVITY. *

LET'S SEE HOW MCCAIN LIKES **POLITICAL** TORTURE!

KARL ROVE

*ELIZABETH DREW, "THOSE WHISPERS ABOUT MCCAIN," *WASHINGTON POST*, NOVEMBER 19, 1999, P. A45

WHILE THE BLAME CANNOT BE PLACED WITH ABSOLUTE CERTAINTY ON GEORGE W. BUSH, WHO HAD REPEATEDLY PLEDGED TO RUN A POSITIVE CAMPAIGN, IT CAN BE PLACED ON BUSH SUPPORTERS AND MEMBERS OF THE BUSH CAMPAIGN.

IT IS THESE SURROGATES WHO ENGAGE IN DIRTY POLITICS SO THAT BUSH DOESN'T HAVE TO GET PERSONALLY INVOLVED, AND IT IS BUSH'S POLITICAL ADVISOR KARL ROVE WHO MANAGES THE MOVES OF MANY OF THESE SURROGATES. *

DESTROY!

*JAMES MOORE AND WAYNE SLATER, *BUSH'S BRAIN: HOW KARL ROVE MADE GEORGE W. BUSH PRESIDENTIAL*, HOBOKEN: JOHN WILEY & SONS, INC., 2003, P. 27.

THE ROWDY RARIN' ROVERS! VS. JOHN MCCAIN

THE ATTACK ON MCCAIN'S MENTAL CAPACITIES FAILED TO SINK HIS CHANCES, AND ACTUALLY SEEMED TO BOOST HIS STANDINGS AMONG THE REPUBLICAN CANDIDATES, AS MANY VOTERS SENSED THAT THE UNBELIEVABLY SLIMY ATTACKS HAD ORIGINATED IN THE BUSH CAMP.

AFTER MCCAIN WON THE REPUBLICAN NEW HAMPSHIRE PRIMARY BY A COMFORTABLE 18 PERCENT MARGIN, BUSH WAS READY TO PULL OUT ALL THE STOPS TO BRING MCCAIN'S CAMPAIGN TO A CRASHING HALT. THE MENTAL INSTABILITY ATTACKS WERE TAME COMPARED TO SOME OF THE OUTRAGEOUS RUMORS THAT WOULD APPEAR IN THE FOLLOWING WEEKS.

BUSH'S STRATEGY OF GAINING SUPPORT FOR HIMSELF FROM THE EXTREME RIGHT WING, WHILE AT THE SAME TIME ALLOWING HIS SUPPORTERS TO TEAR MCCAIN DOWN GOT UNDERWAY THE DAY AFTER THE NEW HAMPSHIRE PRIMARIES.

BUSH SPOKE AT BOB JONES UNIVERSITY, AN ANTI-CATHOLIC INSTITUTION WITH A POLICY AGAINST INTERRACIAL DATING.

LATER, BUSH WOULD OFFICIALLY DISTANCE HIMSELF FROM THE UNIVERSITY'S IDEOLOGY, * BUT ONLY AFTER HE HAD BEATEN MCCAIN IN SOUTH CAROLINA, AND BECAUSE HE NEEDED THE SUPPORT OF MODERATE CONSERVATIVES TO WIN PRIMARIES ELSEWHERE.

*DAVID S. BRODER AND MIKE ALLEN, "BUSH CITES REGRET ON BOB JONES; APOLOGY TO CATHOLICS FOLLOWS FAILURE TO FAULT COLLEGE'S BIASES," *WASHINGTON POST*, FEBRUARY 27, 2000.

NEARLY A MONTH AFTER HIS BOB JONES UNIVERSITY VISIT, BUSH APOLOGIZED PUBLICLY WITH A LETTER TO CARDINAL JOHN O'CONNOR.

WHEN CONFRONTED BY REPORTERS ON HIS CAMPAIGN PLANE AS TO WHETHER HIS LETTER TO THE CARDINAL WAS ENOUGH, BUSH OPENED A PEN KNIFE AND PUT IT TO HIS THROAT.

"WHAT DO YOU WANT? I JUST ATE CROW ON NATIONAL TV?" *

*MOORE AND SLATER, *BUSH'S BRAIN*, P. 260.

ANYWAY, BACK TO THE BUSH CAMPAIGN'S OUTRAGEOUS ATTACKS. HOW LOW WOULD GEORGE W. BUSH AND HIS SURROGATES GO TO SINK JOHN MCCAIN?

AFTER MCCAIN MET WITH MEMBERS OF THE LOG CABIN REPUBLICANS (A GROUP REPRESENTING GAY AND LESBIAN REPUBLICANS), BUSH SURROGATES MOUNTED A MASSIVE PHONE CAMPAIGN IN SOUTH CAROLINA TO PORTRAY MCCAIN AS "THE FAG CANDIDATE." *

BUSH REFUSED TO MEET WITH THE LOG CABIN REPUBLICANS UNTIL AFTER HIS STANDING AS THE REPUBLICAN NOMINEE SEEMED CERTAIN.

*JOHN NICHOLS, "BUSH GOES TO THE EXTREME TO GET VOTES," *WISCONSIN STATE JOURNAL*, FEBRUARY 24, 2000, P. 12A.

ONE BUSH CAMPAIGN WEAPON WAS THE "PUSH POLL."

THE IDEA BEHIND A PUSH POLL IS TO CALL AN INDIVIDUAL WHO MAY BE UNDECIDED ON WHO THEY'RE GOING TO VOTE FOR AND TO ASK LEADING QUESTIONS THAT SUGGEST NEGATIVE THINGS ABOUT A PARTICULAR CANDIDATE.

IF JOHN MCCAIN HAD A HISTORY OF BURNING DOWN ORPHANAGES FULL OF CUTE KIDS AND ADORABLE BABY ANIMALS, WOULD YOU THINK OF HIM AS MORE PRESIDENTIAL OR LESS PRESIDENTIAL?

WHO GAVE YOU THIS NUMBER?!

HERE ARE TWO OF THE PUSH POLL QUESTIONS USED AGAINST MCCAIN IN SOUTH CAROLINA:

"DO YOU KNOW THE MCCAIN TAX PLAN DOES NOT GIVE A SIGNIFICANT TAX CUT TO AVERAGE WORKING FAMILIES?" *

"DO YOU AGREE WITH MCCAIN'S PLAN TO GIVE MORE POWER TO THE MEDIA AND UNIONS TO PICK THE PRESIDENT?" *

*BOTH EXAMPLES FROM "SENATOR MCCAIN ACCUSING GOVERNOR BUSH OF PUSH POLLING IN SOUTH CAROLINA," *CBS EVENING NEWS*, FEBRUARY 10, 2000.

RALPH REED, FORMER LEADER OF THE CHRISTIAN COALITION, JOINED THE BUSH CAMPAIGN TO SPREAD DISINFORMATION ABOUT MCCAIN'S STANCE ON REPRODUCTIVE RIGHTS. THOUGH THE STANDS OF BUSH AND MCCAIN AGAINST ABORTION WERE ACTUALLY QUITE SIMILAR, THE MAILINGS AND PHONE CALLS FROM REED'S GROUP PORTRAYED MCCAIN AS LESS COMMITTED TO THE ANTI-ABORTION MOVEMENT THAN BUSH. *

BUSH LOVES THE UNBORN MORE THAN ANYONE!

*ERIC POOLEY, "READ MY KNUCKLES," *TIME* (CANADIAN EDITION), FEBRUARY 28, 2000, P. 16.

ONE BUSH SUPPORTER, BOB JONES UNIVERSITY PROFESSOR RICHARD HAND, SENT EMAILS TO REPUBLICAN VOTERS IN SOUTH CAROLINA, CLAIMING THAT MCCAIN "CHOSE TO FOCUS HIS LIFE ON PARTYING, PLAYING, DRINKING AND WOMANIZING." *

LOOKING AT THE FIRST THREE POINTS OF THIS OF THE ACCUSATION, ONE MIGHT HAVE THOUGHT HAND WAS TALKING ABOUT A YOUNGER GEORGE W. BUSH.

*ANDREW SULLIVAN, "BUSH REVEALS HIS POISONOUS COLOURS," *SUNDAY TIMES OF LONDON*, FEBRUARY 20, 2000, P. 8.

HEY MA! THE COMPUTER BOX SAY JOHN MCCAIN DID BAD STUFF! GASP! NOW IT SAY IT HAS A CURE FOR MY SMALL PENIS!

BUSH WENT ON TO DEFEAT MCCAIN IN SOUTH CAROLINA, AND SHIFTED TO ACTING LIKE A MORE MODERATE CONSERVATIVE THROUGH THE REMAINDER OF THE PRIMARIES, CONVINCINGLY ENOUGH TO BECOME THE REPUBLICAN PRESIDENTIAL NOMINEE WHO WOULD FACE DEMOCRATIC NOMINEE AL GORE.

THERE'S A CURE?

IN SEPTEMBER, BUSH ALLOWED THE AIRING OF A REPUBLICAN PARTY COMMERCIAL ATTACKING AL GORE'S HEALTH CARE PLAN.

IN THE AD, HOWEVER, WAS SOMETHING THAT MANY DEMOCRATS SAW AS AN INTENTIONAL SUBLIMINAL MESSAGE. FOR A FRACTION OF A SECOND, THE WORD "RATS" FLASHED ACROSS THE SCREEN.

Poo! Poo!

"I SAW IT ON A COMPUTER AND DIDN'T SEE RATS WHEN I SAW IT..." *

*"PROFILE: CONTROVERSY SURROUNDING GEORGE W. BUSH POLITICAL AD IN WHICH THE WORD 'RATS' IS FLASHED ACROSS THE SCREEN," *MORNING EDITION* (NPR), SEPTEMBER 13, 2000.

IT SEEMED A STRETCH WHEN THE BUSH CAMPAIGN CLAIMED THAT THE ERROR WAS ACCIDENTAL. WHEN THE PRESS SOUGHT AN EXPLANATION, BUSH PLED IGNORANCE.

ZOOM! ZOOM!

VOTE FOR ME!

"I WANT TO MAKE IT CLEAR TO PEOPLE THAT, YOU KNOW, THE IDEA OF PUTTING SUBLIMINABLE MESSAGES INTO ADS IS -- IT'S RIDICULOUS." *

*IBID.

GORE IS A RAT!

HEE HEE

IT'S TREW

EEK EEK

MAYBE BUSH REALLY HADN'T CAUGHT THE "RATS" IN THE AD WHEN HE APPROVED IT. BUT TO THINK THAT NO ONE INVOLVED IN THE AD'S CREATION HAD NOTICED THE WORD FLASHING ACROSS THE SCREEN IS WHAT IS TRULY RIDICULOUS.

OR PERHAPS WHEN BUSH INVENTED THE WORD "SUBLIMINABLE," HE WAS SUBLIMINALLY SUGGESTING THAT HIS CAMPAIGN WAS "ABLE" TO USE "SUBLIMINAL" MESSAGES.

THE WORLD MAY NEVER KNOW.

IN SEPTEMBER 2000, THE ISSUE OF A MOLE WITHIN THE BUSH CAMPAIGN AROSE.

THIS MOLE LEAKED A VIDEO OF A BUSH PRACTICE DEBATE SESSION AND SEVERAL DEBATE-RELATED DOCUMENTS TO GORE'S DEBATE COACH, TOM DOWNEY, WHO QUICKLY TURNED THE MATERIAL OVER TO THE FBI WHEN HE REALIZED WHAT IT WAS THAT HE HAD RECEIVED. *

*MIKE ALLEN AND TERRY M. NEAL, "HOMING IN ON A CAMPAIGN 'MOLE?", *WASHINGTON POST*, SEPTEMBER 27, 2000, P. A12.

TECHNOLOGY'S EVIL ANYHOW!

BUSH WAS FURIOUS. HIS CAMPAIGN DEMANDED THAT COMPUTER HARD DRIVES BE CONFISCATED FROM GORE CAMPAIGN HEADQUARTERS SO THAT ANY INCRIMINATING EMAILS THAT MIGHT INDICATE THE PERPETRATOR COULD BE FOUND. *

OF COURSE, SUCH AN ACT WOULD HAVE BEEN SEVERELY DISRUPTIVE TO THE *GORE* CAMPAIGN.

*IBID.

FACTUAL DEPICTION!

BUT IF BUSH AND ROVE HAD EXPECTED THE FBI TO DISRUPT THE GORE CAMPAIGN, THEY HAD BEEN WRONG. INSTEAD, THE FOCUS FELL MAINLY ON THE BUSH CAMPAIGN AND ON THE PEOPLE WHO HAD ACCESS TO THE MATERIAL IN QUESTION.

BUSH WANTED TO CREATE THE IMPRESSION THAT GORE HAD SENT AN OPERATIVE TO STEAL THE DEBATE TAPE AND PAPERS, BUT THERE WAS NO EVIDENCE TO BACK SUCH A CLAIM UP. BUT THE SUGGESTION SERVED THE PURPOSE OF SMEARING THE GORE CAMPAIGN.

IN MARCH 2000, IT WAS DISCOVERED THAT JUANITA YVETTE LOZANO, AN AIDE AT THE MEDIA CONSULTING FIRM THAT HANDLED THE BUSH CAMPAIGN'S ADVERTISING, WAS RESPONSIBLE FOR THE LEAK. * NO DEFINITIVE PROOF EMERGED THAT EITHER CAMPAIGN HAD ANY DIRECT INFLUENCE OVER HER ACTIONS.

BUT BUSH'S CAMPAIGN HAD THE MOTIVE (MAJORLY DISRUPTING GORE'S CAMPAIGN) AND THE ACCESS (THE TAPE WAS IN THE OFFICE OF BUSH'S MEDIA CONSULTANT, MARK MCKINNON; LOZANO WAS MCKINNON'S AIDE). AND WITH KARL ROVE'S HISTORY OF DIRTY TRICKS, THE SENSE THAT IT WAS A POLITICAL MANEUVER BY THE BUSH CAMPAIGN IS NOT EASILY SHAKEN.

*JOANNE ALLEN, "EX-AIDE PLEADS GUILTY TO LEAKING BUSH DEBATE TAPE," REUTERS, JUNE 14, 2001.

ON OCTOBER 3, 2000, IN THE FIRST PRESIDENTIAL DEBATE WITH AL GORE, GEORGE W. BUSH SHOWED THAT HE DIDN'T WANT TO BE HONEST ABOUT HIS OWN POLICIES:

"I WANT TO TAKE ONE HALF OF THE SURPLUS AND DEDICATE IT TO SOCIAL SECURITY, ONE QUARTER OF SURPLUS FOR IMPORTANT PROJECTS. AND I WANT TO SEND ONE QUARTER OF THE SURPLUS BACK TO THE PEOPLE WHO PAY THE BILLS." *

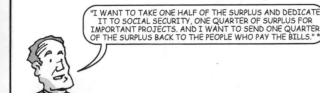

THE PROJECTED SURPLUS AT THE TIME, ACCORDING TO THE CONGRESSIONAL BUDGET OFFICE, WAS CLOSE TO $4.6 TRILLION. ONE QUARTER OF THAT SURPLUS WOULD BE $1.15 TRILLION.

BUSH'S PROPOSED TAX CUTS COST $1.3 TRILLION, WITH ANOTHER 3 BILLION IN INTEREST, TOTALING MORE THAN A THIRD OF THE SURPLUS. *

*PAUL KRUGMAN, "OOPS! HE DID IT AGAIN," *NEW YORK TIMES*, OCTOBER 1, 2000.

VICE PRESIDENT GORE EXPLAINED SOMETHING ABOUT BUSH'S ECONOMIC POLICY THAT BUSH DIDN'T WANT PEOPLE TO KNOW WAS TRUE.

"UNDER GOVERNOR BUSH'S TAX CUT PROPOSAL, HE WOULD SPEND MORE MONEY ON TAX CUTS FOR THE WEALTHIEST 1 PERCENT THAN ALL OF THE NEW SPENDING THAT HE PROPOSES FOR EDUCATION, HEALTH CARE, PRESCRIPTION DRUGS, AND NATIONAL DEFENSE ALL COMBINED." *

*2000 PRESIDENTIAL DEBATE, OCTOBER 3, 2000.

HOW DID BUSH RESPOND? HE TOLD THE AUDIENCE THAT GORE WAS LYING.

"WELL, LET ME JUST SAY, OBVIOUSLY TONIGHT WE'RE GOING TO HEAR SOME PHONY NUMBERS ABOUT WHAT I THINK AND WHAT WE OUGHT TO DO." *

*IBID.

BUT GORE WASN'T READY TO LIE DOWN IN THE FACE OF BUSH'S INSINUATION.

"THE GOVERNOR [BUSH] USED THE PHRASE 'PHONY NUMBERS,' BUT IF YOU -- IF YOU LOOK AT THE PLAN AND ADD THE NUMBERS UP, THESE NUMBERS ARE CORRECT. HE SPENDS MORE MONEY FOR TAX CUTS FOR THE WEALTHIEST 1 PERCENT THAN ALL OF HIS NEW SPENDING PROPOSALS FOR HEALTH CARE, PRESCRIPTION DRUGS, EDUCATION, AND NATIONAL DEFENSE ALL COMBINED." *

*2000 PRESIDENTIAL DEBATE, OCTOBER 3, 2000.

AT THE TIME, BUSH'S TAX CUTS FOR THE WEALTHIEST 1 PERCENT (CONSIDERING BOTH INCOME TAX CUTS AND THE REPEAL OF THE ESTATE TAX) TOTALED $561 BILLION. * BUSH'S NEW SPENDING ON THE AREAS GORE MENTIONED TOTALED ONLY $382 BILLION. SO GORE HAD HIS FACTS RIGHT, BUT THAT DIDN'T STOP BUSH FROM LYING.

WHO PAYS ATTENTION TO NUMBERS ANYWAY?

FUZZY MATH!

HE'S RIGHT!

I'M NO NERD!

*"REVISED ANALYSIS OF BUSH PLAN," CITIZENS FOR TAX JUSTICE, 8/31/00.

LATER IN THE FIRST DEBATE, WITH THE CANDIDATES DISCUSSING THEIR COMPETING PRESCRIPTION DRUG COVERAGE PLANS, BUSH CONTINUED TO BE BEFUDDLED BY GORE'S ABILITY TO COMPREHEND AND SPEAK ABOUT DOLLAR AMOUNTS IN BOTH HIS OWN AND BUSH'S PLANS.

"THIS IS A MAN WHO'S GOT GREAT NUMBERS. HE TALKS ABOUT NUMBERS. I'M BEGINNING TO THINK NOT ONLY DID HE INVENT THE INTERNET BUT HE INVENTED THE CALCULATOR. (LAUGHTER.) IT'S FUZZY MATH."

BUT GORE HAD BEEN DESCRIBING THE DETAILS OF BUSH'S POLICIES ACCURATELY.

MEANWHILE BUSH HAD SIMPLY MADE GENERAL STATEMENTS, AND SOMETIMES OUTRIGHT WRONG STATEMENTS, ABOUT HIS OWN POLICIES.

BUSH WENT CONTINUED TO SPEAK INCORRECTLY ABOUT HIS TAX PLAN, MISLEADING THE PUBLIC WITH BLATANT LIES.

"...BY FAR THE VAST MAJORITY OF THAT HELP [TAX RELIEF] GOES TO PEOPLE AT THE BOTTOM OF THE ECONOMIC LADDER." *

WHERE'S MY FOOD STAMPS?

HE THEN WENT ON TO SPEAK OF FAMILIES OF FOUR MAKING $50,000 AS IF THEY WERE THE ONES "AT THE BOTTOM OF THE ECONOMIC LADDER."

*2000 PRESIDENTIAL DEBATE, OCTOBER 3, 2000.

LOOKING AT THE CITIZENS FOR TAX JUSTICE ANALYSIS OF BUSH'S PLAN, THE FACTS ARE CLEAR:

-THOSE AT THE BOTTOM OF THE ECONOMIC LADDER (THE BOTTOM 20% OF TAXPAYERS) WOULD, ON AVERAGE, GET A TAX CUT OF $42 (A 5.5% TAX REDUCTION), WHILE THE WEALTHIEST 1% OF TAXPAYERS WOULD, ON AVERAGE, HAVE THEIR TAXES CUT BY MORE THAN $46,000 (A 13.6% REDUCTION). *

-THE BOTTOM 20% OF TAXPAYERS WOULD RECEIVE 0.8% OF THE TOTAL BUSH TAX CUTS, WHILE THE WEALTHIEST 1% WOULD RECEIVE 42.6% OF THE BUSH TAX CUTS. *

-ONE IN FOUR TAXPAYERS WOULD RECEIVE NO TAX RELIEF FROM THE BUSH PLAN. *

FUZZY MATH!

*THESE FACTS ARE FROM "REVISED ANALYSIS OF BUSH PLAN," CITIZENS FOR TAX JUSTICE, 8/31/00.

IN RESPONSE TO A QUESTION ABOUT ENERGY, BUSH MADE IT CLEAR THAT HE STOOD FOR FUNDING THE LOW INCOME HOME ENERGY ASSISTANCE PROGRAM (LIHEAP), A PROGRAM WHICH HELPS LOW-INCOME FAMILIES COVER THEIR HEATING AND COOLING COSTS.

BUT WHEN BUSH SUBMITTED HIS FIRST BUDGET (FOR FISCAL YEAR 2002) TO CONGRESS IN APRIL 2001, HE CALLED FOR A CUT OF OVER $500 MILLION IN LIHEAP FROM THE PREVIOUS YEAR'S OVERALL FUNDING, EVEN AS ENERGY COSTS WERE ON THE RISE.

THEN IN HIS FISCAL YEAR 2003 BUDGET, BUSH CALLED FOR ANOTHER $300 BILLION CUT IN LIHEAP FUNDING.

LOW-INCOME FAMILIES MUST'VE MISSED THE MEMO THAT REDEFINED "FULLY FUND" TO MEAN "CUT FUNDING REPEATEDLY"!

"FIRST AND FOREMOST, WE'VE GOT TO MAKE SURE WE FULLY FUND LIHEAP." *

THEY MISQUOTED ME! I MEANT TO SAY LIE HEAP, WHICH IS WHERE I KEEP ALL MY LIES!

*2000 PRESIDENTIAL DEBATE, OCTOBER 3, 2000.

BUSH OUTLINED HIS FEELINGS ABOUT ABORTION, TYING IT TO EUTHANASIA AND TEEN VIOLENCE.

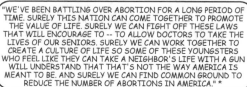

"WE'VE BEEN BATTLING OVER ABORTION FOR A LONG PERIOD OF TIME. SURELY THIS NATION CAN COME TOGETHER TO PROMOTE THE VALUE OF LIFE. SURELY WE CAN FIGHT OFF THESE LAWS THAT WILL ENCOURAGE TO -- TO ALLOW DOCTORS TO TAKE THE LIVES OF OUR SENIORS. SURELY WE CAN WORK TOGETHER TO CREATE A CULTURE OF LIFE SO SOME OF THESE YOUNGSTERS WHO FEEL LIKE THEY CAN TAKE A NEIGHBOR'S LIFE WITH A GUN WILL UNDERSTAND THAT THAT'S NOT THE WAY AMERICA IS MEANT TO BE. AND SURELY WE CAN FIND COMMON GROUND TO REDUCE THE NUMBER OF ABORTIONS IN AMERICA." *

HE'S RIGHT!

*2000 PRESIDENTIAL DEBATE, OCTOBER 3, 2000.

SO, JUST TO BE CLEAR, BUSH WAS SUGGESTING THAT ONCE YOU GET RID OF ABORTION IN AMERICA, VIOLENCE WILL PLUMMET. THE MERE EXISTENCE OF ABORTION SHOWS EVERYONE THAT LIFE IS NOT AT ALL VALUABLE, AND TEACHES CHILDREN TO KILL THEIR NEIGHBORS!

WITH SUCH A RAMPANT CULTURE OF DEATH BORNE OUT OF THE EXISTENCE OF ABORTION, IT IS ONE OF THE GREAT MYSTERIES OF OUR TIME THAT ANYONE IN AMERICA IS ALIVE TODAY.

WHEN THE TOPIC OF SOCIAL SECURITY REFORM WAS BROUGHT UP, GORE PUT OUT THE FACTS, WHICH SHOWED THAT BUSH'S PLAN WOULD TAKE FUNDING FROM SOCIAL SECURITY.

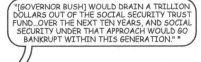

"[GOVERNOR BUSH] WOULD DRAIN A TRILLION DOLLARS OUT OF THE SOCIAL SECURITY TRUST FUND...OVER THE NEXT TEN YEARS, AND SOCIAL SECURITY UNDER THAT APPROACH WOULD GO BANKRUPT WITHIN THIS GENERATION." *

*2000 PRESIDENTIAL DEBATE, OCTOBER 3, 2000.

"THE PAYROLL TAXES ARE YOUR MONEY; YOU OUGHT TO PUT IT IN PRUDENT, SAFE INVESTMENTS SO THAT $1 TRILLION OVER THE NEXT 10 YEARS GROWS TO BE $3 TRILLION. THE MONEY STAYS WITHIN THE SOCIAL SECURITY SYSTEM." *

IT'S SAFE! COME ON IN!

*IBID.

"MY PLAN IS SOCIAL SECURITY PLUS. THE GOVERNOR'S PLAN IS SOCIAL SECURITY 'MINUS.' YOUR FUTURE BENEFITS WOULD BE CUT BY THE AMOUNT THAT'S DIVERTED INTO THE STOCK MARKET, AND IF YOU MAKE BAD INVESTMENTS, THAT'S TOO BAD. BUT EVEN BEFORE THEN, THE PROBLEM HITS BECAUSE THE MONEY CONTRIBUTED TO SOCIAL SECURITY THIS YEAR IS AN ENTITLEMENT. THAT'S HOW IT WORKS, AND THE MONEY IS USED TO PAY THE BENEFITS FOR SENIORS THIS YEAR." *

*2000 PRESIDENTIAL DEBATE, OCTOBER 3, 2000.

"IF YOU CUT THE AMOUNT GOING IN ONE OUT OF EVERY SIX DOLLARS, THEN YOU HAVE TO CUT THE VALUE OF EACH CHECK BY ONE OUT OF EVERY SIX DOLLARS, UNLESS YOU COME UP WITH THE MONEY FROM SOMEWHERE ELSE. I WOULD LIKE TO KNOW FROM THE GOVERNOR -- I KNOW WE'RE NOT SUPPOSED TO ASK EACH OTHER QUESTIONS, BUT I'D BE INTERESTED IN KNOWING -- DOES THAT TRILLION DOLLARS COME FROM THE TRUST FUND, OR DOES IT COME FROM THE REST OF THE BUDGET?" *

TOO MANY WORDS.

*IBID.

GORE HIT THE PROBLEM OF BUSH'S PLAN HEAD ON: YOU CAN'T SPEND THE PAYROLL TAXES BECAUSE THEY ARE NEEDED TO PAY SOCIAL SECURITY BENEFITS TO TODAY'S SENIORS.

SO HOW WAS BUSH GOING TO PAY FOR HIS PROPOSED REFORM OF SOCIAL SECURITY?

"NO. THERE'S ENOUGH MONEY TO PAY SENIORS TODAY IN THE CURRENT AFFAIRS OF SOCIAL SECURITY. THE TRILLION COMES FROM THE SURPLUS. SURPLUS IS MONEY -- MORE MONEY THAN NEEDED." *

SHEESH!

*IBID.

OF COURSE, BUSH'S SOCIAL SECURITY REFORM WENT NOWHERE ONCE HE GOT INTO OFFICE AND THE PROJECTED SURPLUSES TURNED INTO PROJECTED DEFICITS INTO THE FORESEEABLE FUTURE. THE PLAN RESURFACED IN THE 2004 STATE OF THE UNION ADDRESS, BUT WITHOUT ANY WAY TO FUND SUCH A REFORM AT THIS POINT, IT'S JUST A REPEAT OF THE POLITICAL POSTURING IN THE 2000 CAMPAIGN: HEAVY ON HIGH-SOUNDING RHETORIC, LIGHT ON THE DETAILS OF THE COST.

IT'S YOUR MONEY! YOU SHOULD BE ABLE TO INVEST YOUR OWN MONEY!

BUT IT'S GONNA COST YA...

GEORGE W. BUSH WAS VERY CLEAR IN INSISTING THAT WHOEVER BECAME PRESIDENT SHOULD BE RESPONSIBLE FOR THEIR ACTIONS.

"WE NEED TO SAY THAT EACH OF US NEED TO BE RESPONSIBLE FOR WHAT WE DO. AND PEOPLE IN THE HIGHEST OFFICE OF THE LAND MUST BE RESPONSIBLE FOR DECISIONS THEY MAKE IN LIFE. AND THAT'S THE WAY I'VE CONDUCTED MYSELF AS GOVERNOR OF TEXAS, AND THAT'S THE WAY I'LL CONDUCT MYSELF AS PRESIDENT OF THE UNITED STATES..." *

*2000 PRESIDENTIAL DEBATE, OCTOBER 3, 2000.

ONCE HE BECAME PRESIDENT, OF COURSE, BUSH DIDN'T SEEM TO CARE SO MUCH ABOUT PERSONAL RESPONSIBILITY.

THERE ARE AMPLE EXAMPLES OF HIS TAKING CREDIT FOR THINGS PERCEIVED AS GOOD, BUT VERY FEW EXAMPLES OF HIM OWNING UP TO HIS MISTAKES.

I DID IT!

EVEN BEFORE HE FOUND HIMSELF IN THE WHITE HOUSE, BUSH WAS SHOWING THE KIND OF RESPONSIBILITY HE EMBODIED.

WHEN IT WAS REVEALED LESS THAN A WEEK BEFORE THE ELECTION THAT BUSH WAS ARRESTED FOR DRUNK DRIVING IN 1976, BUSH JUST FELL BACK ON THE SAME OLD TIRED EXCUSE HE COULD THROW OUT AT ANY ACCUSATION OR LINE OF QUESTIONING THAT HE DIDN'T LIKE.

"IT'S BECOME CLEAR TO AMERICA OVER THE COURSE OF THIS CAMPAIGN THAT I'VE MADE MISTAKES IN MY LIFE." *

*MIKE ALLEN AND DAN BALZ, "BUSH SEEKS TO MINIMIZE DUI FALLOUT," WASHINGTON POST, NOVEMBER 4, 2000, P. A1.

THIS REVELATION ABOUT BUSH MEANT THAT HE HAD LIED TO DALLAS MORNING NEWS REPORTER WAYNE SLATER IN AN INTERVIEW IN 1998, WHEN BUSH CLAIMED THAT HE HAD NOT BEEN ARRESTED AFTER 1968. *

BUT HEY, AT LEAST BUSH THREW OUT THAT WHOLE "MADE MISTAKES" LINE! IF HE HADN'T SO INFORMED THE VOTERS, PEOPLE MIGHT HAVE THOUGHT THAT HE WAS AN EMBODIMENT OF PERFECTION!

WHEN I SAY MISTAKES, I COULD MEAN 2 OR I COULD MEAN 2 MILLION. ONLY I KNOW!

*IBID.

BUT WHY HADN'T BUSH MENTIONED THE DRUNK DRIVING ARREST WHEN HE WAS DIRECTLY ASKED ABOUT IT IN THE PAST? BUSH'S COMMUNICATIONS MANAGER, KAREN HUGHES, HAD A STRIKINGLY FAMILIAR ANSWER.

"I THINK THAT IS CONSISTENT WITH HIS DESIRE AS A FATHER TO SET A GOOD EXAMPLE FOR HIS OWN DAUGHTERS." *

THERE HE WAS, SETTING AN EXAMPLE AGAIN! COVER YOUR EARS, THE WORLD, FOR IF YOU HEAR THE DETAILS OF BUSH'S MISTAKES, YOU'RE DESTINED TO REPEAT THEM!

*KAREN HUGHES, REMARKS ON BUSH DUI, NOVEMBER 3, 2000.

WHETHER OTHER MISTAKES LURK IN BUSH'S PAST IS NEARLY IMPOSSIBLE TO DISCERN FROM SUCH A BLANKET STATEMENT. IF ANYTHING COMES UP THAT WASN'T PREVIOUSLY REVEALED, BUSH CAN ALWAYS FALL BACK AND SAY HE'S ALREADY COVERED IT WITH HIS REPEATED, "I'VE MADE MISTAKES," AND HE'D EVEN REPEAT IT A FEW MORE TIMES FOR GOOD MEASURE. WHY SHOULD ANYONE BE SATISFIED WITH SUCH A STATEMENT? IT COVERS EVERYTHING FROM THE MINISCULE TO THE MAJOR.

AND THEN TO MAKE THE ARGUMENT, WHEN HE'S CAUGHT IN A LIE, THAT HE WAS DOING THE NOBLE THING BY LYING TO PROTECT THE WORLD'S YOUTH FROM THE INFLUENCE HIS PAST MISTAKES WOULD INEVITABLY HAVE UPON THEM IS JUST TO ADD EVEN MORE INSULT TO THE INITIAL INSULT OF THE INSISTENCE THAT SAYING, "I'VE MADE MISTAKES," ACTUALLY MEANS ANYTHING WHEN SPOKEN BY ANYONE.

OF THE VOTES CAST ON ELECTION DAY -- NOVEMBER 7, 2000 -- NEARLY 51 MILLION PEOPLE CAST THEIR VOTE FOR GORE, THE 2ND-HIGHEST TOTAL IN AMERICAN HISTORY. *

50.5 MILLION CAST THEIR VOTE FOR BUSH.

GORE WON THE POPULAR VOTE BY MORE THAN 500,000 VOTES, WITH THE SECOND-HIGHEST TOTAL IN AMERICAN HISTORY.

BUT BECAUSE THE OUTCOME OF AN AMERICAN PRESIDENTIAL ELECTION IS DECIDED BY THE ELECTORAL COLLEGE, WITH ELECTORS CHOSEN BY EACH STATE, THE POPULAR VOTE HAS NO EFFECT ON THE OUTCOME.

GEORGE W. BUSH RECEIVED 271 ELECTORAL VOTES...

AL GORE RECEIVED 266.

THINGS WOULD HAVE BEEN DIFFERENT IF THE SUPREME COURT HADN'T HANDED FLORIDA'S 25 ELECTORAL VOTES TO BUSH.

*TOOBIN, *TOO CLOSE TO CALL*, P. 275.

IN FLORIDA, BUSH'S FINAL CERTIFIED WINNING LEAD OVER GORE WAS JUST 537 VOTES OUT OF NEARLY 6 MILLION VOTES CAST IN THE STATE.

BUT WITH MASSIVE IRREGULARITIES IN FLORIDA -- SOME BY DESIGN, OTHERS BY COINCIDENCE -- BUSH'S WIN WAS ONE TAINTED BY SIGNS THAT THE MAJORITY OF VOTERS IN FLORIDA HAD NOT INTENDED TO VOTE FOR HIM.

I WON BECAUSE I WON!

FOR ONE THING, THERE WERE VOTERS CONFUSED IN PALM BEACH COUNTY BY THE BUTTERFLY BALLOT USED THERE.

THE BALLOT HAD NAMES ON BOTH THE RIGHT AND LEFT WITH ARROWS POINTING FROM THE NAMES TO HOLES IN THE CENTER OF THE SHEET. GEORGE W. BUSH AND AL GORE WERE THE FIRST NAMES ON THE LEFT SIDE OF THE BALLOT, WITH A VOTE FOR BUSH INDICATED BY PUNCHING THE FIRST HOLE AND A VOTE FOR GORE INDICATED BY PUNCHING THE THIRD HOLE.

THE HOLE BETWEEN BUSH AND GORE REPRESENTED A VOTE FOR PAT BUCHANAN, THE REFORM PARTY CANDIDATE.

BUTTERFLY BALLOT

(REPUBLICAN)
GEORGE W. BUSH
DICK CHENY →

(DEMOCRATIC)
AL GORE
JOE LIEBERMAN →

(LIBERTARIAN)
HARRY BROWNE
ART OLIVER →

(GREEN)
RALPH NADER
WINONA LADUKE

(SUPEROSITY)
ALF MELMAC →

(REFORM)
PAT BUCHANAN
EZOLA FOSTER

(SOCIALIST)
DAVID McREYNO
MARY CAL HOLLIS

← (MILK)
PUT IT IN THE MILK
PUT IT IN THE MILK

← (WEREWOLVES)
LARRY TALBOT
BRITNEY SPEARS

← (TOM ARNOLD)
TAMPON

HOW DO I **NOT** VOTE FOR PAT BUCHANAN?

OLD PERSON

GORE LOST 6,607 NET VOTES IN PALM BEACH COUNTY BECAUSE SOME PEOPLE ACCIDENTALLY VOTED FOR BUCHANAN AND THEN WROTE GORE'S NAME ON THE BALLOT, * CAUSING THEIR BALLOTS NOT TO BE COUNTED AT ALL BECAUSE THE BALLOTS WERE THEN CONSIDERED OVER-VOTES -- BALLOTS WHICH SHOWED MORE THAN ONE VOTE FOR A PRESIDENTIAL CANDIDATE.

SO, WITH THE PALM BEACH COUNTY BUTTERFLY BALLOT OVER-VOTES ACCOUNTED FOR IN THE FINAL TALLY, GORE WON BY MORE THAN 6,000 VOTES.

*"NEWSPAPER: BUTTERFLY BALLOT COST GORE WHITE HOUSE," CNN.COM, MARCH 11, 2001.

ONE WAY THAT GORE WAS CHEATED OUT OF THE ELECTION WAS A BIT MORE DEVIOUS THAN SOMETHING AS INNOCENT AS THE BUTTERFLY BALLOTS IN PALM BEACH COUNTY.

THE INITIAL LEAD BUSH HAD OVER GORE WAS SMALL ENOUGH THAT AN AUTOMATIC MACHINE RECOUNT WAS AUTOMATICALLY ENACTED, AS REQUIRED BY FLORIDA LAW.

THE INITIAL MACHINE RECOUNT REDUCED BUSH'S LEAD FROM 1,784 TO 327 VOTES. *

WHY CAN'T YOU ALL JUST ACCEPT THAT I WON?

MR. WINNER

VOTES

*TOOBIN, *TOO CLOSE TO CALL*, P.36.

BUT THE MACHINE RECOUNT EXCLUDED 1.58 MILLION VOTES IN 18 FLORIDA COUNTIES.

THOSE COUNTIES WERE UNSURE OF WHAT CONSTITUTED A MACHINE RECOUNT AND WERE NOT TOLD THAT ADDING UP THE ORIGINAL VOTE TOTALS FROM EACH MACHINE (WHICH IS WHAT THEY DID) WAS NOT ENOUGH. IT WAS NECESSARY TO REFEED OPTICAL-SCAN BALLOTS INTO THE VOTE-COUNTING MACHINES IN ORDER TO ACTUALLY MEET PREVIOUSLY-ESTABLISHED STANDARDS SET FOR A MACHINE RECOUNT. *

GORE WOULD HAVE NETTED 130 VOTES IN JUST ONE OF THE 18 COUNTIES THAT DIDN'T PROPERLY PERFORM THE MACHINE RECOUNT. *

*BOTH FROM TOOBIN, *TOO CLOSE TO CALL*, P. 66.

PART OF THE REASON FOR THE REMARKABLY INEPT BEHAVIOR OF THE STATE ELECTION OFFICIALS WAS THEIR OWN POLITICAL AFFILIATIONS.

KATHERINE HARRIS, THE FLORIDA'S SECRETARY OF STATE, WAS SUPPOSED TO BE A NONPARTISAN OVERSEER OF FLORIDA'S ELECTIONS WITH THE INTERESTS OF THE VOTERS FIRST AND FOREMOST.

BUT SHE WAS AN ARDENT SUPPORTER OF GEORGE W. BUSH, * FAR MORE INTERESTED IN STEALING THE ELECTION FOR BUSH THAN SHE WAS IN DOING RIGHT BY THE VOTERS OF FLORIDA AND THE REST OF THE NATION.

*TOOBIN, *TOO CLOSE TO CALL*, P. 61.

HARRIS AND HER MINIONS DID ALL THEY COULD TO PREVENT MANUAL RECOUNTS REQUESTED BY GORE IN FOUR COUNTIES.

THEY ALSO WORKED TO UNDERMINE AL GORE'S CHANCES IN FLORIDA EVEN BEFORE THE ELECTION WAS UNDERWAY, TRYING TO MAKE THE STATE AN EASY WIN FOR GEORGE W. BUSH.

HARRIS SOUGHT TO HAVE AS MANY PEOPLE WRONGFULLY DECLARED FELONS, AND THUS UNABLE TO VOTE, AS SHE POSSIBLY COULD. AN OUTSIDE CONTRACTOR, CHOICEPOINT DBT WAS IN CHARGE OF CREATING THE FELON LISTS THAT WOULD BE USED TO PURGE THE VOTER ROLLS. *

*PALAST, *THE BEST DEMOCRACY MONEY CAN BUY*, P. 12.

IN THE END, AS MANY AS 57,700 FLORIDA VOTERS WERE BARRED FROM VOTING BECAUSE THEY WERE WRONGFULLY LISTED AS EX-FELONS. WITH 54% OF THE VOTERS ON THE PURGE LISTS BEING AFRICAN AMERICAN OR HISPANIC, * GROUPS WHICH LEAN DEMOCRATIC, THEIR IMPACT WAS CERTAINLY MORE THAN ENOUGH TO TILT THE ELECTION TO BUSH.

*PALAST, *THE BEST DEMOCRACY MONEY CAN BUY*, PP. 11-12.

OF THOSE ON THE VOTER PURGE LISTS, AT LEAST 325 WERE LISTED WITH CONVICTION DATES IN THE FUTURE. 4,000 HAD BLANK CONVICTION DATES. *

*PALAST, *THE BEST DEMOCRACY MONEY CAN BUY*, PP. 13.

THERE WERE OTHER WAYS THAT GOVERNOR JEB BUSH AND SECRETARY OF STATE KATHERINE HARRIS TOOK VOTING RIGHTS AWAY FROM INDIVIDUALS WHO SHOULD HAVE HAD THE RIGHT TO VOTE.

SECRETARY HARRIS AND GOVERNOR BUSH ILLEGALLY DEMANDED THAT EX-FELONS WHO HAD HAD THEIR VOTING RIGHTS RESTORED IN ANOTHER STATE ASK FOR REINSTATEMENT OF THEIR VOTING RIGHTS WHEN THEY MOVED TO FLORIDA. THIS POLICY MAY HAVE PREVENTED AS MANY AS 40,000 EX-FELONS IN FLORIDA FROM VOTING WHO HAD THE RIGHT TO VOTE. *

*PALAST, *THE BEST DEMOCRACY MONEY CAN BUY*, PP. 36.

EVEN WITHOUT THE BARRING OF NON-FELONS FROM VOTING ENFORCED BY THE SHAMELESSLY PARTISAN HARRIS AND BUSH, FLORIDA'S DISENFRANCHISEMENT OF THE VOTING RIGHTS OF ACTUAL EX-FELONS HAD A MAJOR IMPACT ON THE TOTAL DEMOCRATIC VOTE.

IN 2000, OVER 200,000 BLACK VOTERS -- NEARLY ONE-THIRD OF THE AFRICAN AMERICAN POPULATION IN FLORIDA -- WERE NOT ALLOWED TO VOTE BECAUSE OF PAST FELONY CONVICTIONS. *

*"US: FLORIDA EX-OFFENDERS BARRED FROM VOTE," HUMAN RIGHTS WATCH PRESS RELEASE, NOVEMBER 8, 2000.

CAN'T VOTE!

I ONLY DO THIS IN **WHITE** COUNTIES! TAKE **THAT**, HOPES FOR A FAIR DEMOCRACY!

IN SOME FLORIDA COUNTIES WITH AFRICAN AMERICAN POPULATIONS OF OVER 25%, VOTES WERE LESS LIKELY TO BE COUNTED THAN IN THE WHITEST COUNTIES. IN PART, THIS WAS THE RESULT OF THE VOTING MACHINES HAVING A BALLOT-REJECTION MECHANISM ACTIVATED IN THE WHITE COUNTIES AND NOT ACTIVATED IN THE BLACK COUNTIES. THE MECHANISM WAS DESIGNED TO REJECT BALLOTS THAT WERE MARKED INCORRECTLY, ALLOWING FOR HIGHER RATES OF INVALID, AND THEREFORE UNCOUNTED, BALLOTS IN THE BLACK COUNTIES. *

Proo!

VOTE

*PALAST, *THE BEST DEMOCRACY MONEY CAN BUY*, P. 62-63.

WHEN AL GORE AND HIS CAMPAIGN SOUGHT A RECOUNT IN FLORIDA, GEORGE W. BUSH DELEGATED OTHERS TO DO THE DIRTY WORK FOR HIM, TRYING TO APPEAR ABOVE THE FRAY.

IN ONE INSTANCE, BUSH'S CAMPAIGN SPENT OVER TWO MILLION DOLLARS TO TRANSPORT AND HOUSE NEARLY 250 GOP OPERATIVES POSING AS FLORIDIAN PROTESTORS AGAINST THE RECOUNT. *

I'M FROM FLORIDA!

I'M FROM FLORIDA!

*MOORE AND SLATER, *BUSH'S BRAIN*, P. 14.

IN THE END, THE SUPREME COURT HALTED RECOUNTS WHICH WERE UNDERWAY, ESSENTIALLY HANDING THE ELECTION TO BUSH. THE FIVE CONSERVATIVE JUSTICES SIDED WITH BUSH, WHILE THE LIBERAL JUSTICES WOULD HAVE PREFERRED TO HAVE SEEN THE RECOUNTS CONTINUE AS THE FLORIDA SUPREME COURT HAD RULED.

ONE INTERESTING INSIGHT INTO HOW THE SUPREME COURT DECISION MIGHT HAVE BEEN MADE BEFORE THE RECOUNTS WERE EVEN UNDERWAY IS REVEALED IN A GLIMPSE AT SANDRA DAY O'CONNOR'S REACTION TO WHAT APPEARED TO BE VICTORY FOR GORE ON ELECTION NIGHT.

LOOKS LIKE GORE MIGHT WIN!

"THIS IS TERRIBLE."*

GORE im
BUSH im

PRESIDENT WASHINGTON?!

*TOOBIN, *TOO CLOSE TO CALL*, P. 149.

HAD THE RECOUNTS BEEN ALLOWED TO CONTINUE AS THEY HAD BEEN ESTABLISHED, BUSH STILL WOULD HAVE WON, OFFICIALLY. *

BUT THAT DOESN'T CHANGE THE OBSERVABLE FACT THAT MORE VOTERS SET OUT IN FLORIDA TO VOTE FOR GORE ON ELECTION DAY 2000 THAN FOR BUSH.

RAR! HARRIS HAPPY!

JEB

GORE

*DAN KEATING AND DAN BALZ, "FLORIDA RECOUNTS WOULD HAVE FAVORED BUSH," *WASHINGTON POST*, NOVEMBER 12, 2001, P. A01.

THROUGH A COMBINATION OF INTENTIONAL ILLEGAL VOTER PURGES BY PARTISAN FLORIDA OFFICEHOLDERS AND LIKELY UNINTENTIONAL BALLOT CONFUSION, GORE LOST AN ELECTION IN WHICH HE WOULD HAVE HAD ENOUGH VOTES IN THE ELECTORAL COLLEGE TO BE THE WINNER, HAD CONDITIONS BEEN EVEN SLIGHTLY DIFFERENT IN FLORIDA LEADING UP TO ELECTION DAY.

GEORGE W. BUSH HAD ASCENDED TO THE PRESIDENCY, READY TO GO FULL THROTTLE WITH HIS AGENDA.

MOVE OVER, WASHINGTON D.C.! MR. HUMBLE COMIN' THROUGH!

HOLY CRAP!

IMPEACH BUSH!

RELIGION

SINCE THEN, BUSH HAS WORN HIS RELIGION ON HIS SLEEVE, MIXING PROSELYTIZATION AND POLITICKING TO HIS HEART'S CONTENT.

ONE WAY THAT HE HAS SHOWN THIS IS THROUGH SOME OF HIS POLICY DECISIONS DURING HIS TIME AS GOVERNOR OF TEXAS, AND THROUGH CERTAIN POLICIES HE HAS PROMOTED DURING HIS TIME AS PRESIDENT.

IN TEXAS, BUSH HAD SUCCESSFULLY PUSHED FOR LEGISLATION THAT ALLOWED RELIGIOUS YOUTH REFORM HOMES TO OPERATE OUTSIDE OF THE BOUNDS OF STATE LICENSING, AND THUS OUTSIDE THE PURVIEW OF STATE INSPECTORS, DESPITE A HISTORY OF ABUSE IN SUCH HOMES.

SOME OF THESE YOUTH HOMES WERE FOUND TO HAVE TORTURED THOSE IN THEIR CUSTODY WITH TACTICS NOT UNLIKE THOSE USED AGAINST U.S. P.O.W.S IN VIETNAM AND KOREA, LEADING THE TEXAS LEGISLATURE TO BLOCK THE RENEWAL OF THE LAW EXEMPTING SUCH FACILITIES FROM STATE LICENSING. *

*LIND, *MADE IN TEXAS*, PP.120-122.

IT'S DOUBTFUL YOU'LL HEAR BUSH MENTION THESE UNGODLY INCIDENTS, HOWEVER, WHEN HE'S TOUTING THE VIRTUE OF HIS "FAITH-BASED AND COMMUNITY INITIATIVES" FOR THE ENTIRE COUNTRY.

BUT WHO CAN BLAME HIM? WHO WOULD SUPPORT PROGRAMS THAT DEREGULATE THESE "FAITH-BASED" FACILITIES THAT GO TOO FAR IN ADMINISTERING WHAT THEY BELIEVE TO BE GOD'S WILL?

I WOULD! I SUPPORT 'EM!

BUSH'S FAITH-BASED INITIATIVES AND THE POLICIES OF "COMPASSIONATE CONSERVATISM" SEEK TO SHIFT THE RESPONSIBILITY OF CARING FOR THE NEEDY FROM GOVERNMENT WELFARE PROGRAMS TO RELIGIOUS CHARITIES, WHICH WOULD BE FUNDED BY TAXPAYER DOLLARS.

BUT WOULDN'T THAT VIOLATE THE SEPARATION OF CHURCH AND STATE SET FORTH IN THE ESTABLISHMENT CLAUSE OF THE FIRST AMENDMENT OF THE U.S. CONSTITUTION?

"MY ATTITUDE IS, THE GOVERNMENT SHOULD NOT FEAR FAITH-BASED PROGRAMS -- WE OUGHT TO WELCOME FAITH-BASED PROGRAMS AND WE OUGHT TO FUND FAITH-BASED PROGRAMS. FAITH-BASED PROGRAMS ARE ONLY EFFECTIVE BECAUSE THEY DO PRACTICE FAITH. IT'S IMPORTANT FOR OUR GOVERNMENT TO UNDERSTAND THAT." *

*JENNIFER LOVEN, "BUSH MAKES APPEAL ON FAITH-BASED PROGRAMS," ASSOCIATED PRESS, JANUARY 15, 2004.

"INTRACTABLE PROBLEMS, PROBLEMS THAT SEEM IMPOSSIBLE TO SOLVE, CAN BE SOLVED. THERE IS A MIRACLE OF SALVATION THAT IS REAL, THAT IS TANGIBLE, THAT IS AVAILABLE FOR ALL TO SEE." *

WAIT A MINUTE!!! YOU WANT GOVERNMENT TO SUBSIDIZE RELIGIOUS GROUPS!

*IBID.

THAT'S RIGHT. THE CURRENT HEAD OF BUSH'S OFFICE OF FAITH BASED AND COMMUNITY INITIATIVES, JIM TOWEY, CAN SWEAR UP AND DOWN THAT THE GOVERNMENT WON'T BE SUBSIDIZING RELIGIOUS DISCRIMINATION AND PROMOTION, * BUT WHEN THE PRESIDENT SPEAKS OF FAITH-BASED ORGANIZATIONS AND THEIR "MIRACLE OF SALVATION," IT'S BLATANTLY OBVIOUS THAT HIS PLAN IS TO FUND WHAT ULTIMATELY AMOUNTS TO RELIGIOUS CONVERSION IN THE NAME OF HEALING SOCIETAL ILLS.

GOD CAN DO FOR YOU WHAT HE DID FOR ME!

*RANDALL MIKKELSEN, "WHITE HOUSE MOVES TO ADVANCE 'FAITH-BASED' AID," REUTERS, SEPTEMBER 22, 2003.

FAITH BASED FUN! FAITH BASED FUN! FAITH BASED FUN! FAITH BASED FU
FAITH BASED FUN! FAITH BASED FUN! FAITH BASED FUN! FAITH BASED
FAITH BASED FUN! FAITH BASED FUN! FAITH BASED FUN! FAITH BASED FU

WHEN CONFRONTED WITH THE IDEA THAT THE FAITH-BASED INITIATIVES VIOLATE THE ESTABLISHMENT CLAUSE, JIM TOWEY RESORTS TO ATTACKING HIS CRITICS, AS OPPOSED TO PRESENTING THE MERITS OF GEORGE W. BUSH'S ARGUMENT.

"I THINK IT SMACKS OFTEN OF RELIGIOUS INTOLERANCE." *

*DAVID T. COOK, "MONITOR BREAKFAST: JIM TOWEY," CHRISTIAN SCIENCE MONITOR, MARCH 18, 2004.

PAGANS BITE! PAGANS BITE! PAGANS BITE! PAGANS BITE! PAGANS BITE! PA

MAYBE HE HAS A POINT... RELIGIOUS INTOLERANCE SURELY SHOULDN'T BE TOLERATED IN THIS DAY AND AGE! IT WOULD BE A SHAME IF RELIGIOUS INTOLERANCE WERE PRESENT AT ANY LEVEL ANYWHERE IN MODERN SOCIETY.

ONE PLACE WHERE IT WOULD BE INCREDIBLY SHAMEFUL AND AWFULLY HYPOCRITICAL IS IN THE OFFICE OF FAITH BASED INITIATIVES AT THE WHITE HOUSE.

"I HAVEN'T RUN INTO A PAGAN FAITH-BASED GROUP YET, MUCH LESS A PAGAN GROUP THAT CARES FOR THE POOR! ONCE YOU MAKE IT CLEAR TO ANY APPLICANT THAT PUBLIC MONEY MUST GO TO PUBLIC PURPOSES AND CAN'T BE USED TO PROMOTE IDEOLOGY, THE FRINGE GROUPS LOSE INTEREST. HELPING THE POOR IS TOUGH WORK AND ONLY THOSE WITH LOVING HEARTS SEEM DRAWN TO IT." *

BE MINE (NOT PAGAN)

*ASK THE WHITE HOUSE, NOVEMBER 26, 2003.

PAGANS, IN GENERAL, LACK LOVING HEARTS? LOOK UP "RELIGIOUS INTOLERANCE" IN THE DICTIONARY AND YOU MIGHT JUST FIND A PICTURE OF JIM TOWEY PUNCHING A PAGAN IN THE GUT, WITH GEORGE W. BUSH'S APPROVAL.

R

PAGAN!

OOF!

RELIGIOUS INTOLERANCE

fig. 1: TOWEY DELIVERS RIGHTEOUS PUNCH TO A PAGAN WHO JUST HAS NO COMPASSION FOR THE POOR PEOPLE, AS GEORGE W. BUSH LOOKS ON APPROVINGLY.

BUT WHAT ABOUT EFFECTIVENESS? FAITH-BASED CHARITIES AND ORGANIZATIONS CAN TACKLE THE "INTRACTABLE PROBLEMS" THAT CAN'T BE SOLVED BY THE GOVERNMENT, RIGHT?

IN ONE CASE, ONE FAITH-BASED AFTER-SCHOOL AND SUMMER ACTIVITIES CENTER IN WASHINGTON, D.C., RUN BY FORMER PRO FOOTBALL PLAYER DARRELL GREEN, HAS RECEIVED $1.3 MILLION FUNDING FROM AMERICAN TAXPAYERS SINCE 2001 BECAUSE OF BUSH'S FAITH-BASED INITIATIVES. SERVING ONLY 38 CHILDREN, THAT WORKS OUT TO OVERALL SPENDING OF $34,000 PER CHILD, COMPARED TO $1,000 PER CHILD IN THE LARGEST FEDERALLY-FUNDED NON-FAITH-BASED AFTER-SCHOOL PROGRAM. *

SUCH INEFFICIENCY DOLLAR-FOR-DOLLAR CERTAINLY DOESN'T SEEM TO JUSTIFY BUSH'S EBULLIENCE FOR FAITH-BASED INSTEAD OF FEDERAL PROGRAMS.

YOUR LICORICE ALBATROSS, YOUNG SIR.

IT BETTER BE RED LICORICE THIS TIME!

*JIM MYERS, "FOOTBALL STAR SCORES IN WASHINGTON," *YOUTH TODAY*, JULY/AUGUST 2003.

IN ANOTHER CASE, A PURDUE UNIVERSITY STUDY SHOWED THE DIFFERENCES BETWEEN THOSE IN SECULAR AND FAITH-BASED JOB PLACEMENT PROGRAMS. THOUGH THE JOB PLACEMENT RATE WAS EQUAL FOR BOTH PROGRAMS, THOSE IN THE FAITH-BASED PROGRAMS WERE MORE LIKELY TO WORK FEWER HOURS AND LACK HEALTH INSURANCE. *

YOU PROBABLY WON'T HEAR BUSH TALKING ABOUT THIS STUDY ANY TIME SOON!

HEY! LOOK OVER THERE! IT'S A GUY DRESSED LIKE **JESUS** AND HE'S PRAISING FAITH-BASED ORGANIZATIONS!

LO, THE FAITH-BASED INSTITUTIONS' CUPS SHALL FLOWETH OVER WITH TAXPAYER DOLLARS!

*ALAN COOPERMAN, "FAITH-BASED CHARITIES MAY NOT BE BETTER, STUDY INDICATES," *WASHINGTON POST*, MAY 25, 2003, P. A07.

WWW.FAT-JESUS.COM

IN YET ANOTHER INSTANCE, ONE OF BUSH'S FAVORITE FAITH-BASED PROGRAMS -- CONVICTED WATERGATE CRIMINAL AND BORN AGAIN EVANGELICAL CHARLES COLSON'S INNERCHANGE FREEDOM INITIATIVE -- SEEKS TO PUT PRISONERS ON THE PATH OF RIGHTEOUSNESS, SO THAT THEY DON'T END UP BACK IN JAIL AFTER THEY'RE RELEASED.

BUT A PENN STATE STUDY SHOWED THAT THE RECIDIVISM RATE -- THE NUMBER OF RELEASED PRISONERS WHO ARE REARRESTED -- AMONG THOSE IN THE INNERCHANGE PROGRAM WAS ACTUALLY HIGHER THAN THAT OF THOSE NOT IN THE PROGRAM. BUSH AND OTHER SUPPORTERS OF THE PROGRAM SIMPLY IGNORE THE FAILURES AND POINT TO THE SUCCESSES, * HOPING TO SWAY PUBLIC OPINION IN THEIR DIRECTION BY LEAVING OUT ALL OF THE PERTINENT FACTS.

ALL FAITH-BASED PROGRAMS HAVE A 100% SUCCESS RATE; ALL SECULAR PROGRAMS HAVE A 100% FAILURE RATE! THESE AND OTHER LIES... ER... FACTS, I MEAN, FACTS... ARE REASONS THAT THE FAITH BASED INITIATIVES ARE SO IMPORTANT TO MY POLITICAL BASE... UM... I MEAN AMERICA... IMPORTANT TO AMERICA.

*MARK A.R. KLEIMAN, "FAITH-BASED FUDGING," SLATE.MSN.COM, AUGUST 5, 2003, VIEWABLE ONLINE AT (HTTP://SLATE.MSN.COM/ID/2086617).

ONE MORE THING ABOUT THE FAITH-BASED INITIATIVES BEFORE MOVING ON:

BUSH SOUGHT TO ALLOW RELIGIOUS GROUPS RECEIVING TAXPAYER DOLLARS UNDER THE FAITH-BASED INITIATIVES TO DISCRIMINATE IN HIRING ON THE BASIS OF RELIGION, WHILE NON-RELIGIOUS GROUPS WOULD NOT BE GRANTED THE SAME ABILITY, DUE TO THE INCREDIBLE WRONGNESS OF SUCH A RIGHT. BUT TO BUSH, IT'S RIGHT FOR RELIGIOUS GROUPS TO DISCRIMINATE!

IF I CAN'T KEEP PAGANS OUT OF THE WORKFORCE, ALL OF AMERICA'S GOOD HEARTS ARE **DOOMED!**

"IF THERE IS DISCRIMINATION BASED ON RELIGION, THERE CAN EFFECTIVELY BE DISCRIMINATION BASED ON RACE. SUNDAY AT 11 A.M. IS STILL THE MOST SEGREGATED HOUR IN AMERICA. CHURCHES CAN DISCRIMINATE WITH THEIR OWN MONEY, BUT NOT WITH FEDERAL TAXPAYERS' MONEY." *

Rep. Robert C. "Bobby" Scott (D-VA)

*JOSEPH L. CONN, "PREACHING THE GOP GOSPEL?", *CHURCH AND STATE*, SEPTEMBER 1, 2003, P. 8.

WHEN IT COMES TO SCIENCE POLICY, BUSH'S RELIGIOSITY THREATENS TO UNDERMINE THE VERY FABRIC OF TIME AND SPACE!

IN 2000, BUSH SPOKE ABOUT HIS THOUGHTS ON EVOLUTION BEING TAUGHT IN PUBLIC SCHOOLS.

"I HAVE NO PROBLEM EXPLAINING THAT THERE ARE DIFFERENT THEORIES ABOUT HOW THE WORLD WAS FORMED. I MEAN, AFTER ALL, RELIGION HAS BEEN AROUND A LOT LONGER THAN DARWINISM... I BELIEVE GOD DID CREATE THE WORLD. AND I THINK WE'RE FINDING OUT MORE AND MORE AND MORE AS TO HOW IT ACTUALLY HAPPENED." *

*STEVE BENEN, "CHURCH, STATE AND THE BUSH ADMINISTRATION," *CHURCH AND STATE*, FEBRUARY 1, 2001, P. 8.

OF COURSE, THERE IS NOTHING WRONG WITH A PERSON HAVING THEIR OWN BELIEFS REGARDING THE CREATION OF THE WORLD OR ANYTHING ELSE, FOR THAT MATTER.

WHILE EVOLUTION IS BASED ON OBSERVATIONAL EVIDENCE, CREATIONISM AND ITS OFFSHOOTS CLAIM THAT THEIR OWN IDEAS ARE WORTHY OF CONSIDERATION IN THE CLASSROOM THROUGH THE USE OF SPECIOUS ARGUMENTS THAT AMOUNT TO LITTLE MORE THAN ATTACKS ON THE VALIDITY OF EVOLUTION, USING UNSCIENTIFIC RHETORIC TO PROMOTE THEIR OWN CREATIONIST VIEWS.

THE EVOLUTION VS. CREATIONISM DEBATE IS MUCH MORE ABOUT POLITICS AND MINGLING RELIGIOUS IDEAS WITH PUBLIC EDUCATION THAN IT IS ABOUT "EXPLAINING THAT THERE ARE DIFFERENT THEORIES."

IT'S REALLY QUITE SIMPLE!

WINK!

IN AUGUST 2001, GEORGE W. BUSH ANNOUNCED A PROGRAM INVOLVING FEDERAL FUNDING FOR RESEARCH USING HUMAN EMBRYONIC STEM CELL LINES, SURPRISING BOTH THOSE OPPOSED TO AND SUPPORTIVE OF SUCH RESEARCH.

"AS A RESULT OF PRIVATE RESEARCH, MORE THAN 60 GENETICALLY DIVERSE STEM CELL LINES ALREADY EXIST. THEY WERE CREATED FROM EMBRYOS THAT HAVE ALREADY BEEN DESTROYED, AND THEY HAVE THE ABILITY TO REGENERATE THEMSELVES INDEFINITELY, CREATING ONGOING OPPORTUNITIES FOR RESEARCH. I HAVE CONCLUDED THAT WE SHOULD ALLOW FEDERAL FUNDS TO BE USED FOR RESEARCH ON THESE EXISTING STEM CELL LINES, WHERE THE LIFE AND DEATH DECISION HAS ALREADY BEEN MADE." *

*BUSH REMARKS ON STEM CELL RESEARCH, AUGUST 9, 2001.

BUSH WAS SAYING THAT THERE IS A MORAL DILEMMA IN DESTROYING A WEEK-OLD EMBRYO FROM AN IN VITRO FERTILIZATION CLINIC -- AN EMBRYO WHICH WOULD OTHERWISE BE DISCARDED -- TO EXTRACT STEM CELLS WHICH HAVE THE POTENTIAL TO REVOLUTIONIZE MEDICAL SCIENCE.

IT WAS A FALLACIOUS ARGUMENT. BUSH WAS, IN FACT, PANDERING TO HIS RELIGIOUS CONSTITUENTS WITH LANGUAGE WHICH TREATED THE DESTRUCTION OF AN EMBRYO TO EXTRACT STEM CELLS AS THOUGH IT WERE THE SAME THING AS ABORTION.

BUSH DIDN'T EVEN HAVE THE DECENCY TO TELL THE TRUTH, MAKING HIS PROPOSED "COMPROMISE" WITH SCIENTISTS SOUND FAR MORE GENEROUS THAN IT ACTUALLY WAS:

MORE THAN TWO YEARS AFTER BUSH'S SPEECH, ONLY 15 STEM CELL LINES WERE AVAILABLE FOR GOVERNMENT-FUNDED RESEARCH, * DESPITE HIS CLAIM OF FOUR TIMES THAT AMOUNT BEING AVAILABLE IN 2001.

JUST 'CAUSE I AIN'T NO MATH-A-MAGICIAN DON'T MEAN I'M A LIAR!

*STEPHANIE NANO, "SCIENTISTS GIVE ACCESS TO STEM CELL LINES," ASSOCIATED PRESS, MARCH 3, 2004.

IN ADDITION, THE EMBRYONIC STEM CELL LINES ALLOWED FOR USE IN FEDERALLY-FUNDED RESEARCH MAY BE CONTAMINATED WITH MOUSE FEEDER CELLS, RAISING DOUBTS THAT THEY COULD BE SAFELY USED TO EVENTUALLY TREAT HUMANS. *

OH MY GOD, IT'S FULL OF MICE!

*LAURA MECKLER, "BUSH STEM CELL RESEARCH POLICY COMES UNDER FIRE IN SENATE," ASSOCIATED PRESS, MAY 22, 2003.

BUSH'S STEM CELL DECISION WAS AT ODDS WITH SOME PROMINENT REPUBLICANS, INCLUDING NANCY REAGAN, WIFE OF FORMER PRESIDENT AND ALZHEIMER'S SUFFERER RONALD REAGAN.

"A LOT OF TIME IS BEING WASTED. A LOT OF PEOPLE WHO COULD BE HELPED ARE NOT BEING HELPED." *

NANCY REAGAN

*ALESSANDRA STANLEY, "NANCY REAGAN FIGHTS BUSH OVER STEM CELLS," *NEW YORK TIMES*, SEPTEMBER 29, 2002.

AT LEAST THIS WOULDN'T STOP PRIVATELY FUNDED RESEARCH WITHIN THE U.S. AND RESEARCH IN OTHER NATIONS FROM MAKING UP FOR THE LOSS OF FEDERALLY-FUNDED RESEARCH IN THE U.S.

BUT WAIT, THERE'S MORE!

WHAT, YOU REALLY THOUGHT THAT WAS IT? THERE'S PLENTY MORE!

BUSH WORKED WITH REPUBLICANS IN THE HOUSE OF REPRESENTATIVES TO CRAFT A BILL THAT WOULD BAN ALL FORMS OF CLONING, INCLUDING "THERAPEUTIC" CLONING, WHICH WOULD RESULT IN A COMPLETE BAN ON THE CREATION OF EMBRYONIC STEM CELL LINES IN THE U.S. * THE BILL WAS DEFEATED IN THE SENATE, BUT IT LEAVES NO UNCERTAINTY AMONG SCIENTISTS THAT BUSH WANTS TO STOP EMBRYONIC STEM CELL RESEARCH.

*JIM MORAN, "EMBRYONIC STEM CELL RESEARCH" HUMANIST, JULY 1, 2003, P. 41.

AS WAS LEARNED BY ALL IN THE LEAD-UP TO THE WAR WITH IRAQ, BECAUSE BUSH'S VIEWS ON ANY ISSUE TRUMP THE ENTIRE WORLD, THE U.S. PUSHED FOR AN INTERNATIONAL ANTI-CLONING TREATY AT THE UNITED NATIONS. AGAIN, SUCH A BAN WOULD OUTLAW THERAPEUTIC CLONING WHICH ALLOWS FOR THE CREATION OF NEW LINES OF EMBRYONIC STEM CELLS. FORTUNATELY, THE MEASURE WAS DEFEATED BY A MARGIN OF ONE VOTE, WITH THE ISSUE TO BE REVISITED IN 2005. *

*IRWIN ARIEFF, "UN PANEL DERAILS BUSH DRIVE FOR BROAD CLONING BAN," REUTERS, NOVEMBER 6, 2003.

IF BUSH IS STILL PRESIDENT IN 2005, EXPECT FOR A SIMILAR PUSH AT THE U.N. TO BAN ALL FORMS OF CLONING, WITH THE AIM OF PLEASING THE POLITICALLY POWERFUL ANTI-ABORTION MOVEMENT, AND EFFECTIVELY TELLING THE WORLD TO KISS THE PROMISE OF MEDICAL ADVANCEMENTS AS A RESULT OF EMBRYONIC STEM CELL RESEARCH GOODBYE.

ON THE ISSUE OF ABORTION, BUSH OFTEN CITES HIS SOLIDARITY WITH ANTI-ABORTION ACTIVISTS. IN 2003, HE SIGNED A BAN ON "PARTIAL BIRTH" ABORTION. THE BAN WAS IMMEDIATELY CHALLENGED IN 3 FEDERAL COURTS, WITH SOME DOCTORS ARGUING THAT OTHER, MORE COMMON PROCEDURES COULD FALL UNDER THE VAGUE WORDING OF THE BAN, AND THAT THE BAN DOES NOT INCLUDE AN EXCEPTION TO PROTECT A WOMAN'S HEALTH. *

THE CASES WILL LIKELY FIND THEIR WAY TO THE SUPREME COURT, AS IT'S UNLIKELY THAT EITHER SIDE OF THE DEBATE WILL ACCEPT A LOWER FEDERAL COURT RULING AGAINST THEM.

*DAVID KRAVETS, "COURTS TO HEAR 3 ABORTION-BAN CHALLENGES," ASSOCIATED PRESS, MARCH 27, 2004.

NOT CONTENT TO LIMIT REPRODUCTIVE RIGHTS IN AMERICA, ONE OF BUSH'S FIRST ACTS AS PRESIDENT WAS TO REINSTATE A TERRIBLE POLICY KNOWN AS THE "GLOBAL GAG RULE," WHICH WITHHOLDS FUNDING FROM ANY FAMILY PLANNING CENTER THAT OFFERS ABORTIONS, OR EVEN ADVISES PATIENTS ON ABORTION AS A FAMILY-PLANNING OPTION. AS A RESULT OF THE RULE, MANY AFRICAN COMMUNITIES LACK ACCESS TO HEALTH CARE FACILITIES. *

I'M JUST PROTECTING THE UNBORN VICTIMS OF ABORTION!

*"US ABORTION RULE 'HITS AFRICA WOMEN,'" BBC NEWS, SEPTEMBER 26, 2003.

THE OBSERVABLE CONSEQUENCES OF THE GLOBAL GAG RULE ARE AN INCREASE IN THE NUMBER OF UNSAFE ABORTIONS IN AFRICA ALONG WITH AN INCREASE IN THE NUMBER OF DEATHS FROM THOSE ABORTIONS, AND IN LESS ACCESS TO CONTRACEPTION IN PARTS OF AFRICA WHERE HIV/AIDS IS A PERVASIVE THREAT. *

APPARENTLY, THE LIVES OF AFRICANS ARE LESS IMPORTANT TO GEORGE W. BUSH THAN ARE THE VOTES OF THE ANTI-ABORTION MOVEMENT IN THE U.S.

I'M JUST SAVING BABIES! I'M A GOOD GUY!

INCREASED DEATH RATE FROM UNSAFE ABORTIONS DUE TO GLOBAL GAG RULE

*IBID.

BUSH ALSO PROMOTES ABSTINENCE-ONLY SEX EDUCATION TO THE EXCLUSION OF CONTRACEPTION-BASED SEX-ED.

ONE STUDY OF 12,000 ADOLESCENTS FOUND THAT OF THOSE WHO HAD TAKEN PLEDGES OF ABSTINENCE, 88% ADMITTED TO HAVING SEX BEFORE MARRIAGE. IT ALSO FOUND THAT THOSE WHO TOOK SUCH PLEDGES WERE AS LIKELY AS OTHER TEENS TO CONTRACT SEXUALLY TRANSMITTED DISEASES, AND THAT THEY WERE LESS LIKELY THAN OTHERS TO RECOGNIZE THAT THEY HAD AN STD. *

*KRYSTAL OVERMYER, "WANING SEX EDUCATION HAS SOME WORRIED," DAILY NEBRASKAN, APRIL 2, 2004.

ON SAME-SEX MARRIAGE, BUSH DANCED AROUND ADDRESSING THE ISSUE DIRECTLY FOR QUITE A WHILE, BUT WHEN HE SAW THINGS TAKING A TURN THAT INDICATED THAT HIS BRAND OF RELIGIOUS JUSTICE WASN'T GOING TO WIN OVER IN STATE COURTS, HE TOOK A STAND IN SUPPORT OF A CONSTITUTIONAL AMENDMENT DEFINING MARRIAGE.

"I BELIEVE MARRIAGE HAS SERVED SOCIETY WELL, AND I BELIEVE IT IS IMPORTANT TO AFFIRM THAT...THAT MARRIAGE BETWEEN A MAN AND A WOMAN IS THE IDEAL. AND THE JOB OF THE PRESIDENT IS TO DRIVE POLICY TOWARD THE IDEAL." *

*SCOTT LINDLAW, "BUSH STANDS BY DECISION TO SUPPORT AMENDMENT PROHIBITING SAME-SEX MARRIAGE," ASSOCIATED PRESS, FEBRUARY 27, 2004.

THE CHANCES OF SUCH AN AMENDMENT SUCCESSFULLY BEING ENACTED INTO LAW, HOWEVER, WERE IMMEDIATELY SEEN BY POLITICAL EXPERTS TO BE EXCEEDINGLY LOW. THE REASONING BEHIND BUSH'S SUPPORT OF SUCH A LOSING CAUSE IS SIMPLY POLITICAL: HE WANTS TO SHOW THAT HE'S WITH THE CHRISTIAN CONSERVATIVES ON THE ISSUE OF SAME-SEX MARRIAGE, WITH THEIR SUPPORT OF HIS STAND REFLECTED IN THEIR TURNOUT ON ELECTION DAY. *

BY SUPPORTING AN AMENDMENT THAT DISCRIMINATES, I CAN ACTUALLY GAIN POLITICAL SUPPORT? COUNT ME IN!

*ALAN EISNER, "MARRIAGE AMENDMENT MAY BOOST BUSH BUT NOT PASS," REUTERS, FEBRUARY 24, 2004.

SPEAKING OF THE SUPPORT OF CHRISTIAN CONSERVATIVES, IT'S WORTH MENTIONING ONE OF BUSH'S MOST FERVENT SUPPORTERS, PAT ROBERTSON. WHEN ROBERTSON, FOR THE SECOND TIME IN THE YEAR, SUGGESTED IN OCTOBER 2003 THAT BLOWING UP THE U.S. STATE DEPARTMENT WOULD BE "THE ANSWER," THE WHITE HOUSE REFUSED TO DISTANCE ITSELF FROM ROBERTSON. *

PRAY FOR IT RIGHT NOW!

SEND IN MONEY!

*"ROBERTSON SUGGESTS LOBBING NUCLEAR BOMB AT U.S. STATE DEPARTMENT," *CHURCH AND STATE*, NOVEMBER 1, 2003.

IT WASN'T LONG BEFORE IT BECAME APPARENT WHY THE WHITE HOUSE WOULD PUT UP WITH TERRORIST TALK FROM SOMEONE AS LOONY AS ROBERTSON.

"I THINK GEORGE BUSH IS GOING TO WIN IN A WALK. I REALLY BELIEVE I'M HEARING FROM THE LORD IT'S GOING TO BE LIKE A BLOWOUT ELECTION IN 2004. IT'S SHAPING UP THAT WAY."*

FOR THE SAKE OF THE FUTURE OF AMERICA AND THE WORLD, LET'S HOPE THAT HE'S HEARING FROM THE SAME "GOD" THAT TOLD HIM HE WOULD WIN IN HIS OWN 1988 PRESIDENTIAL BID.

HEY!

PAT

*SONJA BARISIC, "PAT ROBERTSON: GOD TOLD HIM IT'S BUSH IN A 'BLOWOUT' IN NOVEMBER ELECTIONS," ASSOCIATED PRESS, JANUARY 2, 2004.

A 1997 MANIFESTO FOUNDING AN INSTITUTION BY THE NAME OF PROJECT FOR THE NEW AMERICAN CENTURY EXPANDED ON WOLFOWITZ'S 1992 CONCEPTS, BUT HAD GENERALLY THE SAME UNILATERALIST U.S.-CENTRIC THRUST, WITH THE U.S. ENGAGING IN PREEMPTIVE WARS TO MODEL THE WORLD AFTER ITSELF. *

STAMP!

NEW AMERICA

*RUPERT CORNWELL, " IRAQ CRISIS: WAR IS ALMOST UPON US - BUT HOW DID IT COME TO THIS?", *INDEPENDENT* (UK), MARCH 6, 2003.

SIGNATORIES TO THE PROJECT FOR THE NEW AMERICAN CENTURY DOCUMENT INCLUDED WOLFOWITZ AND CHENEY, AS WELL AS A FEW OTHERS SCATTERED THROUGHOUT THE ADMINISTRATION OF GEORGE W. BUSH: *

(A) SECRETARY OF DEFENSE DONALD RUMSFELD,

(B) VICE PRESIDENT CHENEY'S CHIEF OF STAFF LEWIS LIBBY,

AND (C) NATIONAL SECURITY COUNCIL MIDDLE EAST SECTION CHIEF ELLIOT ABRAMS.

THE NEW AMERICAN CENTURIONS!

*IBID.

A 1998 LETTER TO THEN-PRESIDENT BILL CLINTON URGED THE REMOVAL OF SADDAM HUSSEIN FROM POWER IN IRAQ. SIGNATORIES TO THIS LETTER INCLUDED WOLFOWITZ, RUMSFELD, ABRAMS, AND THESE OTHER MEMBERS OF GEORGE W. BUSH'S ADMINISTRATION: *

(A) FORMER CHAIRMAN OF THE DEFENSE POLICY BOARD RICHARD PERLE,

(B) DEPUTY SECRETARY OF STATE RICHARD ARMITAGE,

(C) DEFENSE UNDERSECRETARY FOR POLICY DOUGLAS FEITH,

(D) UNDERSECRETARY OF STATE FOR GLOBAL AFFAIRS PAULA J. DOBRIANSKY,

AND (E) UNDERSECRETARY OF STATE FOR ARMS CONTROL AND INTERNATIONAL SECURITY JOHN BOLTON.

THE NEW AMERICAN CENTURIONS: SADDAMICIDE SQUAD!

*OPEN LETTER TO PRESIDENT CLINTON FROM THE COMMITTEE FOR PEACE AND SECURITY IN THE GULF, FEBRUARY 19, 1998.

BUSH'S PLACEMENT OF THESE INDIVIDUALS WITHIN HIS ADMINISTRATION SUGGESTS THAT HE WANTED FOR THEIR IDEOLOGY TO BE THE GUIDE FOR U.S. POLICY AGAINST IRAQ, AND PERHAPS FOR DEFENSE AND FOREIGN POLICY IN GENERAL.

ACCORDING TO BUSH'S FORMER TREASURY SECRETARY PAUL O'NEILL, ONLY 10 DAYS AFTER INAUGURATION, BUSH AND HIS ADVISORS WERE PLANNING WAYS TO REMOVE SADDAM HUSSEIN FROM POWER. *

LET'S SEE.. HIM.. AND HIM... AND HIM. THEY WILL DO NICELY TO ADVANCE AMERICAN HEGEMONIC TENDENCIES THROUGHOUT THE WORLD FOR THE DURATION OF MY PRESIDENCY AND BEYOND...

BUT SIR.. THIS IS JUST A CHILDREN'S BOOK WITH PICTURES OF ZOO ANIMALS!

BUT I WANT A GIRAFFE!!

ZOO

"IT WAS ALL ABOUT FINDING A WAY TO DO IT. THAT WAS THE TONE OF IT." *

*"BUSH SOUGHT 'WAY' TO INVADE IRAQ?", 60 MINUTES, JANUARY 11, 2004.

LESS THAN TWO WEEKS AFTER BUSH TOOK OFFICE IN 2001, AN ANONYMOUS ADVISOR TO THE IRAQI NATIONAL CONGRESS, A GROUP OF IRAQI EXILES, TOLD REUTERS THAT "IRAQ IS PRETTY HIGH ON THE [WHITE HOUSE] AGENDA RIGHT NOW," ALSO SAYING THAT "CHENEY AND RUMSFELD ARE IN OUR CORNER." *

YAY!
YAY!
YAY!

INC

*JONATHAN WRIGHT, "IRAQI OPPOSITION COMING TO U.S. WITH HIGH HOPES," REUTERS, JANUARY 31, 2001.

ON FEBRUARY 24, 2001, SECRETARY OF STATE COLIN POWELL, ONE OF THE LESS HAWKISH MEMBERS OF THE BUSH ADMINISTRATION, SAID THAT IRAQ WAS NO LONGER A THREAT AFTER TEN YEARS OF SANCTIONS.

"AND FRANKLY THEY [SANCTIONS] HAVE WORKED. HE HAS NOT DEVELOPED ANY SIGNIFICANT CAPABILITY WITH RESPECT TO WEAPONS OF MASS DESTRUCTION. HE IS UNABLE TO PROJECT CONVENTIONAL POWER AGAINST HIS NEIGHBORS." *

COLIN

THIS WAS A RARE GLIMPSE FROM THE ADMINISTRATION THAT SADDAM WASN'T THE THREAT HE ONCE HAD BEEN AND THAT THEY WOULD LATER MAKE HIM OUT TO BE.

*PRESS REMARKS WITH FOREIGN MINISTER OF EGYPT AMRE MOUSSA.

AFTER THE TERRORIST ATTACKS ON SEPTEMBER 11, 2001, IRAQ WAS ONE OF THE FIRST TARGETS DISCUSSED, DESPITE THE LACK OF ANY EVIDENCE OF IRAQI INVOLVEMENT.

"RUMSFELD WAS SAYING THAT WE NEED TO BOMB IRAQ." *

FORMER ANTI-TERRORISM ADVISOR RICHARD CLARKE

*"CLARKE'S TAKE ON TERROR," *60 MINUTES*, MARCH 21, 2004.

ALSO SHORTLY AFTER 9/11, BUSH HIMSELF APPROACHED CLARKE ABOUT MAKING AN IRAQ CONNECTION.

"THE PRESIDENT...SAID, 'I WANT YOU TO FIND WHETHER IRAQ DID THIS.' NOW HE NEVER SAID, 'MAKE IT UP.' BUT THE ENTIRE CONVERSATION LEFT ME IN ABSOLUTELY NO DOUBT THAT GEORGE BUSH WANTED ME TO COME BACK WITH A REPORT THAT SAID IRAQ DID THIS." *

CONNECTION!

*IBID.

I SAID, 'MR. PRESIDENT... THERE'S NO CONNECTION'" *

"HE CAME BACK AT ME AND SAID, 'IRAQ! SADDAM! FIND OUT IF THERE'S A CONNECTION.' AND IN A VERY INTIMIDATING WAY." *

9-11

SADDAM

*IBID.

AFTER CLARKE WROTE UP A REPORT REVIEWING THE AVAILABLE INFORMATION AND CONCLUDING THAT THERE WAS NO AL QAEDA--SADDAM CONNECTION, THE REPORT WAS REJECTED BY THE NATIONAL SECURITY ADVISOR OR DEPUTY. *

IT DIDN'T FIT THE AGENDA OF GEORGE W. BUSH.

REPORT

REJECTED

*IBID.

BUT IRAQ WASN'T THE IMMEDIATE TARGET. WITH THE PUBLIC AWARE THAT OSAMA BIN LADEN'S AL QAEDA ORGANIZATION WAS BEHIND THE ATTACKS, ATTACKING IRAQ AS IMMEDIATE RETALIATION WOULD HAVE BEEN A TOUGH SELL.

WHAT I PORTRAY AS IMPORTANT TO THE SAFETY OF THE AMERICAN PEOPLE IS MORE IMPORTANT THAN SOMETHING AS INCONSEQUENTIAL AS TELLING THE TRUTH!

JUST BECAUSE IT WASN'T IMMEDIATELY FEASIBLE DIDN'T MEAN THE PLAN TO INVADE IRAQ HAD TO BE SHELVED FOREVER. INSTEAD, FROM SHORTLY AFTER SEPTEMBER 11, 2001, BUSH AND MEMBERS OF HIS ADMINISTRATION PREPARED THE PEOPLE OF THE UNITED STATES AND THE REST OF THE WORLD FOR WAR AGAINST IRAQ, PORTRAYING THREATS AND CONNECTIONS THAT HAD PREVIOUSLY NOT BEEN REASON ENOUGH TO INVADE, AND WHICH IN SEVERAL CASES WERE BLATANTLY MISLEADING OR WRONG.

BIG WORDS IN THAT ONE!

EAGLE

SANKYS WORK.

OUT! OUT OF THE DISCUSSION! SHOO!

COLIN

DNA

GONE FROM THE DISCUSSION ON IRAQ WAS THE EARLIER SUGGESTION BY COLIN POWELL THAT SANCTIONS HAD WORKED.

GONE, ESPECIALLY, WAS CONCERN FOR WHAT THE REST OF THE WORLD THOUGHT. BUT THAT HADN'T REALLY BEEN A PRIORITY TO BUSH DURING HIS TIME IN THE WHITE HOUSE. HE HAD A STRATEGY THAT WAS READY TO ENACT, WORLD OPINION BE DAMNED.

IN THE 2002 STATE OF THE UNION, GEORGE W. BUSH MADE CLEAR THAT HIS POLICY HAD CHANGED. SANCTIONS ALONE WERE SUDDENLY NOT ENOUGH.

LATER IN THE SAME SPEECH, BUSH GROUPED IRAQ, IRAN, AND NORTH KOREA INTO THE NOW-FAMOUS TRIO THAT WAS OUT TO DESTROY THE WORLD.

"IRAQ CONTINUES TO FLAUNT ITS HOSTILITY TOWARD AMERICA AND TO SUPPORT TERROR. THE IRAQI REGIME HAS PLOTTED TO DEVELOP ANTHRAX, AND NERVE GAS, AND NUCLEAR WEAPONS FOR OVER A DECADE. THIS IS A REGIME THAT HAS ALREADY USED POISON GAS TO MURDER THOUSANDS OF ITS OWN CITIZENS... THIS IS A REGIME THAT AGREED TO INTERNATIONAL INSPECTIONS -- THEN KICKED OUT THE INSPECTORS. THIS IS A REGIME THAT HAS SOMETHING TO HIDE FROM THE CIVILIZED WORLD."

"STATES LIKE THESE, AND THEIR TERRORIST ALLIES, CONSTITUTE AN AXIS OF EVIL, ARMING TO THREATEN THE PEACE OF THE WORLD. BY SEEKING WEAPONS OF MASS DESTRUCTION, THESE REGIMES POSE A GRAVE AND GROWING DANGER. THEY COULD PROVIDE THESE ARMS TO TERRORISTS, GIVING THEM THE MEANS TO MATCH THEIR HATRED. THEY COULD ATTACK OUR ALLIES OR ATTEMPT TO BLACKMAIL THE UNITED STATES. IN ANY OF THESE CASES, THE PRICE OF INDIFFERENCE WOULD BE CATASTROPHIC."

HOLY CRAP!

AXIS of EVIL!

IT GOES WITHOUT SAYING THAT BUSH AND HIS SPEECHWRITERS ARE CERTAINLY ADEPT AT WEAVING RHETORIC.

NOW FOR A QUICK SIDESTEP TO EXPLAIN THE NON-IRAQ MEMBERS OF THE AXIS OF EVIL:

IRAN IS AN ISLAMIC REPUBLIC CONTROLLED BY CONSERVATIVE CLERICS WHO REPRESS DEMOCRATIC ASPIRATIONS OF THE IRANIAN PUBLIC. IRAN IS BELIEVED TO ALREADY POSSESS CHEMICAL AND BIOLOGICAL WEAPONS, AND LIKELY HAS AN ACTIVE NUCLEAR WEAPONS PROGRAM.

IT'S ALSO WORTH NOTING THAT IRAN AND IRAQ WERE AT WAR THROUGH MUCH OF THE 1980S, WITH THE U.S. BACKING IRAQ.

NORTH KOREA IS RULED BY TYRANNICAL COMMUNIST DICTATOR KIM JONG-IL, WHO ALLOWS FOR THE LARGE MAJORITY OF NORTH KOREA'S POPULATION OF NEARLY 22.5 MILLION TO STARVE IN ORDER TO FUND THE COUNTRY'S MILITARY. IN 1994, NORTH KOREA HAD HALTED A NUCLEAR WEAPONS DEVELOPMENT PROGRAM UNDER AN AGREEMENT WITH THE UNITED STATES.

SHORTLY AFTER BUSH BECAME PRESIDENT, HIS SUSPICIONS ABOUT NORTH KOREA'S NONCOMPLIANCE WITH THE 1994 AGREEMENT LED HIM TO PULL BACK U.S. DIALOGUE WITH NORTH KOREA, JUST AS SOUTH KOREA WAS MAKING AN EFFORT TO EXPAND THEIR OWN DIALOGUE WITH JONG-IL'S RECLUSIVE REGIME. *

I'M CLOSIN' THE DOOR ON DIALOGUE WITH NORTH KOREA

SLAM!

*BEN FENTON, "BUSH SOURS RELATIONS WITH NORTH KOREA," *DAILY TELEGRAPH*, MARCH 9, 2001.

IN OCTOBER 2002, NORTH KOREA ACKNOWLEDGED THAT IT HAD A SECRET URANIUM ENRICHMENT PROGRAM TO U.S. OFFICIALS. LATER, IT RESTARTED ITS REACTOR AT PYONGYANG, WHICH WOULD PRODUCE WEAPONS-GRADE PLUTONIUM AND KICKED OUT INTERNATIONAL INSPECTORS. BUSH INSISTED THAT THE UNITED STATES WOULD NOT NEGOTIATE DIRECTLY WITH NORTH KOREA, BUT WOULD PARTICIPATE IN 6-WAY TALKS IN WHICH, TO DATE, LITTLE OF NOTE HAS BEEN ACCOMPLISHED, EXCEPT FOR POSSIBLY GRANTING NORTH KOREA THE TIME IT NEEDS TO ADD A FEW MORE NUKES TO ITS ARSENAL.

"I WILL NOT WAIT ON EVENTS, WHILE DANGERS GATHER. I WILL NOT STAND BY AS PERIL DRAWS CLOSER AND CLOSER." *

PERIL!

KOREA

MAYBE HE SHOULD HAVE ADDED SOMETHING ABOUT NORTH KOREA BEING THE EXCEPTION?

*2002 STATE OF THE UNION ADDRESS, JANUARY 29, 2002.

BUSH'S GROUPING OF THESE THREE NATIONS INTO A MARRIAGE OF CONVENIENCE IN THE "AXIS OF EVIL" HAS AS MUCH TO DO WITH DEFINING THESE NATION'S WHICH BUSH PERCEIVES ONLY AS TARGETS AS "EVIL" (WITH THE U.S., OBVIOUSLY, BEING THE UNIVERSAL "GOOD") AS IT DOES WITH ALLUDING TO THE AXIS POWERS OF WWII, RECALLING IMAGERY THAT WAS UNMISTAKABLY EVIL.

BUSH WASN'T JUST NAMING THESE NATIONS TO GET THEM TO CHANGE THEIR WAYS. HIS SUGGESTION SEEMED TO BE THAT THESE WERE THE NEXT TARGETS IN THE WAR ON TERRORISM. NOT SURPRISINGLY, ANY HOPE FOR REFORM FROM WITHIN OR WITHOUT WENT COMPLETELY DOWN THE DRAIN AS IRAN AND NORTH KOREA DECIDED TO ACCELERATE THEIR WEAPONS PROGRAMS, NOW UNDER THE MANTLE OF DETERRENCE AGAINST A U.S. INVASION.

IRAQ WAS A SPECIAL CASE. IT WAS OBVIOUS THAT SADDAM HUSSEIN HADN'T PERSONALLY CHANGED MUCH SINCE 1989, WHEN HE GASSED IRAQI KURDS, OR 1991, WHEN HE INVADED KUWAIT, BUT THERE WAS PLENTY OF EVIDENCE, INCLUDING FROM BUSH'S OWN ADMINISTRATION, THAT SADDAM WAS NO LONGER A THREAT TO HIS NEIGHBORS IN THE REGION, AS SECRETARY OF STATE COLIN POWELL HAD INDICATED IN THE FIRST MONTHS OF THE ADMINISTRATION.

A MAJOR PART OF GEORGE W. BUSH'S LEAD UP TO A WAR WITH IRAQ, AND PERHAPS TO MANY FUTURE WARS, WAS THE NATIONAL SECURITY STRATEGY, RELEASED IN 2002.

IN THIS DOCUMENT, BUSH LAID OUT A DANGEROUS NEW DIRECTION FOR AMERICAN FOREIGN POLICY. THE ARGUMENT MADE, IN SHORT, IS THAT THE UNITED STATES SHOULD RESHAPE THE WORLD IN ITS OWN IMAGE. THE STRATEGY'S GOALS BORE A STRIKING RESEMBLANCE TO THOSE OF THE PROJECT FOR THE NEW AMERICAN CENTURY, THE GROUP WITH AN OUTLOOK SHARED BY NUMEROUS BUSH ADVISORS.

SO IT WAS THAT U.S. DEFENSE POLICY WAS EXPANDED TO INCLUDE PREEMPTION, "EVEN IF UNCERTAINTY REMAINS AS TO THE TIME AND PLACE OF THE ENEMY'S ATTACK." *

THE WORLD IS GONNA LOOK A LOT MORE LIKE MY AMERICA!

SLURP!

*NATIONAL SECURITY STRATEGY OF THE UNITED STATES OF AMERICA, SEPTEMBER 2002.

SEPTEMBER 2002 SAW THE ADMINISTRATION GO FROM BEHIND THE SCENES PLANNING OF AN OPERATION AGAINST IRAQ TO A BLARING, NONSTOP PRO-INVASION PR BARRAGE THAT ONLY LET UP WHEN THE WAR WAS UNDERWAY.

ON SEPTEMBER 12, 2002, BUSH SPOKE BEFORE THE U.N. GENERAL ASSEMBLY, WITH IRAQ AS HIS CENTRAL TOPIC.

BUSH MENTIONED IRAQ'S HISTORY OF NON-COMPLIANCE WITH U.N. RESOLUTIONS ON EVERYTHING FROM HUMAN RIGHTS TO WEAPONS OF MASS DESTRUCTION. BUT THE WEAPONS WERE HIS MAIN POINT OF JUSTIFICATION FOR A NEW RESOLUTION.

"WE KNOW THAT SADDAM HUSSEIN PURSUED WEAPONS OF MASS MURDER EVEN WHEN INSPECTORS WERE IN HIS COUNTRY. ARE WE TO ASSUME THAT HE STOPPED WHEN THEY LEFT? THE HISTORY, THE LOGIC, AND THE FACTS LEAD TO ONE CONCLUSION: SADDAM HUSSEIN'S REGIME IS A GRAVE AND GATHERING DANGER."

THEN BUSH WENT EVEN FURTHER, THOUGH THIS TIME, THE TARGET OF HIS RHETORIC WAS THE LEGITIMACY OF THE UNITED NATIONS.

"ARE SECURITY COUNCIL RESOLUTIONS TO BE HONORED AND ENFORCED, OR CAST ASIDE WITHOUT CONSEQUENCE? WILL THE UNITED NATIONS SERVE THE PURPOSE OF ITS FOUNDING, OR WILL IT BE IRRELEVANT?" *

SO BUSH HAD ESSENTIALLY TOLD THE U.N. THAT THEY WERE EITHER WITH HIM OR AGAINST HIM IN GOING TO WAR WITH IRAQ. AND IF THEY WERE AGAINST HIM, THE U.N. WAS IRRELEVANT.

*GEORGE W. BUSH REMARKS TO U.N. GENERAL ASSEMBLY, SEPTEMBER 12, 2002.

BUSH WAS ALWAYS GLAD TO POINT OUT THE OPTIONS ON THE TABLE. OF COURSE, THEY WEREN'T THE REAL OPTIONS, BUT WHEN YOU'RE AS GOOD AT CONSTRUCTING FALSE ARGUMENTS AS BUSH AND HIS SPEECHWRITERS, YOU JUST GO WITH IT!

"THERE IS NO RISK-FREE COURSE OF ACTION. SOME HAVE ARGUED WE SHOULD WAIT -- AND THAT'S AN OPTION. IN MY VIEW, IT'S THE RISKIEST OF ALL OPTIONS, BECAUSE THE LONGER WE WAIT, THE STRONGER AND BOLDER SADDAM HUSSEIN WILL BECOME. WE COULD WAIT AND HOPE THAT SADDAM DOES NOT GIVE WEAPONS TO TERRORISTS, OR DEVELOP A NUCLEAR WEAPON TO BLACKMAIL THE WORLD." *

"I'M NOT WILLING TO STAKE ONE AMERICAN LIFE ON TRUSTING SADDAM HUSSEIN." *

*GEORGE W. BUSH SPEAKING IN CINCINNATI, OCTOBER 7, 2002.

WHO WAS ARGUING THAT THE WORLD JUST SIT BACK AND WAIT?

NO ONE WAS SAYING, "LET'S GIVE SADDAM SOME TIME! WE TRUST SADDAM HUSSEIN!" WITH THE POSSIBLE EXCEPTION OF SADDAM HUSSEIN HIMSELF.

THE ACTUAL ARGUMENT AGAINST INVASION WAS THAT SANCTIONS AND THE RETURN OF WEAPONS INSPECTORS TO IRAQ COULD WORK TO CONTAIN SADDAM JUST AS THEY HAD THROUGHOUT MOST OF THE 1990S.

BUT THE TRUTH WASN'T CONVENIENT FOR THE HAWKS OF THE BUSH ADMINISTRATION.

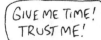

GIVE ME TIME! TRUST ME!

THE ADMINISTRATION PAINTED A TERRIFYING PICTURE OF IRAQ AS A THREAT TO AMERICA AND THE WORLD.
IRAQ POSSESSED TONS OF CHEMICAL, BIOLOGICAL, AND NUCLEAR WEAPONS.
HA! KILLED IT UP!
POW!
IRAQ HARBORED, TRAINED, AND FUNDED TERRORISTS WHO WERE OUT TO GET AMERICA.
IRAQ WOULD GIVE THEIR CHEMICAL, BIOLOGICAL, AND NUCLEAR WEAPONS TO TERRORISTS IN ORDER TO STRIKE AT AMERICA.
AMIDST ALL OF THESE TERRIFYING REVELATIONS, THE U.S. CONGRESS PASSED A RESOLUTION AUTHORIZING THE USE OF FORCE AGAINST IRAQ. THE U.N. SECURITY COUNCIL PASSED A RESOLUTION WHICH WOULD SEND WEAPONS INSPECTORS TO IRAQ, WITH THE INTENT OF ENSURING THAT SADDAM WAS DISARMED.

IN ANOTHER INSTANCE, BUSH LAID OUT WHY SADDAM AND AL QAEDA WOULD WORK TOGETHER.

"THE WAR ON TERROR, YOU CAN'T DISTINGUISH BETWEEN AL QAEDA AND SADDAM WHEN YOU TALK ABOUT THE WAR ON TERROR. AND SO IT'S A COMPARISON THAT IS -- I CAN'T MAKE BECAUSE I CAN'T DISTINGUISH BETWEEN THE TWO, BECAUSE THEY'RE BOTH EQUALLY AS BAD, AND EQUALLY AS EVIL, AND EQUALLY AS DESTRUCTIVE." *

SOFT!?

EQUAL!

SUCH A STRONG ARGUMENT MIGHT HAVE SLIPPED UNDER SOME REPORTERS' RADARS, BUT IT'S PRESENTED HERE FOR ALL TO SEE THE IMPRESSIVE DELIBERATIVE PROCESS THAT LED PRESIDENT GEORGE W. BUSH TO DRAW LINKS BETWEEN TWO OBVIOUSLY UNRELATED THINGS.

*REMARKS BY PRESIDENT BUSH, SEPTEMBER 25, 2002.

IN THE MONTHS LEADING UP TO THE WAR, BUSH WOULD PUSH IRAQ'S THREAT AS THE JUSTIFICATION FOR WAR. BUT IT WOULD LATER BECOME CLEAR THAT HE AND OTHERS IN HIS ADMINISTRATION WERE OFTEN OMITTING IMPORTANT FACTS FROM THEIR PUBLIC PRESENTATIONS, AND IN SOME CASES, LYING OUTRIGHT.

OMITTING RELEVANT FACTS ISN'T THE SAME AS LYING!

WHAT A HERO YOU ARE!

FOX NEWS

MY NAME IS JOHN KERRY.

THUSLY..

BASTARD LIAR!

FOX NEWS

IN THEIR ATTEMPT TO PROVE THAT SADDAM WAS PURSUING NUCLEAR CAPABILITIES, BUSH AND HIS NATIONAL SECURITY TEAM REPEATEDLY CLAIMED THAT SADDAM HAD TRIED TO ACQUIRE ALUMINUM TUBES THAT COULD ONLY BE USED FOR GAS CENTRIFUGES USED TO ENRICH URANIUM.

THEY SHOULD BE CALLED EVIL-UMINUM!

HEH.

NOT MENTIONED BY ADMINISTRATION OFFICIALS WAS THE FACT THAT ANALYSTS AT OAK RIDGE NATIONAL LABORATORY -- AS EARLY AS 2001 -- HAD CONCLUDED THAT THE TUBES WERE INTENDED FOR CONVENTIONAL ROCKETS. *

TUBES

DESPITE THIS ASSESSMENT, THE TUBES WERE MENTIONED IN THE 2003 STATE OF THE UNION ADDRESS, AND IN COLIN POWELL'S FEBRUARY 5, 2003 PRESENTATION AT THE UNITED NATIONS.

*"THE MAN WHO KNEW," 60 MINUTES II, FEBRUARY 4, 2004.

THE OTHER KEY ELEMENT IN BUSH'S ASSERTION THAT SADDAM WAS ATTEMPTING TO GO NUCLEAR WAS THE AFRICA URANIUM CLAIM, INEXPLICABLY IN THE 2003 STATE OF THE UNION ADDRESS, DESPITE A WARNING FROM CIA DIRECTOR GEORGE TENET MONTHS EARLIER THAT THE CLAIM WAS NOT RELIABLE. THE ADMINISTRATION WOULD LATER ADMIT THAT THE CLAIM SHOULD NOT HAVE BEEN IN THE SPEECH. *

"THE BRITISH GOVERNMENT HAS LEARNED SADDAM HUSSEIN HAS RECENTLY SOUGHT SIGNIFICANT QUANTITIES OF URANIUM FROM AFRICA." *

GROOVY BABY!

*WALTER PINCUS, "BUSH TEAM KEPT AIRING ALLEGATION," *WASHINGTON POST*, AUGUST 8, 2003.

THOUGH BEFORE U.N. WEAPONS INSPECTORS WERE ALLOWED BACK INTO IRAQ, IT WAS EASILY ARGUED THAT SADDAM HUSSEIN LIKELY POSSESSED CHEMICAL AND BIOLOGICAL WEAPONS STOCKPILES AND THE CAPACITY TO PRODUCE MORE, IT BECAME INCREASINGLY DIFFICULT TO HOLD ONTO SUCH BELIEFS UNLESS ONE CHOSE TO IGNORE THE RELEVANT FACTS ON THE GROUND.

BUT BUSH DIDN'T LIKE WHAT THE INSPECTORS HAD TO SAY, SO HE AND HIS FELLOW WAR-MONGERS CHOSE TO QUESTION THE VALIDITY OF THEIR FINDINGS, AND TO MISREPRESENT THEIR CONCLUSIONS.

WARMONGERS FORUM

LET'S MISRREPRESENT!

STUPID IDIOTS!

DAMN FINDINGS!

FACTS

IN 731 INSPECTIONS IN SEARCH OF CHEMICAL AND BIOLOGICAL WEAPONS CONDUCTED BY U.N. INSPECTORS UNDER THE LEADERSHIP OF HANS BLIX, NO STOCKPILES OR ACTIVE DEVELOPMENT PROGRAMS WERE UNCOVERED. *

NUMBER OF INSPECTIONS:

731

NUMBERS!

NUMBER OF CHEM/BIO WEAPONS DISCOVERED:

0

*FAREED ZAKARIA, "WE HAD GOOD INTEL--THE U.N.'S," *NEWSWEEK*, FEBRUARY 9, 2004.

WHAT ABOUT IRAQ'S TIES TO AL QAEDA?

BUSH SPOKE OF "HIGH-LEVEL CONTACTS THAT GO BACK A DECADE" BETWEEN AL QAEDA AND IRAQ, BUT FAILED TO MENTION THAT INTELLIGENCE SHOWED NO CONTINUATION OF SUCH CONTACTS INTO THE LATE 90S TO THE PRESENT. *

*WALTER PINCUS, "REPORT CAST DOUBT ON IRAQ-AL QAEDA CONNECTION," *WASHINGTON POST*, JUNE 22, 2003, P. A01.

BUSH AND OTHER ADMINISTRATION OFFICIALS ALSO PERSISTENTLY INSISTED THAT PROOF OF SADDAM'S TIES TO AL QAEDA WERE EVIDENCED IN HIS ALLOWING ABU MUSSAB ZARQAWI, A JORDANIAN TERRORIST, TO BE TREATED AT A HOSPITAL IN BAGHDAD. THOUGH BUSH AND OTHERS WOULD REPEATEDLY CLAIM THAT ZARQAWI WAS A HIGH-RANKING AL QAEDA LEADER, THERE WAS A LACK OF CONSENSUS IN THE U.S. INTELLIGENCE COMMUNITY THAT HE WAS AFFILIATED WITH AL QAEDA, AS HE WAS THE LEADER OF A SEPARATE TERRORIST GROUP WHO MAY HAVE ONLY HAD INFREQUENT CONTACT WITH AL QAEDA. *

*WALTER PINCUS, "REPORT CAST DOUBT ON IRAQ-AL QAEDA CONNECTION," *WASHINGTON POST*, JUNE 22, 2003, P. A01.

AS FOR THE ALLEGATION THAT IRAQ HAD PROVIDED BOMB-MAKING AND WEAPONS TRAINING TO AL QAEDA MEMBERS, THAT INFORMATION HAD BEEN GLEANED FROM AL QAEDA TERRORISTS HELD BY THE U.S. *

THIS IS EXACTLY THE SORT OF ALLEGATION THAT COULD BE MADE IN ORDER TO LEAD THE U.S. INTO A WAR THAT WOULD RESULT IN INCREASED ANTI-AMERICANISM, LEADING TO INCREASED RECRUITMENT OF INDIVIDUALS BY TERRORIST GROUPS.

*IBID.

ON TOP OF EVERYTHING ELSE, BUSH HAD SEEN IN THE NATIONAL INTELLIGENCE ESTIMATE THAT THE LIKELIHOOD OF SADDAM PASSING CHEMICAL OR BIOLOGICAL WEAPONS TO A TERRORIST GROUP LIKE AL QAEDA WOULD INCREASE IF HE WERE ATTACKED AND FACED WITH THE PROSPECT OF BEING REMOVED FROM POWER. *

OH CRAP. PROBABLY SHOULDN'T BE HANDLING THIS WITHOUT SOME RADIATION SUITS ON!

NOW YOU SAY THAT!!!

*WALTER PINCUS, "OCT. REPORT SAID DEFEATED HUSSEIN WOULD BE THREAT," *WASHINGTON POST*, JULY 21, 2003, P. A01.

THAT BUSH WAS ALERTED THAT A DEFEATED SADDAM WOULD PASS THE MOST DANGEROUS OF WEAPONS TO TERRORISTS LEAVES TWO UNSETTLING POSSIBILITIES:

IF BUSH AND HIS ADVISORS BELIEVED THE INTELLIGENCE WHICH SAID SADDAM DIDN'T HAVE WEAPONS OF MASS DESTRUCTION, THEY KNEW THAT HE COULDN'T PASS THEM TO AL QAEDA. BUT THIS WOULD ALSO MEAN THAT THEY WERE LYING TO THE PUBLIC IN MAKING THE CASE FOR WAR.

IT'S ONLY A LIE IF I **SAY** IT'S A LIE!

FAIR AND WHATNOT!

BOING!

FOX NEWS

IF BUSH ACTUALLY BELIEVED THAT SADDAM DID HAVE WMDS, HE WAS DOING THE ONE THING THAT HIS OWN INTELLIGENCE AGENCIES WERE SAYING WOULD LIKELY RESULT IN SADDAM HANDING THE MOST DANGEROUS WEAPONS TO TERRORISTS, RISKING THE LIVES OF COUNTLESS AMERICANS.

WELL, IT'S LIKE I ALWAYS SAY, ANOTHER ATTACK ON AMERICA IS IMMINENT, AND WITH MY POLICIES, IT MIGHT HAPPEN SOONER THAN LATER!

THIS IS HOW NANCY REAGAN DOES IT.

WITH VIRTUALLY NO SOLID EVIDENCE THAT IRAQ HAD ANY WEAPONS OF MASS DESTRUCTION OR TIES TO TERRORIST GROUPS THAT THREATENED THE UNITED STATES, BUSH TOOK AMERICA AND A FEW ALLIES -- WITHOUT THE BACKING OF THE UNITED NATIONS SECURITY COUNCIL -- TO WAR WITH IRAQ.

THIS'LL MAKE A GREAT AD FOR MY RE-ELECTION CAMPAIGN!

SLIGHTLY MORE THAN A MONTH AFTER THE INVASION, PRESIDENT BUSH LANDED ON AN AIRCRAFT CARRIER IN A FIGHTER JET. HE THEN STOOD IN FRONT OF A MISSION ACCOMPLISHED BANNER, AND PROCLAIMED THAT "MAJOR COMBAT OPERATIONS" IN IRAQ WERE OVER.

BUT AT WHAT COST?

BETTER THAN THE AWOL ONE

THROUGHOUT THE SIX-WEEK INVASION, 150 U.S. TROOPS WERE KILLED, WITH ESTIMATES OF BETWEEN 4,000 TO 10,000 IRAQI CIVILIANS KILLED DURING THAT PERIOD. *

FROM THE START OF MILITARY OPERATIONS TO THE END OF MARCH 2004, THE TOTAL NUMBER OF U.S. AND COALITION FORCES KILLED IN IRAQ WAS 685.*

PROBABLY GONNA LEAVE THAT BIT OUT OF THE AD.

DAMN THAT MEDIA FILTER! ALWAYS SHOWING THE BAD STUFF!

AID WORKERS AND IRAQI CIVILIANS ARE ALSO OFTEN THE TARGET OF IRAQI INSURGENTS AND TERRORISTS WHO SEEK TO DRIVE U.S. FORCES OUT OF IRAQ.

AND THE NUMBERS CONTINUE TO RISE.

*"THE INVASION OF IRAQ," FRONTLINE, WEB RESOURCES, VIEWABLE AT: (HTTP://WWW.PBS.ORG/WGBH/PAGES/FRONTLINE/SHOWS/INVASION/THEMES/CIVILIAN.HTML)

*"A LOOK AT U.S. MILITARY DEATHS IN IRAQ," ASSOCIATED PRESS, MARCH 29, 2004.

DON'T EXPECT TO SEE ANY NEWS COVERAGE OF THE RETURN OF DEAD SOLDIERS TO AMERICAN BASES. JUST BEFORE THE START OF THE WAR IN IRAQ, BUSH'S ADMINISTRATION BANNED THE AIRING OF IMAGES OF FLAG-DRAPED CASKETS AS THEY ARRIVED AT AMERICAN MILITARY BASES. *

DON'T NEED TO SEE *THAT!*

*DANA MILBANK, "CURTAINS ORDERED FOR MEDIA COVERAGE OF RETURNING COFFINS," *WASHINGTON POST*, OCTOBER 21, 2003, P. A23.

AND AS OF JANUARY 2004, BUSH HADN'T ATTENDED EVEN ONE FUNERAL FOR ANY OF THE SOLDIERS KILLED IN IRAQ. *

WELL I OBVIOUSLY CAN'T FUNDRAISE FOR RE·ELECTION *AND* TRY TO APPEAR HUMAN!

*"GEORGE W. BUSH AND THE REAL STATE OF THE UNION," *INDEPENDENT/UK*, JANUARY 20, 2004.

LOOKING FOR THE NUMBER OF WOUNDED TROOPS? GOOD LUCK!

OFFICIALLY, THE PENTAGON REPORTED 3,433 INJURED U.S. TROOPS AS A RESULT OF BOTH HOSTILE AND NON-HOSTILE ACTION IN IRAQ AT THE END OF MARCH 2004. *

I ALSO GOT SHOT IN THE BUTT!

SHUT UP, FORREST GUMP!

*"A LOOK AT U.S. MILITARY DEATHS IN IRAQ," ASSOCIATED PRESS, MARCH 29, 2004.

BUT SOME HAVE ACCUSED THE PENTAGON OF OBSCURING THE ACTUAL NUMBER OF WOUNDED TROOPS.

AS OF JANUARY 2004, THE U.S. ARMY ALONE HAD MADE 8,848 MEDICAL EVACUATIONS FROM IRAQ RESULTING FROM NON-COMBAT ILLNESSES AND INJURIES. *

THEY CAN HAVE FRANK BURNS!

HEY!

BOOM!

4077

*DANIEL ZWERDLING, "ANALYSIS: ELUSIVE NUMBERS OF US TROOPS EVACUATED FROM IRAQ DUE TO SERIOUS INJURY OR ILLNESS," *ALL THINGS CONSIDERED*, JANUARY 7, 2004.

AND WHAT OF THE MONETARY COST OF REBUILDING AND POLICING IRAQ?

ANDREW NATSIOS, THE ADMINISTRATOR FOR THE U.S. AGENCY FOR INTERNATIONAL DEVELOPMENT, APPEARED ON NIGHTLINE ON APRIL 23, 2003, WITH AN AMAZINGLY OPTIMISTIC ESTIMATION OF THE COST OF POST-WAR RECONSTRUCTION IN IRAQ.

"1.7 BILLION IS THE LIMIT ON RECONSTRUCTION FOR IRAQ." *

NIGHTLINE, APRIL 23, 2003.

WHEN NATSIOS FIRST MENTIONED THE AMOUNT, TED KOPPEL SEEMED INCREDULOUS.

"YOU'RE NOT SUGGESTING THAT THE REBUILDING OF IRAQ IS GONNA BE DONE FOR $1.7 BILLION?" *

*IBID.

"IN TERMS OF THE AMERICAN TAXPAYERS CONTRIBUTION...THIS IS IT FOR THE U.S. THE REST...WILL BE DONE BY OTHER COUNTRIES WHO HAVE ALREADY MADE PLEDGES...AND IRAQI OIL REVENUES, EVENTUALLY IN SEVERAL YEARS...WILL FINISH THE JOB... THEY'RE GOING TO GET $20 BILLION A YEAR IN OIL REVENUES." *

*IBID.

IN FACT, ESTIMATES FOR THE COST OF THE RECONSTRUCTION OF IRAQ OVER THE NEXT FEW YEARS RUN FROM $50 BILLION TO OVER $100 BILLION, WITH ANY IRAQI OIL REVENUES NOW EXPECTED TO BE USED TO FUND THE OPERATION IRAQ'S NEW GOVERNMENT. U.S. TAXPAYERS WILL SHOULDER THE MAJORITY OF THIS BURDEN. *

*"INCREASED COSTS OF IRAQ DEMAND INCREASED ACCOUNTABILITY," OPEN SOCIETY INSTITUTE, WEB REPORT, VIEWABLE AT: (HTTP://WWW.IRAQREVENUEWATCH.ORG/REPORTS/091803.PDF).

BEFORE THE WAR, BUSH'S ECONOMIC ADVISOR LAWRENCE LINDSAY HAD ESTIMATED THE COST OF WAR WITH IRAQ TO BE BETWEEN $100 TO $200 BILLION. *

SUCH A HIGH ESTIMATE DIDN'T SIT WELL WITH BUSH, WHO FIRED LINDSAY A SHORT WHILE LATER.

BY MARCH 2004, THE WAR IN IRAQ HAD ALREADY COST MORE THAN $100 BILLION, WITH THE COST OF OCCUPYING IRAQ THROUGH 2013 ESTIMATED AT UP TO $200 BILLION MORE, AND PRESIDENT BUSH PUTTING OFF ASKING FOR MORE MONEY UNTIL AFTER THE NOVEMBER 2004 ELECTIONS. *

I WON'T HAVE MEMBERS OF MY ADMINISTRATION TELLING THE PUBLIC ANYTHING EVEN **CLOSE** TO THE TRUTH!!

LARRY LINDSAY

EXIT

*VINCENT CABLE, "STING IN THE TAIL," *THE WORLD TODAY*, FEBRUARY 1, 2003, P. 12.

OCCUPYING IRAQ IS **FREE** UNTIL AFTER I'M RE-ELECTED! THIS IS HOW I DEMONSTRATE MY PERSONAL SENSE OF RESPONSIBILITY!

No MONEY DOWN!

HERO

YAY!

FREE

CHEAP!

*PAULINE JELINEK, "PENTAGON PRESSED FOR IRAQ'S WAR COSTS," ASSOCIATED PRESS, MARCH 10, 2004.

A CENTER FOR PUBLIC INTEGRITY REPORT SHOWED THAT SOME OF THE COMPANIES GRANTED U.S. GOVERNMENT CONTRACTS -- WORTH BILLIONS OF DOLLARS -- TO WORK IN IRAQ HAD GIVEN HUNDREDS OF THOUSANDS OF DOLLARS TO BUSH'S 2000 PRESIDENTIAL CAMPAIGN. *

WHAT? I'M NOT **REWARDING** THEM, I'M JUST GIVIN' THEM A REASON TO SUPPORT ME IN **2004**!

*"STUDY LINKS US RECONSTRUCTION DEALS IN IRAQ, AFGHANISTAN TO BUSH BACKERS," AGENCE FRANCE PRESSE, OCTOBER 30, 2003.

PARTICULARLY WORTHY OF NOTE IN THE RECONSTRUCTION OF IRAQ IS VICE PRESIDENT DICK CHENEY'S OLD COMPANY, HALLIBURTON. WITH AS MUCH AS $6 BILLION IN RECONSTRUCTION CONTRACTS GOING TO HALLIBURTON AND ITS SUBSIDIARIES IN POST-WAR IRAQ, THERE SEEMS TO BE NO END TO THEIR MONEY-MAKING PROSPECTS THERE, EVEN AMID MULTIPLE ALLEGATIONS OF OVERCHARGING THE U.S. GOVERNMENT FOR EVERYTHING FROM FOOD FOR U.S. TROOPS TO GASOLINE SHIPPED INTO IRAQ FROM KUWAIT. *

SMIRK!

NOT EVIL!

HALLIBURTON

*MATT KELLEY, "IRAQ CONTRACTS GIVE HALLIBURTON HEADACHES," ASSOCIATED PRESS, MARCH 30, 2004.

AS FOR THE CREDIBILITY OF THE PRESIDENCY, THE INTELLIGENCE COMMUNITY, AND THE DEFENSE COMMUNITY OF THE UNITED STATES, THE COST IS FAR-REACHING.

THE WEAPONS ARE **HIDING!!**

YET EVEN AS IT BECAME INCREASINGLY APPARENT THAT WEAPONS OF MASS DESTRUCTION OR ACTIVE WMD DEVELOPMENT PROGRAMS WOULD NOT BE FOUND IN IRAQ, THE ADMINISTRATION HELD TO ITS STORY.

MEOW!

WHEN CRITICS OF THE PRESIDENT EXPRESSED THEIR DISTASTE THAT THE WAR AGAINST IRAQ HAD BEEN LAUNCHED TO ELIMINATE THE WMDS THAT DIDN'T EXIST, BUSH BRUSHED ASIDE THEIR CONCERNS, AND CLAIMED THAT THEY WERE REWRITING HISTORY.

BUT OBVIOUSLY, IT WAS BUSH HIMSELF THAT WAS REWRITING HISTORY BY SUGGESTING THAT IRAQ'S ALLEGED POSSESSION OF WMDS HAD NOT BEEN HIS MAIN JUSTIFICATION FOR WAR!

"WE MADE IT CLEAR TO THE DICTATOR OF IRAQ THAT HE MUST DISARM. WE ASKED OTHER NATIONS TO JOIN US IN SEEING TO IT THAT HE WOULD DISARM, AND HE CHOSE NOT TO DO SO, SO WE DISARMED HIM. AND I KNOW THERE'S A LOT OF REVISIONIST HISTORY NOW GOING ON, BUT ONE THING IS CERTAIN. HE IS NO LONGER A THREAT TO THE FREE WORLD, AND THE PEOPLE OF IRAQ ARE FREE." *

*REMARKS BY GEORGE W. BUSH IN ANNANDALE, VIRGINIA, JUNE 17, 2003.

ONE OF THE FAVORITE SUGGESTIONS OF THE ADMINISTRATION IS THAT SADDAM PASSED HIS WEAPONS OFF TO SYRIA, * LEAVING THE DOOR OPEN TO MAKE THE SAME TYPES OF ALLEGATIONS AGAINST SYRIA THAT WERE MADE AGAINST IRAQ, AND TO AN INVASION WITH SIMILAR JUSTIFICATION.

ZOOM ZOOM ZOOM ZOOM

WELL, WE HAVE TO DEFEND OURSELVES AGAINST **EVIL**, SO MAYBE JUST **ONE** MORE INVASION......

*"SYRIA SCOFFS AT U.S. CLAIM IT HAS IRAQI WEAPONS," REUTERS, JANUARY 25, 2004.

BY THE TIME OF THE 2004 STATE OF THE UNION ADDRESS, BUSH WAS PRACTICALLY INSULTING THE INTELLIGENCE OF THE AMERICAN PEOPLE, ADJUSTING HIS RATIONALE TO A FINAL, UTTERLY RIDICULOUS STATEMENT.

"WE'RE SEEING ALL THE FACTS - ALREADY THE KAY REPORT IDENTIFIED DOZENS OF WEAPONS OF MASS DESTRUCTION-RELATED PROGRAM ACTIVITIES AND SIGNIFICANT AMOUNTS OF EQUIPMENT THAT IRAQ CONCEALED FROM THE UNITED NATIONS." *

*2004 STATE OF THE UNION ADDRESS, JANUARY 20, 2004.

BUT DAVID KAY, THE U.S. CHIEF WEAPONS INSPECTOR IN IRAQ, RESIGNED IN THE SAME WEEK THAT BUSH REFERRED TO KAY'S REPORT AS PROOF OF "WEAPONS OF MASS DESTRUCTION-RELATED PROGRAM ACTIVITIES."

AND IN TESTIMONY BEFORE THE SENATE ARMED SERVICES COMMITTEE, KAY PUT IT VERY DIFFERENTLY THAN BUSH HAD IN THE STATE OF THE UNION ADDRESS.

"WE WERE ALL WRONG." *

"I BELIEVE THAT THE EFFORT THAT HAS BEEN DIRECTED TO THIS POINT HAS BEEN SUFFICIENTLY INTENSE THAT IT IS HIGHLY UNLIKELY THAT THERE WERE LARGE STOCKPILES OF DEPLOYED, MILITARIZED CHEMICAL WEAPONS THERE." *

*BOTH QUOTES FROM "US WEAPONS EXPERT: 'WE WERE ALL WRONG,'" AGENCE FRANCE PRESSE, JANUARY 28, 2004.

IT WAS ONLY A MATTER OF TIME BEFORE THE PRESIDENT OF THE UNITED STATES STARTED TO ACT LIKE THE WEAPONS OF MASS DESTRUCTION IN IRAQ WERE JUST A FUN JOKE ON THE OTHERWISE DEAD SERIOUS PATH TO WAR. HOW ELSE COULD SOMEONE LIKE GEORGE W. BUSH KEEP HIMSELF ENTERTAINED?

IN MARCH 2004, AT A DINNER PARTY, BUSH SHOWED PHOTOGRAPHS OF HIMSELF LOOKING FOR WEAPONS OF MASS DESTRUCTION BEHIND WHITE HOUSE FURNITURE, PROVIDING COMMENTARY AND GETTING A HEARTY CHUCKLE FROM HIS AUDIENCE. *

"THOSE WEAPONS OF MASS DESTRUCTION HAVE GOT TO BE HERE SOMEWHERE... NOPE, NO WEAPONS OVER THERE... MAYBE UNDER HERE?" *

WHY SHOULD HE ATTEND THE FUNERALS OF SOLDIERS WHEN HE CAN ENTERTAIN AT PARTIES INSTEAD?

COULD YOU GUYS SHUT UP? I WANNA HEAR IF THERE ARE WMDS IN THAT CABINET!

AND BY MAKING FUN OF THE REASON THAT THEY DIED, EVEN! SUCH BARRELS OF FUN!

DON'T YOU MEAN BARRELS OF OIL? TEE HEE!

*"BUSH'S JOKE ABOUT WMD DRAWS CRITICISM," ASSOCIATED PRESS, MARCH 26, 2004.

BUSH CARED SO MUCH ABOUT THE SOLDIERS HE HAD SENT TO IRAQ TO DEPOSE SADDAM THAT HE CHOSE TO MAKE A PERSONAL SACRIFICE TO SHOW SOLIDARITY WITH THE TROOPS.

STEPHEN MANSFIELD, IN HIS BOOK THE FAITH OF GEORGE W. BUSH, WRITES, "AIDES FOUND [BUSH] FACE DOWN ON THE FLOOR IN PRAYER IN THE OVAL OFFICE. IT BECAME KNOWN THAT HE REFUSED TO EAT SWEETS WHILE AMERICAN TROOPS WERE IN IRAQ, A PARTIAL FAST SELDOM REPORTED OF AN AMERICAN PRESIDENT." *

NO CANDY TIL' THEY'RE ALL SAFE!

*EXCERPT FROM THE FAITH OF GEORGE W. BUSH, QUOTED IN SYDNEY H. SCHANBERG, "THE WIDENING CRUSADE," VILLAGE VOICE, OCTOBER 15-21, 2003.

LIL' ANGEL

SUCH DEDICATION!

SUCH MORAL CLARITY!

SUCH A LOAD OF HOOEY!

TURNS OUT THAT PRESIDENT BUSH WASN'T ALL THAT COMMITTED TO HIS OWN GOALS. IN OCTOBER, A REPORT SHOWED BUSH DOING THE UNTHINKABLE.

YUMMY CANDY MAKES EVERY DEATH IN IRAQ THAT MUCH EASIER TO STOMACH!

"BUSH WAS IN AN EXPANSIVE MOOD ON THE FLIGHT FROM INDONESIA TO AUSTRALIA, WEARING AN AIR FORCE ONE FLIGHT JACKET, SNACKING NOISILY ON A BUTTERSCOTCH SWEETS AND CHOPPING THE AIR FOR EMPHASIS." *

SO MUCH FOR THE ILLUSIONS OF BUSH AS A MAN OF MORAL CLARITY!

*STEVE HOLLAND, "BUSH SAYS KIM LET HIS PEOPLE STARVE, SHRINK," REUTERS, OCTOBER 22, 2003.

WITH U.S. TROOPS IN IRAQ FOR THE FORESEEABLE FUTURE, THE COST IN DOLLARS AND LIVES WILL LIKELY CONTINUE FOR YEARS TO COME.

BUT WHAT ARE THE TANGIBLE RESULTS THAT THE WAR IN IRAQ HAVE BROUGHT ABOUT?

SADDAM HUSSEIN IS NOW IN CUSTODY AND IS NO LONGER BRUTALIZING THE PEOPLE OF IRAQ. HOW THIS MAKES AMERICA SAFER IS CERTAINLY DEBATABLE, CONSIDERING HE HAD NO WMDS TO USE AGAINST THE U.S. OR TO PASS TO TERRORISTS.

SIGH.

ROADSIDE BOMBS AND SUICIDE BOMBERS ARE NOW A CONSTANT THREAT TO THE LIVES OF NORMAL IRAQIS, INTERNATIONAL AID WORKERS, AND U.S. AND COALITION TROOPS.

BY MID-MARCH 2004, BETWEEN 660 AND 760 PEOPLE HAD BEEN KILLED IN 24 SUICIDE ATTACKS IN IRAQ SINCE THE U.S. INVASION. *

*TAREK AL-ISSAWI, "AP TALLY: IRAQ SUICIDE BOMBS KILLED 660," ASSOCIATED PRESS, MARCH 18, 2004.

U.S. DEPUTY DEFENSE SECRETARY PAUL WOLFOWITZ ACTUALLY VIEWS ATTACKS ON IRAQIS AND U.S. TROOPS AS A SIGN OF AMERICA'S SUCCESS IN THE REGION.

"THE MORE SUCCESSFUL WE ARE THE MORE WE CAN EXPECT THEM TO GO AFTER THOSE THINGS THAT REPRESENT SUCCESS." *

APPARENTLY, HE WASN'T CONSIDERING THAT CONTINUED LOSS OF INNOCENT LIVES IN TERRORIST ATTACKS REPRESENTS SOMETHING OF A FAILURE. STOP THE TERRORIST ATTACKS, THEN CALL IT A SUCCESS.

*TABASSUM ZAKARIA, "WOLFOWITZ: IRAQ ATTACKS SHOW U.S. EFFORTS SUCCEEDING," FEBRUARY 2, 2004.

THE MANY ETHNIC DIVISIONS IN IRAQI SOCIETY MAY LEAD THE COUNTRY INTO CIVIL WAR IF DIFFERENCES BECOME TOO DIVISIVE. *

*WARREN P. STROBEL AND JONATHAN S. LANDAY, "CIA OFFICERS WARN OF IRAQ CIVIL WAR, CONTRADICTING BUSH'S OPTIMISM," KNIGHT-RIDDER, JANUARY 22, 2004.

ADDITIONALLY, SOME U.S. POLICY IN POST-WAR IRAQ DOESN'T EXACTLY EXUDE THE FREEDOM-CENTRIC VIEW THAT BUSH SO LOUDLY AND PROMINENTLY PROCLAIMS.

ONE EXAMPLE WAS THE RECRUITMENT OF FORMER IRAQI INTELLIGENCE SERVICE AGENTS TO AID IN THE HUNT FOR ANTI-U.S. FIGHTERS. THESE ARE THE SAME AGENTS WHO RELIED ON TORTURE AND THE FEAR WHICH THE INTELLIGENCE SERVICE STRUCK IN THE HEARTS OF IRAQIS UNDER SADDAM HUSSEIN'S RULE. *

BUT HEY, WITH SADDAM GONE, LET HIS FORMER THUGS RUN FREE, AND ON THE U.S. PAYROLL, AT THAT!

WHO'D HAVE THOUGHT THAT **AMERICA** WOULD PAY ME INSTEAD OF IMPRISON ME?!

*ANTHONY SHADID AND DANIEL WILLIAMS, "U.S. RECRUITING HUSSEIN'S SPIES," *WASHINGTON POST*, AUGUST 24, 2003, P. A01.

WHILE SADDAM'S FORMER THUGS GO FREE, IRAQIS WHO ARE TRYING TO MAKE A DIFFERENCE IN POST-WAR IRAQ ARE ARRESTED BY U.S. FORCES WITHOUT BEING CHARGED WITH ANY CRIME.

POLICE

NON-BA'ATHISTS NEED NOT APPLY

IN ONE PARTICULARLY DISTURBING CASE, INDIVIDUALS ELECTED TO CITY COUNCIL POSITIONS BY THE CITIZENS OF KARBALA WERE THREATENED WITH ARREST WHEN ONE OF THEM COMPLAINED TO AMERICAN TROOPS ABOUT THE REINSTATEMENT, BY THE AMERICANS, OF A BA'ATH PARTY (SADDAM HUSSEIN'S RULING PARTY) OFFICIAL IN THE LOCAL POLICE DEPARTMENT. *

*"OPERATION IRAQI FREEDOM,"*60 MINUTES*, DECEMBER 4, 2003.

ANOTHER INDIVIDUAL ARRESTED BY U.S. FORCES, NAJEEB AL SHAMI, WAS A CITY COUNCILOR IN KARBALA, REPLACED BY A SADDAM LOYALIST ALSO AT THE INSISTENCE OF U.S. FORCES. AFTER REPORTERS WITH 60 MINUTES WERE GIVEN A TOUR OF THE PRISON WHERE AL SHAMI WAS BEING HELD, AND A U.S. GENERAL ASSURED THE REPORTER THAT NO ONE WAS BEING HELD THERE WITHOUT CHARGES OR ACCESS TO FAMILY AND A LAWYER, THE SAME GENERAL DISCOVERED THAT AL SHAMI WAS BEING HELD WITHOUT CHARGES (IT HAD BEEN FOR OVER A MONTH AT THAT POINT), AND COULD NOT BE ALLOWED TO SEE HIS FAMILY OR A LAWYER BECAUSE HE WAS SUSPECTED OF CRIMES AGAINST THE COALITION, AND WOULD 60 MINUTES PLEASE TURN OFF THEIR CAMERAS. *

SOUNDS LIKE THINGS ARE GOING SWIMMINGLY... FOR THE BA'ATHISTS THAT HAVE FOR SOME COMPLETELY INEXPLICABLE REASON BECOME AMERICA'S SWEETHEARTS, AT LEAST.

SO LONG AS **TERROR** EXISTS, IT'S JUSTIFIABLE TO LOCK PEOPLE UP **ALL** AROUND **THE WORLD** WITHOUT CHARGING THEM WITH ANYTHING!

NO!

*IBID.

IN A SIGN OF THE HOPES OF FREEDOM OF SPEECH, THE U.S. APPOINTED IRAQI GOVERNING COUNCIL HAS REPEATEDLY BANNED CERTAIN TELEVISION STATIONS FROM ACCESS TO GOVERNING COUNCIL EVENTS. *

AFTER THE INVASION, AND ESPECIALLY AFTER THE CAPTURE OF SADDAM HUSSEIN, SIGNS BEGAN TO INCREASINGLY POINT AWAY FROM ANY LINK BETWEEN HUSSEIN'S REGIME AND AL QAEDA.

WHEN SADDAM WAS CAPTURED, A DOCUMENT HE HAD WITH HIM WARNED HIS LOYALISTS TO AVOID JOINING UP WITH FOREIGN ARAB TERRORISTS. *

IRAQI GOVERNING COUNCIL

SEE, SADDAM IS SO LINKED TO THE TERRORISTS THAT HE WROTE THE WORD "TERRORISTS" IN THIS DOCUMENT!

*"IRAQI GOVERNING COUNCIL LIMITS AL JAZEERA COVERAGE," REUTERS, JANUARY 31, 2004.

*JAMES RISEN, "HUSSEIN WARNED IRAQIS TO BEWARE OUTSIDE FIGHTERS, DOCUMENT SAYS," NEW YORK TIMES, JANUARY 13, 2004.

LATER, A LETTER WAS DISCOVERED ASKING OSAMA BIN LADEN TO SEND ISLAMIC RADICALS TO HELP FIGHT IRAQ'S AMERICAN OCCUPIERS. IT STATED THAT IRAQI INSURGENTS WERE NOT COOPERATING WITH FOREIGN FIGHTERS, AND THAT IRAQIS WERE NOT PARTICIPATING IN SUICIDE ATTACKS, SOMETHING THAT THE FOREIGN FIGHTERS TAKE PRIDE IN. *

*HAMZA HENDAWI, "IRAQ LETTER SEEKS AID FROM AL-QAIDA," ASSOCIATED PRESS, FEBRUARY 11, 2004.

YET THIS LETTER WHICH SHOWED THAT IRAQI INSURGENTS LOYAL TO SADDAM WERE NOT HELPING THE FOREIGN TERRORISTS IN IRAQ WAS LATCHED ONTO BY BUSH AND HIS NATIONAL SECURITY TEAM AS PROOF OF THE LINK BETWEEN SADDAM AND TERRORISTS BEFORE THE WAR.

"IT CERTAINLY LENDS, I THINK, SOME CREDENCE TO WHAT WE SAID AT THE U.N. LAST YEAR, THAT [ZARQAWI] WAS ACTIVE IN IRAQ IN DOING THINGS THAT SHOULD HAVE BEEN KNOWN TO THE IRAQIS." *

COLIN POWELL

*"POWELL SAYS AL-QAEDA MEMO GIVES 'CREDENCE' TO US CLAIMS," AGENCE FRANCE PRESSE, FEBRUARY 9, 2004.

GREG THIELMANN, A FORMER STATE DEPARTMENT EXPERT IN WEAPONS OF MASS DESTRUCTION, MADE AN IMPORTANT OBSERVATION OF THE LINK BETWEEN IRAQ AND FOREIGN TERRORISTS.

"THE U.S. ATTACK ON IRAQ HAS NOW MADE A TERRORIST CONNECTION A SELF-FULFILLING PROPHECY. WE REALLY FOUND ONE FORMULA THAT MAXIMIZES AL-QAIDA'S CHANCES OF INCREASING THEIR OPERATIONS IN IRAQ." *

*JOHN SOLOMON, "U.S. SEES SOME IRAQ CONTACT WITH AL-QAIDA," ASSOCIATED PRESS, SEPTEMBER 13, 2003.

AND SUCH IS THE CONDITION OF IRAQ AS AMERICA PREPARES TO HAND THE COUNTRY OVER TO SOME FORM OF A GOVERNING COUNCIL ON JUNE 30, 2004, WITH U.S. TROOPS STAYING SO LONG AS THE THEN-SOVEREIGN IRAQI LEADERS SEE THAT THEY'RE NEEDED, OR UNTIL GEORGE W. BUSH DECIDES THAT HE'S ACCOMPLISHED THAT WHICH HE SET OUT TO DO OR DECIDES TO SEND THEM ELSEWHERE.

I'M DEDICATED TO DEMOCRACY IN IRAQ, JUST LIKE I'M DEDICATED TO DEMO-CRACY IN AFGHANISTAN! THEN WHEN I'M SAFELY RE-ELECTED, I'LL LET YOU KNOW HOW MUCH THAT'S ALL GOING TO COST YOU!
- OINK!

WITH IT BEING AN ELECTION YEAR, BUSH HAS PUT BACK ON HIS BEST DIPLOMATIC FACE AFTER ALL OF HIS JUSTIFICATIONS FOR WAR TURNED OUT TO BE FALSE. IN AN ADDRESS TO AMBASSADORS FROM 83 NATIONS, HE SOUGHT TO PUT THE WHOLE AFFAIR BEHIND THEM.

"THERE HAVE BEEN DISAGREEMENTS IN THIS MATTER AMONG OLD AND VALUED FRIENDS. THOSE DIFFERENCES BELONG IN THE PAST. ALL OF US CAN NOW AGREE THAT THE FALL OF THE IRAQI DICTATOR HAS REMOVED A SOURCE OF VIOLENCE, AGGRESSION AND INSTABILITY IN THE MIDDLE EAST." *

YOU'LL NOTICE THAT BUSH DIDN'T SAY HE HAD BEEN WRONG, JUST THAT THERE HAD BEEN "DISAGREEMENTS." SO MUCH FOR PERSONAL RESPONSIBILITY.

*STEVE HOLLAND, "BUSH TELLS WORLD IRAQ DIFFERENCES ARE IN THE PAST," REUTERS, MARCH 19, 2004.

RICHARD CLARKE IDENTIFIED THE PROBLEM WITH THE INVASION OF IRAQ, AND HOW IT HAS ACTUALLY SERVED TO COUNTER THE GOAL OF FIGHTING INTERNATIONAL TERRORISTS.

"OSAMA BIN LADEN HAD BEEN SAYING FOR YEARS, 'AMERICA WANTS TO INVADE AN ARAB COUNTRY AND OCCUPY IT... SO WHAT DID WE DO AFTER 9/11? ... WE STEPPED RIGHT INTO BIN LADEN'S PROPAGANDA. AND THE RESULT OF THAT IS THAT AL QAEDA AND ORGANIZATIONS LIKE IT... HAVE BEEN GREATLY STRENGTHENED."

TIME WILL TELL IF CLARKE'S GRAVE CONCLUSION IS TRUE.

*"CLARKE'S TAKE ON TERROR," 60 MINUTES, MARCH 21, 2004.

AFTER RUNNING A CAMPAIGN WHICH INCLUDED SURROGATE ATTACKS ON JOHN KERRY AND CONSTANT REMINDERS AND DISTORTIONS OF THE EVENTS OF SEPTEMBER 11, 2001, GEORGE W. BUSH FOUND HIMSELF ENTERING A SECOND TERM WITH 286 ELECTORAL VOTES AND 51% OF THE POPULAR VOTE.*

*www.cnn.com/ELECTION/2004/pages/results/president/

BUT A WIND OF CHANGE WAS BLOWING. EVEN AS BUSH BASKED IN HIS NARROW VICTORY, AND IN THE INCREASED REPUBLICAN PRESENCE IN BOTH THE HOUSE OF REPRESENTATIVES AND SENATE, PUBLIC SENTIMENT WAS TURNING AGAINST HIM.

THE SITUATION IN IRAQ WAS STILL FAR FROM SECURE.

AFGHANISTAN'S RECONSTRUCTION WAS GOING MORE SLOWLY THAN PLANNED (IF IT CAN BE SAID THAT THERE EVER WAS ANY REALISTIC PLANNING THAT WENT ON WITH REGARDS TO AFGHANISTAN).

IRAN AND NORTH KOREA WERE INTENT ON BUILDING THEIR OWN NUCLEAR ARSENALS.

ALL THE WHILE, BUSH RELIED MORE ON THE SAME TIRED RHETORIC THAN ON SUBSTANTIVE ACTION.

ON OCTOBER 9, 2004, A PRESIDENTIAL ELECTION WAS HELD THROUGHOUT AFGHANISTAN WITH HAMID KARZAI, THE MAN PREVIOUSLY APPOINTED INTERIM AFGHAN PRESIDENT, EMERGING THE VICTOR.

DESPITE THE PASSING OF THIS IMPORTANT MILESTONE, IT REMAINED CLEAR THAT THREATS AND INTIMIDATION INFLUENCED THE DECISIONS OF MANY POTENTIAL VOTERS, LEADING SOME TO VOTE AS DIRECTED BY LOCAL WARLORDS AND OTHERS TO REFRAIN FROM VOTING AT ALL.*

WE'RE VOTING FOR **THAT GUY.**

POLLS

*"THE RULE OF THE GUN: HUMAN RIGHTS ABUSES AND POLITICAL REPRESSION IN THE RUN UP TO AFGHANISTAN'S PRESIDENTIAL ELECTION," HUMAN RIGHTS WATCH, SEPTEMBER 2004.

THE SAME INTIMIDATION AND THREATS LIKELY INFLUENCED THE DECISIONS OF VOTERS AND POTENTIAL CANDIDATES IN AFGHANISTAN'S PARLIAMENTARY ELECTIONS, WHICH WERE HELD ON SEPTEMBER 18, 2005.

WILL REGIONAL WARLORDS ELECTED TO PARLIAMENT DESTROY THE DREAMS OF PEACE IN THE HEARTS OF THE PEOPLE OF AFGHANISTAN?

THIS IS THE CHART THAT I WILL SHOOT TO DEMONSTRATE WHAT I WILL DO TO YOU IF YOU DO NOT VOTE FOR ME.

ELECTION

IN THE FIRST 6 MONTHS OF 2005, 200 AFGHAN CIVILIANS HAD BEEN KILLED IN FIGHTING THROUGHOUT THE COUNTRY, IN ADDITION TO ABOUT 100 MEMBERS OF AFGHAN SECURITY FORCES.* SOME OF THIS VIOLENCE WAS A DIRECT RESULT OF THE TALIBAN CAMPAIGN TO INTIMIDATE VOTERS AHEAD OF THE SEPTEMBER PARLIAMENTARY ELECTIONS.

*JUSTIN HUGGLER, "THE 5-MINUTE BRIEFING; TURMOIL IN AFGHANISTAN," *THE INDEPENDENT*, AUGUST 24, 2005.

ACCORDING TO THE U.S. DEPARTMENT OF DEFENSE, BY THE END OF DECEMBER 2005, OVER 250 U.S. TROOPS HAD BEEN KILLED IN OR AROUND AFGHANISTAN, WITH OVER 650 WOUNDED IN ACTION.

IN JUST THE FIRST 7 MONTHS OF 2005, 47 U.S. TROOPS HAD BEEN KILLED IN COMBAT IN AFGHANISTAN,* A NUMBER SUGGESTING THAT PERHAPS THINGS AREN'T GOING AS SMOOTHLY AS SOME IN WASHINGTON WOULD LIKE THE WORLD TO BELIEVE.

WE'RE WINNING THE WAR ON TERROR!

JUST IGNORE THOSE NUMBERS!

*"U.S. SAYS 16 MILITANTS KILLED IN AFGHAN FIGHTING," REUTERS, AUGUST 25, 2005.

WHAT ABOUT THE PACE OF REBUILDING THE INFRASTRUCTURE OF AFGHANISTAN?

ACCORDING TO A REPORT BY THE U.S. GOVERNMENT ACCOUNTABILITY OFFICE, AFGHANISTAN'S ECONOMY WAS STIFLED BY A RISE IN OPIUM PRODUCTION, WHILE THE SECURITY SITUATION MEANT THAT AID COULDN'T GET TO WHERE IT WAS MOST NEEDED.*

*"SECURITY, DRUG, FUNDING WOES HINDER U.S. REBUILDING IN AFGHANISTAN," AGENCE FRANCE PRESSE, JULY 29, 2005.

THE U.S. AGENCY FOR INTERNATIONAL DEVELOPMENT INTENDED TO COMPLETE WORK ON 286 SCHOOLS THROUGHOUT 2004. IT ONLY COMPLETED WORK ON EIGHT.*

$286 - 8 = ?$

*IBID.

WITH THE WORLD'S ATTENTION FOCUSED ELSEWHERE, WILL AFGHANISTAN RECEIVE THE ATTENTION IT NEEDS TO BECOME A BRIGHT BEACON OF DEMOCRACY? FOR THE SAKE OF THE AFGHAN PEOPLE, WE CAN ONLY HOPE.

WITH PUBLIC OPINION SO STRONGLY TURNING AGAINST BUSH AND THE WAR, EVEN SOME REPUBLICAN MEMBERS OF CONGRESS STARTED TURNING THEIR BACKS ON BUSH AND HIS POLICIES.

IN THE HOUSE OF REPRESENTATIVES, WALTER JONES OF NORTH CAROLINA, WHO COINED THE TERM "FREEDOM FRIES" TO STICK IT TO THE FRENCH FOR OPPOSING GOING TO WAR WITH IRAQ, HAD SOUGHT TO SEEK A RESOLUTION THAT CALLED ON BUSH TO ANNOUNCE A WITHDRAWAL STRATEGY BEFORE THE END OF 2005, WITH ACTUAL WITHDRAWAL TO BEGIN NO LATER THAN OCTOBER 1, 2006.*

"IF I HAD KNOWN THEN WHAT I KNOW NOW, I WOULDN'T HAVE SUPPORTED THE RESOLUTION [AUTHORIZING USE OF FORCE IN IRAQ]."*

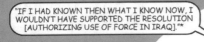

GOD BLESS AMERICA

SLURP

*STEVE HARTSOE, "SUPPORT SAID GROWING FOR IRAQ EXIT PLAN," ASSOCIATED PRESS, AUGUST 18, 2005.

SENATOR CHUCK HAGEL OF NEBRASKA, A VIETNAM WAR VETERAN AND POTENTIAL REPUBLICAN PRESIDENTIAL CANDIDATE IN 2008, ALSO SPOKE ABOUT THE NEED FOR A WITHDRAWAL PLAN FROM IRAQ.

"BY ANY STANDARD, WHEN YOU ANALYZE TWO AND A HALF YEARS IN IRAQ... WE'RE NOT WINNING."*

HAGEL DIDN'T STOP AT CALLING FOR WITHDRAWAL.

"WE'RE PAST THAT STAGE [OF NEEDING A STRONGER MILITARY FORCE IN IRAQ] NOW, BECAUSE WE ARE LOCKED INTO A BOGGED-DOWN PROBLEM NOT UNSIMILAR, DISSIMILAR TO WHERE WE WERE IN VIETNAM. THE LONGER WE STAY, THE MORE PROBLEMS WE'RE GOING TO HAVE."*

*DOUGLASS K. DANIEL, "HAGEL SAYS IRAQ WAR LOOKING LIKE VIETNAM," ASSOCIATED PRESS, AUGUST 21, 2005.

WITH THE PUBLIC AND SOME MEMBERS OF HIS OWN PARTY TURNING SOUR ON BUSH'S LACK OF A STRATEGY IN IRAQ, BUSH WENT ON THE OFFENSIVE. THIS MEANT MORE OF THE SAME RHETORIC THE AMERICAN PEOPLE HAD GROWN ACCUSTOMED TO HEARING SINCE 9/11.

"IRAQ IS A CENTRAL FRONT IN THE WAR ON TERROR. IT IS A VITAL PART OF OUR MISSION."*

*CAREN BOHAN, "BUSH: U.S. MUST FINISH JOB IN IRAQ TO HONOR THE FALLEN," REUTERS, AUGUST 22, 2005.

AND, AS IS OFTEN THE CASE, BUSH PRESENTED A REPULSIVE, COMPLETELY DISTORTED AND BACKWARDS NEW ARGUMENT AS TO WHY AMERICANS HAD TO STAY IN IRAQ.

"WE OWE [THE FALLEN SOLDIERS] SOMETHING. WE WILL FINISH THE TASK THAT THEY GAVE THEIR LIVES FOR. WE'LL HONOR THEIR SACRIFICE BY STAYING ON THE OFFENSIVE AGAINST THE TERRORISTS AND BUILDING STRONG ALLIES IN AFGHANISTAN AND IRAQ THAT WILL HELP US WIN AND FIGHT THE WAR ON TERROR."*

*IBID.

BUSH WAS NOW OVERTLY USING THE FALLEN TROOPS AS AMMUNITION IN HIS POLITICAL OFFENSIVE.

NEVERMIND THAT THE WAR WAS BASED ON FALSE INFORMATION, THAT THE STORIES TOLD BY THE BUSH ADMINISTRATION BEFORE THE WAR OF ALUMINUM TUBES, MOBILE BIO-WEAPONS LABS, AND UNMANNED AERIAL VEHICLES CAPABLE OF REACHING THE U.S. WERE ALL COMPLETE FICTION, AND IN MANY -- IF NOT MOST CASES -- THE ADMINISTRATION HAD IGNORED FACTS IN ORDER TO PRESENT THE LIES THAT PAVED THE PATH TO WAR WITH IRAQ.

WE CAN'T LEAVE IRAQ NOW BECAUSE... UH.. BECAUSE THEN.. I'D HAVE TO SAY I WAS WRONG.

AND THAT'S NOT A SACRIFICE I'M WILLING TO MAKE!

SO THE SOLDIERS WHO HAVE BEEN KILLED, THEY'RE NOW THE JUSTIFICATION TO STAY. WE WENT THERE FOR WEAPONS THAT DIDN'T EXIST, AND NOW WE'RE TOLD THAT WE'RE STAYING TO DEFEND THE HONOR OF THOSE WHO DIED SERVING A PRESIDENT WHO DOESN'T KNOW THE MEANING OF THE PHRASE "PERSONAL SACRIFICE."

JOSEPH WILSON, A FORMER AMBASSADOR WHO HAD GONE TO NIGER TO INVESTIGATE CLAIMS THAT IRAQ HAD SOUGHT URANIUM THERE, WENT ON A MEDIA OFFENSIVE IN JULY OF 2003, COUNTERING BUSH'S 2003 STATE OF THE UNION ADDRESS CLAIM:*

EVEN BEFORE WILSON HAD PUBLICLY VOICED HIS CONCERNS, CERTAIN INDIVIDUALS IN THE WHITE HOUSE WERE RESEARCHING WILSON AND HIS WIFE, VALERIE PLAME, FINDING THAT SHE WAS AN UNDERCOVER OPERATIVE WITH THE CIA. WITH THIS INFORMATION, THEY PLANNED TO UNDERMINE JOSEPH WILSON'S CREDIBILITY, PERHAPS BY PORTRAYING HIM AS FAVORED WITH THE NIGER TRIP DESPITE A LACK OF QUALIFICATIONS BECAUSE OF HIS WIFE'S CONNECTIONS?

"SADDAM HUSSEIN RECENTLY SOUGHT SIGNIFICANT QUANTITIES OF URANIUM FROM AFRICA."

IT'S IRONIC THAT THIS ADMINISTRATION WOULD SEEK TO DISCREDIT SOMEONE FOR MAKING USE OF CONNECTIONS WHEN THE PRESIDENT HIMSELF HAD LIVED HIS LIFE NOT NEEDING ANYTHING OTHER THAN CONNECTIONS AND MONEY TO GET ANYTHING HE WANTED.

HEY! AREN'T YOU THAT SECRET AGENT I'VE READ ABOUT?

*TOM HAMBURGER AND SONNI EFRON, "THE CIA LEAK: INFIGHTING, GRUDGES, JUSTIFYING A WAR," *LOS ANGELES TIMES*, AUGUST 25, 2005.

IN WILSON'S CASE, IF IT MEANT EXPOSING AN UNDERCOVER OPERATIVE FOR THE CIA TO SMEAR WILSON, SO BE IT. THE BUSH WHITE HOUSE DOESN'T PLAY NICE.

ROBERT NOVAK, WHO FIRST PUBLISHED PLAME'S NAME -- AND DISCLOSED HER AS AN OPERATIVE -- ON JULY 14, 2003, WROTE THAT 2 ADMINISTRATION OFFICIALS HAD TOLD HIM THAT IT WAS PLAME WHO HAD SUGGESTED WILSON FOR THE NIGER MISSION.*

DESPITE NOVAK'S COLUMN, PRESS SECRETARY SCOTT MCCLELLAN MADE A STATEMENT REGARDING THE LEAK THAT WOULD COME BACK TO HAUNT THE PRESIDENT AND HIS ADMINISTRATION.

HE NEEDED A LADY TO SEND HIM ON A MISSION! HAW!

AND THAT HAS WHAT TO DO WITH ANYTHING AT ALL?

"I'M TELLING YOU, FLATLY, THAT THAT IS NOT THE WAY THIS WHITE HOUSE OPERATES."

LEAKS

*IBID.

*IBID.

CARL ROVE!

KARL ROVE, GEORGE W. BUSH'S PERSONAL POLITICAL STRATEGIST, IS NOW KNOWN TO HAVE DISCUSSED VALERIE PLAME'S IDENTITY WITH SOME MEMBERS OF THE PRESS AND OTHER ADMINISTRATION OFFICIALS. BY THE END OF OCTOBER 2005, HE HAD NOT BEEN INDICTED IN THE CIA LEAK INVESTIGATION HEADED BY U.S. ATTORNEY PATRICK FITZGERALD, THOUGH THE POSSIBILITY OF FUTURE CHARGES REMAINS.*

*JOHN SOLOMON, "CHENEY ADVISOR RESIGNS AFTER INDICTMENT," ASSOCIATED PRESS, OCTOBER 29, 2005.

THE OTHER BUSH WHITE HOUSE OFFICIAL WHO IS KNOWN TO HAVE PASSED ALONG INFORMATION ABOUT PLAME TO REPORTERS WAS LEWIS "SCOOTER" LIBBY -- VICE PRESIDENT DICK CHENEY'S TOP AIDE.

ON OCTOBER 28, 2005, LIBBY WAS CHARGED WITH OBSTRUCTING JUSTICE, PERJURY, AND LYING TO FBI AGENTS. HE FACES UP TO 30 YEARS IN PRISON AND $1.25 MILLION IN FINES ON THESE CHARGES IF FOUND GUILTY. HE RESIGNED FROM HIS WHITE HOUSE POSITION SHORTLY AFTER THE INDICTMENT WAS ANNOUNCED.

NOT FOR SYMPATHY!

*IBID.

FIRED

"...IF THE COMMITTED A CRIME..." "...WITH A GOAT."

DESPITE A PROMISE BY THE WHITE HOUSE BEFORE THE START OF THE LEAK INVESTIGATION THAT ANYONE INVOLVED IN LEAKING PLAME'S NAME WOULD BE FIRED, ONCE IT BECAME CLEAR THAT SOME HIGH-RANKING OFFICIALS WERE INVOLVED, BUSH BACKPEDALED, SAYING THAT HE WOULD ONLY RESORT TO FIRING IF "SOMEONE COMMITTED A CRIME."*

*TOM HAMBURGER AND SONNI EFRON, "THE CIA LEAK: INFIGHTING, GRUDGES, JUSTIFYING A WAR," LOS ANGELES TIMES, AUGUST 25, 2005.

WILL KARL ROVE BE KEPT ON EVEN IF INDICTED AT A LATER DATE? WITH THE WAY THIS WHITE HOUSE OPERATES, IT'S HARD TO SAY, THOUGH IT WOULD BE HARD TO IMAGINE GEORGE W. BUSH OPERATING WITHOUT THE MAN WHO ORGANIZED THE STRATEGY THAT BROUGHT SO MUCH POWER TO THE REPUBLICAN PARTY, AND BROUGHT BUSH TO THE WHITE HOUSE IN THE FIRST PLACE.

GOOD WORK, TURD BLOSSOM!

I AM NOT FECAL MAYIM BIALIK!

SMAK!

THROUGHOUT HIS TIME IN OFFICE, BUSH HAS SPENT AN INORDINATE AMOUNT OF TIME AWAY FROM THE WHITE HOUSE.

MOMMY?

BY THE END OF AUGUST 2005, HE HAD SPENT 20 PERCENT OF HIS PRESIDENCY IN CRAWFORD, TEXAS, AT HIS RANCH, SURPASSING RONALD REAGAN'S PREVIOUS RECORD FOR TIME SPENT ON VACATION FROM THE MOST IMPORTANT JOB IN THE WORLD,* THOUGH IT TOOK REAGAN 8 YEARS TO RACK UP SUCH NUMBERS.

*JOSH BUREK, "THE WORK-LIFE BALANCE FOR 'NATION'S CEO,'" *CHRISTIAN SCIENCE MONITOR*, AUGUST 24, 2005.

SO, AFTER JUST 5 YEARS IN OFFICE, BUSH HAD SPENT ALMOST ONE FULL YEAR AT HIS RANCH.

PERHAPS IT WOULDN'T BE SO STARTLING HAD BUSH NOT BEEN ON VACATION AT HIS RANCH WHEN HE RECEIVED THE AUGUST 2001 BRIEFING ABOUT THE POSSIBILITY OF TERRORISTS USING PLANES AS WEAPONS.

ZZZ.. ULTRA SERIOUS. ...ZZZ

AFTER SEPTEMBER 11, WHICH BUSH IS QUICK TO MENTION IN SO MANY SPEECHES TO STIR THE EMOTIONS OF THE PUBLIC, AFTER LEADING THE NATION TO WAR IN IRAQ, IS SO MUCH TIME AWAY FROM WASHINGTON JUSTIFIABLE?

IN LATE AUGUST 2005, AS ONE OF BUSH'S VACATIONS WAS WINDING DOWN TO ITS FINAL DAYS, ONE OF THE WORST NATURAL DISASTERS IN THE NATION'S HISTORY STRUCK THE GULF COAST, LEAVING A TRAIL OF DEATH AND DEVASTATION IN ITS WAKE.

THE OFFICIAL DEATH TOLL FOR HURRICANE KATRINA BY THE END OF NOVEMBER 2005 WAS 1,306 IN LOUISIANA AND MISSISSIPPI, WITH THOUSANDS STILL UNACCOUNTED FOR.*

WITH A MORE EXPEDITIOUS FEDERAL RESPONSE, MIGHT THIS NATURAL DISASTER HAVE RESULTED IN FEWER DEATHS?

*KEVIN JOHNSON, "6,644 ARE STILL MISSING AFTER KATRINA; TOLL MAY RISE," *USA TODAY*, NOVEMBER 21, 2005.

DURING BILL CLINTON'S PRESIDENTIAL ADMINISTRATION, THE FEDERAL EMERGENCY MANAGEMENT AGENCY (FEMA) HAD BEEN TRANSFORMED INTO A FUNCTIONAL AGENCY, EMPLOYING PEOPLE WITH EXPERIENCE IN EMERGENCY RESPONSE, AS OPPOSED TO THE PREVIOUS PRACTICE OF PACKING THE AGENCY WITH POLITICAL APPOINTEES WITH LITTLE OR NO PRACTICAL EXPERIENCE.*

GEORGE W. BUSH OPTED TO UNDO CLINTON'S CHANGES, HOWEVER, APPOINTING HIS PRESIDENTIAL CAMPAIGN MANAGER, JOE ALLBAUGH, WHO HAD NO EMERGENCY RESPONSE EXPERIENCE, TO HEAD THE AGENCY. ALLBAUGH'S MAIN OBJECTIVE AS HEAD OF FEMA WAS TO DOWNSIZE IT, ULTIMATELY LEADING TO THE AGENCY'S INEFFECTIVENESS IN THE FACE OF HURRICANE KATRINA.*

IT ALSO DIDN'T HELP THAT THE AGENCY'S FUNDING HAD BEEN REDUCED AFTER IT HAD BECOME PART OF THE DEPARTMENT OF HOMELAND SECURITY.*

IT'S NOT LIKE THERE'S GONE BE ANY EMERGENCY ON **MY** WATCH ANYWAYS!

WHAT'S A MERGENSIE?

*FRONTLINE: THE STORM, DIRECTED BY TIM MANGINI (BOSTON, MASSACHUSETTS: WGBH BOSTON, 2005).

WHEN ALLBAUGH RESIGNED AND WAS REPLACED BY MICHAEL BROWN (A CLOSE FRIEND OF ALLBAUGH'S, ALSO WITH NO PRACTICAL EMERGENCY MANAGEMENT EXPERIENCE), BROWN'S LEADERSHIP OF THE AGENCY CONTINUED THE TREND OF DOWNSIZING THE ORGANIZATION AND USING HIS POSITION FOR POLITICAL PURPOSES.

FOR EXAMPLE, UNDER HIS WATCH, AFTER HURRICANE FRANCES STRUCK FLORIDA IN SEPTEMBER OF 2004, FEMA DISTRIBUTED LARGE SUMS OF MONEY TO AREAS VIRTUALLY UNAFFECTED BY THE STORM, REPORTEDLY FOR THE BENEFIT OF GEORGE W. BUSH'S REELECTION PROSPECTS IN THE BATTLEGROUND STATE OF FLORIDA. OTHERS WITHIN THE DEPARTMENT OF HOMELAND SECURITY WENT SO FAR AS TO SAY THAT BROWN WAS POSITIONING HIMSELF TO BE CHOSEN AS TOM RIDGE'S REPLACEMENT AS SECRETARY OF HOMELAND SECURITY.*

LOOK WHAT I CAN DO!

THANKS, BROWNIE!

GOLD LIMO

*JOHN MINTZ, "REPORT CALLS PAYMENTS BY FEMA QUESTIONABLE," WASHINGTON POST, MAY 19, 2005, A25.

BROWN'S PAST ATTEMPTS TO WIN POLITICAL POINTS WITH BUSH WEREN'T THE ONLY DETAIL THAT RAISED SOME EYEBROWS AFTER HURRICANE KATRINA STRUCK. FEMA'S TOP THREE LEADERS ALL HAD TIES TO BUSH'S 2000 PRESIDENTIAL CAMPAIGN, AND 5 OF THE 8 TOP FEMA OFFICIALS HAD NO PRIOR EMERGENCY MANAGEMENT EXPERIENCE.*

HARDLY THE PEOPLE YOU'D WANT IN CHARGE OF HANDLING A DISASTER OF SUCH ENORMOUS PROPORTIONS.

*SPENCER S. HSU, "LEADERS LACKING DISASTER EXPERIENCE," *WASHINGTON POST*, SEPTEMBER 9, 2005, A01.

IT'S NOT MY FAULT!

EVEN WITH SPECIFIC AID REQUESTS SENT TO FEMA FROM VARIOUS CITY AND STATE OFFICIALS, BROWN FAILED TO ACT IN A DECISIVE FASHION IN THE DAYS IMMEDIATELY FOLLOWING THE HURRICANE, WHEN AID MATTERED MOST.

LATER, HE WOULD GO SO FAR AS TO DENY THAT HE HAD RECEIVED SUCH REQUESTS, DESPITE PHYSICAL EVIDENCE TO THE CONTRARY.*

*FRONTLINE: THE STORM, DIRECTED BY TIM MANGINI (BOSTON, MASSACHUSETTS: WGBH BOSTON, 2005).

EARLY ON, BROWN WAS ASSIGNING BLAME FOR ANY DEATHS THE HURRICANE CAUSED TO AN UNBELIEVABLE SOURCE.

"UNFORTUNATELY, [THE HIGH DEATH TOLL] IS GOING TO BE ATTRIBUTABLE A LOT TO PEOPLE WHO DID NOT HEED THE ADVANCE WARINGS."*

*"FEMA CHIEF: VICTIMS BEAR SOME RESPONSIBILITY," CNN.com, SEPTEMBER 1, 2005, LOCATED AT http://www.cnn.com/2005/WEATHER/09/01/katrina.fema.brown/index.html.

OF COURSE, BROWN KNEW THAT THE NECESSARY RESOURCES WEREN'T IN PLACE TO GET EVERYONE OUT OF NEW ORLEANS, INCLUDING THE ELDERLY AND THOSE WITHOUT VEHICLES. DIDN'T MATTER. HE WASHED HIS HANDS OF THEM AT THAT MOMENT. IT WAS THEIR OWN FAULT FOR BEING TOO POOR, TOO OLD, OR JUST UNLUCKY.

WHAT WAS MICHAEL BROWN DOING WHILE NEW ORLEANS WAS BESIEGED BY HURRICANE KATRINA AND THE STORM'S AFTERMATH? HE WAS SPENDING MORE TIME WORRYING ABOUT HIS OWN AND THE FEDERAL GOVERNMENT'S IMAGE AS OPPOSED TO THE CITIZENS IN DIRE NEED OF FEDERAL ASSISTANCE.

DO YOU SERVE CRABS?

WELL, YOU'RE HERE SO I GUESS THE ANSWER IS "YES."

IN THE AFTERMATH OF THE STORM, BROWN VIRTUALLY IGNORED COMMUNICATIONS FROM A REGIONAL FEMA DIRECTOR, REPLYING TO URGENT EMAIL MESSAGES WITH USELESS INFORMATION ABOUT HIS RESTAURANT DINING SITUATION AND HIS NEED TO APPEAR ON TELEVISION.*

MENU

*"FEMA OFFICIAL IN NEW ORLEANS BLASTS AGENCY'S RESPONSE," CNN.com, OCTOBER 20, 2005, LOCATED AT http://www.cnn.com/2005/POLITICS/10/20/FEMA.Katrina.ap/index.

BROWN'S TENURE AS HEAD OF FEMA CAME TO A CLOSE AFTER HIS INCOMPETENCE PUSHED PUBLIC OPINION EVEN MORE STRONGLY AGAINST THE BUSH WHITE HOUSE. IT MAY ALSO HAVE BEEN USED AS AN OPPORTUNITY FOR BUSH TO DRAW SOME PUBLIC ATTENTION AWAY FROM HIS OWN ACTIONS DURING AND IN THE AFTERMATH OF KATRINA.

WHILE KATRINA WREAKED HAVOC ALONG THE COAST, GEORGE W. BUSH WAS ACCEPTING A SIGNED GUITAR FROM SINGER MARK WILLS. IN THE FACE OF MOUNTING CRITICISM REGARDING HIS ABSENCE FROM WASHINGTON DURING SUCH AN IMMENSE DISASTER, BUSH FINALLY CUT HIS VACATION SHORT BY TWO DAYS,* NOT QUITE GETTING THE FULL FIVE WEEKS HE'D INITIALLY INTENDED.

AFTER THE STORM, BUSH'S POLITICAL TIES MADE THEMSELVES EVIDENT ONCE AGAIN, AS MUCH OF THE RECONSTRUCTION WORK IN NEW ORLEANS WAS HANDED OUT IN SECRETIVE NO BID CONTRACTS TO COMPANIES WITH TIES TO THE PRESIDENT AND HIS POLITICAL ALLIES, INCLUDING KELLOGG BROWN & ROOT (A SUBSIDIARY OF HALLIBURTON, WHICH WAS ONCE HELMED BY VICE PRESIDENT DICK CHENEY) AND THE SHAW GROUP, WHICH JUST HAPPENS TO BE A CLIENT OF BUSH'S FIRST FEMA HEAD AND LONGTIME POLITICAL ALLY, JOE ALLBAUGH.*

AND I PICK.. YOU!

AN' YOU! AN' YOU!

DONOR DONOR DONOR

THANKS FOR THE GUITAR, ELVIS.

*DANIEL BOFFEY, "BUSH TWANGS.. WHILE NEW ORLEANS SINKS," THE MIRROR (UK), SEPTEMBER 1, 2005.

*PHILIP SHENON, "OFFICIAL VOWS INVESTIGATION OF NO-BID RELIEF CONTRACTS," NEW YORK TIMES, SEPTEMBER 14, 2005.

HOW ELSE COULD BUSH FURTHER HURT THE REGION AFFECTED BY THE STORM WHILE CLAIMING ONLY GOOD INTENTIONS? HE COULD TRY TO SCORE SOME POINTS WITH HIS CONSERVATIVE BASE, OF COURSE!

AS RECONSTRUCTION WORK BEGAN IN THE AREAS AFFECTED BY THE STORM, BUSH REPEALED THE DAVIS-BACON WAGE PROTECTION LAW, ALLOWING COMPANIES CONTRACTED TO REBUILD FOR THE GOVERNMENT TO PAY LESS THAN A FAIR WAGE. THE ADMINISTRATION CLAIMED THAT THIS WOULD SOMEHOW REDUCE COSTS. WHAT WAS OBVIOUS IS THAT IT WOULD RESULT IN LESS PAY FOR ANYONE WORKING ON RECONSTRUCTION, AND A BIGGER PROFIT FOR THE COMPANIES DOING THE HIRING.

MUNCH! MUNCH!

DAVIS-BACON WAGE PROTECTION LAW

THIS BACON IS DELICIOUS!

HOWEVER, AFTER 2 MONTHS OF DAVIS-BACON SUSPENSION DEMONSTRATED THAT THERE WAS NO COST REDUCTION TO BE SEEN -- AND AFTER LABOR SUPPORTERS IN BOTH PARTIES EXPRESSED ANGER AND CONCERN OVER BUSH'S DECISION -- THE LAW WAS REINSTATED.*

*DEVLIN BARRETT, "BUSH REINSTATING WAGES FOR KATRINA WORK," ASSOCIATED PRESS, OCTOBER 26, 2005.

HURRICANE KATRINA ALSO OFFERED BUSH THE OPPORTUNITY TO ATTEMPT TO USE SOME OF HIS PET PROGRAMS ON A REGIONAL LEVEL THAT HAD FAILED TO BE ENACTED AT THE NATIONAL LEVEL.

IT'S A MICROCOSM OF COMPASSIONATE CONSERVATISM!

WHO TAUGHT HIM TO SAY 'MICROCOSM'?

???

THIS INCLUDED TEMPORARILY WAIVING CLEAN AIR AND WATER STANDARDS, ATTEMPTING TO ENACT A SCHOOL VOUCHER PROGRAM, AND GIVING TAXPAYER DOLLARS TO RELIGIOUS CHARITIES.

IN HIS REMAINING TIME IN OFFICE, BUSH HAS MANY DECISIONS TO MAKE. WILL HE BE MORE OF A MODERATE IN HIS REMAINING TIME IN OFFICE?

NOT VERY LIKELY. IF HISTORY IS ANY INDICATION, HE'LL CONTINUE TO PRESS FOR THE LEGISLATION HE WANTS, FOR WARS HE WANTS, AND FOR BASICALLY ANYTHING THAT HE WANTS.

WILL THERE BE A SUDDEN WITHDRAWAL FROM IRAQ, LEAVING THE COUNTRY IN THE CLUTCHES OF THE TERRORIST THREAT THAT FILLED THE VACUUM LEFT BY SADDAM'S DEFEAT?

WILL AFGHANISTAN'S PROBLEMS CONTINUE TO BE IGNORED IN FAVOR OF THE FANTASY REALITIES PAINTED BY THE PRESIDENT AND LAURA BUSH?

WILL BUSH GET HIS WAY AND TIP THE SUPREME COURT TO THE EXTREME RIGHT?

WILL THERE BE MORE TERRORIST ATTACKS ON U.S. SOIL?

IF SO, WILL BUSH BLAME THE DEMOCRATS?

ONLY TIME WILL TELL.

AND IN 2008, BARRING UNEARTHLY INTERVENTION, A NEW PRESIDENT WILL BE ELECTED. THE DAMAGE DONE BY BUSH AND HIS POLICIES CAN BE UNDONE, EVENTUALLY, THOUGH IT WILL CLEARLY TAKE MORE TIME TO FIX THAN THE TIME IT TOOK FOR HIM TO DESTROY.

WITH A CLEAR EYE TO THE FUTURE, PERHAPS AMERICA WILL PICK A PRESIDENTIAL CANDIDATE WHOSE RESUME INCLUDES HONESTY, INTEGRITY, AND A STRONG WILL TO SET THINGS RIGHT. ONLY FOR REAL, UNLIKE ALL THE OTHER CANDIDATES WHO ALWAYS MAKE SIMILAR CLAIMS.

OR MORE LIKELY, THE AMERICAN POPULACE WILL ELECT SOME OTHER OVERPRIVILEGED JACKASS WHO WANTS TO MOLD THE WORLD INTO HIS OWN PERVERTED VERSION OF UTOPIA, DAMN THE OPPOSITION.

EITHER WAY, AT LEAST IT WON'T BE GEORGE W. BUSH.

BUT IT *COULD* BE JEB!

SOMEDAY...

SOMEDAY...

BIBLIOGRAPHY OF BOOKS AND BOOK LENGTH SOURCES

FOR 9/11 CHAPTER:

CHISTI, MUZAFFAR A., DORIS MEISSNER, DEMETRIOS G. PAPADEMETRIOU, JAY PETERZELL, MICHAEL J. WISHNIE, AND STEPHEN W. YALE-LOEHR. *AMERICA'S CHALLENGE: DOMESTIC SECURITY, CIVIL LIBERTIES, AND NATIONAL UNITY AFTER SEPTEMBER 11.* WASHINGTON: MIGRATION POLICY INSTITUTE, 2003.

FRANKEN, AL. *LIES (AND THE LYING LIARS WHO TELL THEM): A FAIR AND BALANCED LOOK AT THE RIGHT.* NEW YORK: DUTTON, 2003.

MILLER, JOHN, MICHAEL STONE, AND CHRIS MITCHELL. *THE CELL: INSIDE THE 9/11 PLOT, AND WHY THE FBI AND CIA FAILED TO STOP IT.* NEW YORK: HYPERION, 2002.

POSNER, GERALD. *WHY AMERICA SLEPT: THE FAILURE TO PREVENT 9/11.* NEW YORK: RANDOM HOUSE, 2003.

FOR ALL OTHER CHAPTERS:

IVINS, MOLLY, AND LOU DUBOSE. *SHRUB: THE SHORT BUT HAPPY POLITICAL LIFE OF GEORGE W. BUSH.* NEW YORK: RANDOM HOUSE, 2000.

LIND, MICHAEL. *MADE IN TEXAS: GEORGE W. BUSH AND THE SOUTHERN TAKEOVER OF AMERICAN POLITICS.* NEW YORK: BASIC BOOKS, 2003.

MOORE, JAMES, AND WAYNE SLATER. *BUSH'S BRAIN: HOW KARL ROVE MADE GEORGE W. BUSH PRESIDENTIAL.* HOBOKEN: JOHN WILEY & SONS, 2003.

PALAST, GREG. *THE BEST DEMOCRACY MONEY CAN BUY: THE TRUTH ABOUT CORPORATE CONS, GLOBALIZATION, AND HIGH-FINANCE FRAUDSTERS.* NEW YORK: PLUME, 2003.

TOOBIN, JEFFREY. *TOO CLOSE TO CALL: THE THIRTY-SIX-DAY BATTLE TO DECIDE THE 2000 ELECTION.* NEW YORK: RANDOM HOUSE, 2001.

BLATANT